Dave Matthews Band FAQ

Dave Matthews Band FAQ

All That's Left to Know About the Most Popular Jam Band

Stephen Thomas Erlewine

Guilford, Connecticut

Published by Backbeat Books
An imprint of The Rowman & Littlefield Publishing Group, Inc.
4501 Forbes Blvd., Ste. 200
Lanham, MD 20706
www.rowman.com

Distributed by NATIONAL BOOK NETWORK

The FAQ series was conceived by Robert Rodriguez and developed with Stuart Shea.

All images are from the author's collection unless otherwise noted.

Book design and composition by Snow Creative

Library of Congress Cataloging-in-Publication Data available

ISBN 978-1-61713-651-1

∞™ The paper used in this publication meets the minimum requirements of American National Standard for Information Sciences—Permanence of Paper for Printed Library Materials, ANSI/NISO Z39.48-1992

To Stephanie.
Without her, I may never have completed this book.

Contents

Introduction

Read enough about Dave Matthews Band—or listen to enough interviews with the group—and one thing keeps coming up: this is a band unlike any other.

Fans, musicians, and sometimes critics have repeated this often enough that it has turned into something of a cliché, but, like so many clichés, this one endures because it is rooted in truth: there really are no other bands that sound like Dave Matthews Band. Chalk that up to the unique instrumentation, perhaps: no other band blends a violinist with an acoustic-strumming front man, a saxophonist, and a jazz rhythm section. That very combination sounds unique, but Dave Matthews Band—understandably often called DMB in shorthand—also pulls from unexpected musical inspirations without ever fully sounding like any one thing. Introspective folk intertwines with moody rock, exuberant bluegrass, funk vamps, and soul, with certain sounds ebbing and flowing within the course of one song.

This is especially true of Dave Matthews Band in concert, where the musicians have the time and inclination to jam until they've seemingly exhausted all possibilities for one song, but this is not strictly a "jam band," either. Jam bands usually can't harness their live power in the studio, but Dave Matthews Band could do that from the start, which is one of the reasons DMB transcended the jam-band scene that was its home and became one of the most popular American rock bands of the '90s.

Thanks to the alternative-rock gold rush that followed the rise of grunge, the '90s was a boom time for American rock bands, but among the dozens of major acts that surfaced during that decade, Dave Matthews Band is one of the few to sustain its popularity for a quarter-century. Each of the seven studio albums the band has released between 1998 and 2018 entered the *Billboard* 200 at #1—a consecutive streak no other band of its generation can claim—and DMB remains an in-demand concert draw, selling out its annual summer tours of the United States while launching satellite events such as the traveling festival Dave Matthews Band Caravan, not to mention Dave's regular tours with his guitarist idol, Tim Reynolds.

Part of the reason that Dave Matthews Band earned such a large audience is that it bucked the trend of grunge and alternative-rock in the '90s by offering fluid, adventurous and positive music that connected to a counterculture *outside* of the counterculture. DMB didn't arise from nowhere. The band benefited from the tape-trading, grassroots fan culture cultivated by the Grateful Dead, but was also so forward-thinking that it wound up defying the conventional definition of a "jam band," showing that this music could have broad appeal and hit singles, and be the rarest of things in rock: a reliable institution that remains ever-changing.

Like any band of long standing, Dave Matthews Band has had its share of squabbles and tragedy, but the group's story defies the conventional VH1 *Behind the Music* narrative arc of rags to riches to turmoil to redemption. Some of the backstage drama has seeped out into the public, particularly during the first half of the 2000s—a period that essentially amounts to an awkward adolescence, during which the band members were figuring out how to grow up in public. After a period when they flirted with pop production, they wound up steering back to their strengths and settling into a groove even after the tragic loss of founding member LeRoi Moore, the saxophonist who sometimes was called the heart and soul of the band.

In lieu of tabloid gossip and strife, Dave Matthews Band can seem to be something of a known quantity: something that always was and will always be, arriving fully formed and never changing. That, of course, isn't true, but it goes to the heart of why Dave Matthews Band inspires such devotion among its fans: the band itself is loyal. Dave Matthews Band is loyal to its idiosyncratic musical vision; to its home in Charlottesville, Virginia; to the band members' artistic peers; to their sense of social justice; and to their fans—fans who began to flock to the band in 1992 and then grew exponentially in number over the next decade.

Often, it seemed like Dave Matthews Band itself was almost tangential to the community that surrounds them. To be sure, the band provided the focal point—a reason for fans to gather, or perhaps to travel across the country to get to such destinations as the Gorge, an open-air venue in George, Washington, that essentially functions as the band's own annual Woodstock—but the world of Dave Matthews Band encompasses much more than the five musicians who had their first hit album in 1994. There were the fans, who found such sustenance in the music that they loved to talk about the particulars of individual set lists, or perhaps create art inspired by the music; then there were all the auxiliary projects, including musical busman's holidays, but also food, movies, and philanthropic works, that helped keep the world of DMB vibrant for over twenty-five years.

Also, this particular dynamic—where the band is a constant, the sun around which so much else revolves—makes DMB ideal for a book such as this, which isn't a strict biography (although history is certainly here). By examining the band's career, art, and culture from so many different angles—by looking at the history, the albums, the concerts, the fans, and everything else in the band's orbit—it's easier to appreciate just how far-reaching its impact has been, and also how unlikely its success is. Not for nothing have people been saying that there is no other band like Dave Matthews Band. That's not a matter of opinion. It's a fact that is proven time and time again over the course of this book.

1

Dive In

A Brief History of Dave Matthews Band

Pre-History

Dave Matthews Band may draw from many different cultures—and its leader may hail from South Africa—but this is a uniquely American band, a group that exists at the crossroads of many different strands of American life. It's a multiracial band that also crosses demographics: Carter Beauford, the band's oldest member, was born in 1957, while the youngest, Stefan Lessard, was born in 1974—an age gap great enough that Beauford could've fathered his companion in DMB's rhythm section. The band members blend many different styles of music, sharing a common vocabulary of classic rock and '80s college rock; of the many covers they play in concert, they often return to Bob Dylan, Neil Young, Peter Gabriel, and Talking Heads. Nevertheless, much of their shared language belongs to the idiom of jazz-fusion, their elongated jams finding space not just for lengthy solos but also for elastic rhythms.

This penchant for improvisation means DMB is often called a jam band, but the group doesn't share many musical similarities with its patchouli'd peers, despite often winding up on the same stage as these jammers. Despite having different musical origins, Dave Matthews Band has cannily appropriated the grassroots infrastructure pioneered by the Grateful Dead, using hardcore fans both as guerrilla marketers and as a regenerating life source capable of keeping the band flush with cash even in the years when there's no new album. DMB has stood at the precipice of the mainstream and the counterculture, benefitting from the currents of the underground but operating with the currency of big corporations, carving its own niche at the major labels and finding ways to make concerts in giant sheds named after banks still feel like communal gatherings.

All these coexisting contradictions means that Dave Matthews Band doesn't fit into any particular niche yet appeals to many different audiences. Some listeners may find the band too positive and poppy, as if constructed to cross over into the mainstream. Others might view the band as self-indulgent virtuosos, content to turn simple songs into showcases for extended instrumentals. Millions of fans believe the band speaks directly to them: DMB's music is lively, unpredictable, and soulful, shifting shapes within familiar parameters; music that means different things at different points of life. This multi-dimensionality means that it's difficult to pigeonhole Dave Matthews Band, and, when a group defies easy categories, it can be hard for it to make a large, lasting impact. Once an idiosyncratic band finds an audience, it often turns into an institution, but the trick is finding listeners willing to give a band a break. Fortunately, Dave Matthews Band surfaced in the early '90s, during the thick, heady heyday of alternative rock and grunge—a time when listeners and labels were willing to give a shot to music that didn't fit into a prescribed box.

Alternative rock had its deepest roots in punk, but the scene manifested during the back half of the '80s, fostered by underground press, college radio, and the slow emergence of specialty shows on MTV, like *Post-Modern MTV*. Most of these bands were ragged, ornery, or noisy, but Jane's Addiction—a proudly Dionysian scuzz-rock band from the grimiest quarters of Los Angeles—was led by ex-hippie Perry Farrell, who was enough of a Deadhead to launch a traveling rock-and-roll carnival called Lollapalooza. The first of these tours arrived in the summer of 1991, just a few months prior to the September release of Nirvana's major-label debut, *Nevermind*. These two events had far-reaching repercussions for American rock music in the '90s, establishing that there was a large audience hungry for new rock music that would purchase concert tickets and buy albums in the millions.

During the fallout of *Nevermind*, it often seemed as though all new American rock music was rooted in punk, the sound of an angst-ridden generation finally pushing its tortured voice into the mainstream. All that noisy sludge obscured how, underneath that turbulent outsider rock, there existed a *counter*-counterculture: a brighter, more expansive, and more positive sound; one also bred on American college campuses but created by true believers whose worldview wasn't limited to alienated American suburbanites or misfits roaming the council homes of gloomy, rainy England. These acts would soon be grouped under the "jam band" umbrella, but, like alternative rock, this scene started earlier, existing for years before it even had a name.

Call this scene the children of the Grateful Dead—bands under the sway of the San Franciscan titans of grass-roots rock. During the '80s, the Dead's gradually escalating popularity culminated in a first-ever *Billboard* Top 10 hit in 1987, when the ebullient "Touch of Grey" climbed to #9, but by that point there were legions of bands emulating the loose-limbed, improvisatory groove of the Grateful Dead. Every college campus in the United States seemed to have at least one of these groups, and, by the early '90s, these acts started to transition from local to national level. The first to do so was Blues Traveler, the granddaddy of the jam band scene, laying the foundation for everything that came next by being the first of its kind to sign to a major label. Quickly following were Phish, a band who embraced every nerdy element of this counterculture; and the Spin Doctors, who did the opposite: they managed to package this hippie rock into a pair of major hits in 1992 and 1993, "Little Miss Can't Be Wrong" and "Two Princes."

The Formation

All three of these bands, with their varying levels of tangible success, cleared a pathway for Dave Matthews Band. Hailing from Charlottesville, Virginia, the quintet of Dave Matthews (guitar, vocals), Carter Beauford (drums), LeRoi Moore (saxophone), Stefan Lessard (bass), and Boyd Tinsley (violin) didn't have the Grateful Dead in their DNA—not in the way that their peers did. Theirs was a unique hybrid of introspective folk, classic rock, and jazz-fusion; their improvisation came not from noodling but from focused grooves.

The band's unusual composition wasn't intentional. Matthews told Charlie Rose in 1999, "What attracted me to all these guys wasn't so much the instruments that they played but what came through their instruments. LeRoi would leave me weeping and Carter would leave me dancing and Boyd would just leave me like a fireball."

Dave Matthews Band both belonged to the nascent jam band scene but stood apart from it, possessing a different—yet compatible—sound and aesthetic to its peers, but also working the word-of-mouth, tape-trading culture like no other band did. This was the genius of Dave Matthews Band's manager, Coran Capshaw. Of all the people affiliated with DMB, he was the true Deadhead, having learned to love the group through its live performances—on a 2001 segment of *60 Minutes II*, he claimed, "They're the best live band I've ever seen, bar none." He realized that the homemade live tapes traded through underground taper networks had

One of the first Dave Matthews Band publicity photos released by RCA. *Author's collection*

helped build the Dead's audience in the '70s, and this was an infrastructure he was determined to impose on his fledgling band because he was sure that it would develop lifelong fans of the group.

These two diverging elements—the traditional jam band career path, tempered by a sound that couldn't quite be called jam band—defined Dave Matthews Band, turning it into a group that was marketable to two distinct audiences: the hardcore, who would collect recordings of every performance; plus the fans who would show up simply because they were guaranteed a good time. It's this second group that helped Dave Matthews Band become such a significant band in '90s rock, because they helped DMB's albums sell in the millions, while also coughing up a few crossover hits. Through these sales, Dave Matthews Band became the act that brought jam bands into the American mainstream, opening doors for others to follow, while expanding the post-alternative world so it was no longer beholden to the dark, murky churn of grunge.

Consider the timing of the release of Dave Matthews Band's debut album, *Under the Table and Dreaming*, in September 1994. The record arrived just five months after Nirvana's front man, Kurt Cobain, committed suicide, bringing a violent end to a musician and band that changed the landscape of '90s rock. At the time of Cobain's death, Nirvana wasn't the biggest band in America—it had been eclipsed by Pearl Jam, a band that shared Seattle as a home city and many of the same influences—but remained the defining group in American rock, transforming the definition of success for underground rock while strangling metal in its crib. Such a tragic ending for such a major figure caused sorrowful shockwaves throughout rock and roll, leaving fans and musicians weary and ready for a restorative tonic, and the open-hearted music of Dave Matthews Band certainly provided that. Nominally a roots band but never oriented toward a particular earthy aesthetic, the group encompassed rock, jazz, folk, world-beat, and pop, often channeling all these styles into one loose-limbed song. If grunge looked inward, DMB looked outward, generating a positive vibe that didn't shun darkness—death is an undercurrent that runs throughout Matthews's songs—but felt as bright and messy as life itself.

By embracing so many sensibilities, Dave Matthews Band wound up attracting large audiences. Initially, those fans were college kids—the kind who had the time and enthusiasm to make a band their world, listening to nothing but DMB tapes and communicating with fellow travelers—but new listeners were attracted to the band's brightness and pop skills. The group was certainly aided by the heavy support of RCA, a major label that was in need of a superstar act in 1994 and got one with Dave Matthews Band. RCA worked *Under the Table and Dreaming* hard at both radio and MTV. "What Would You Say," the album's lead single, became an MTV "Buzz Clip" and helped the group gain a foothold across America, but Dave Matthews Band wound up conquering the United States the way it did its native Virginia, along with a good segment of the Eastern Seaboard: through the long, hard work of steady performing.

In the Beginning

Live performances are imprinted in the DNA of Dave Matthews Band, particularly as regards two of its founding members, drummer Carter Beauford and saxophonist LeRoi Moore. Both musicians were fixtures within the jazz scene of Charlottesville, Virginia, the town Dave Matthews made his home after emigrating from his native South Africa. Matthews often heard Moore play with the John D'Earth Quintet at Miller's Bar, where the fledgling singer/songwriter tended bar. At Miller's, the amateur actor Matthews slowly dipped his toe into the town's musical scene, striking up a friendship in 1987 with guitarist/songwriter Tim Reynolds—sometimes he'd jam with Reynolds's band TR3—and eventually starting to pen songs of his own.

Matthews started to write in earnest in 1990, building up a small but sturdy repertoire of songs. One of the reasons he began to compose music was the encouragement of his friend Ross Hoffman, a Charlottesville lawyer who looked at the bartender and saw some musical promise. Matthews later told Richard Harrington of the *Washington Post*, "I was not really sure what I was going to do. I didn't think of myself as much of a singer at all, but then it sort of became evident with what I was writing that there weren't a hell of a lot of people who were going to sing it. So I thought I might have to do it myself for it to go anywhere." Hoffman suggested polishing these songs by recording with other musicians; he also financed the recordings. Hoffman brought Beauford into the fold, and then Matthews brought in LeRoi.

At this point, Matthews told Harrington, he conceived the group as nothing more than a trio "with sort of a quiet, laid-back feel to it. A little funky, maybe, with elements of freedom in the music that would keep it lively for the players." Matthews, Beauford, and Moore started to jam on Dave's originals, and while their initial attempts were unsteady—in retrospect, the singer dubbed them "heinously bad," while Beauford told Charlie Rose "it was the worst thing I've ever heard in my life"—they eventually started to gel. Soon, they sought to expand the band. Upon the advice of John D'Earth, the trio recruited teenager Stefan Lessard, who was then playing bass in a student jazz band. In short order, keyboardist Peter Griesar—a coworker of Matthews's at Miller's—came aboard, and this lineup cut a full demo early in 1991, then made its debut on March 14, 1991, at Trax, a club that would soon become the epicenter of the Dave Matthews Band universe.

Fishing around for an appropriate moniker, the musicians settled on Dave Matthews Band. The name's origin is apocryphal: one legend claims LeRoi Moore called up a venue to book a show for "Dave Matthews" and the club merely added a "Band" to its ledger, while Matthews says Boyd Tinsley—a violinist who joined the group full-time in 1992—wrote "Dave Matthews Band" on a band flyer. Either way, the die had been cast: this group, so egalitarian in so many respects, would forever be seen as a front man and his supporting group.

Over the next year, regular gigs at Charlottesville club Eastern Standard and frat parties expanded to shows at Trax and the Flood Zone. Soon, the owner of the latter, Coran Capshaw, became the group's manager and began expanding its territory out to Richmond, Virginia. With the band poised to go national, Griesar bailed out on in March 1993; he was not replaced. Seven months later, the band self-released *Remember Two Things*, a hybrid of live and studio recordings that became a local hit. It helped widen the band's following, but so too did the live tapes recorded by fans at local gigs. These cassettes were spread far and wide, sometimes sent to college campuses on the other side of the country, acting as calling cards for Dave Matthews Band.

The Glory Years

Eventually, the concerts and fan chatter wound up attracting the attention of major labels, with the band deciding to sign with RCA Records. The group signed with the label on November 1, 1993—a move that coincided with the release of *Remember Two Things*. RCA teamed Dave Matthews Band with Steve Lillywhite—the producer of U2's landmark *War*, among many other classic college-rock albums of the '80s—and the band began recording its first major-label album in early 1994. *Under the Table and Dreaming* duly appeared in September of 1994 (only a few months after *Recently*, a live EP that was nominally independent), and received a heavy push from the label, which helped land "What Would You Say" and "Ants Marching" on radio and MTV. DMB—as the band was soon known on the internet message boards that brought its fervent fan community outside the East Coast—toured hard behind the album, laying the groundwork for the successful launch of its second album, 1996's *Crash*.

Crash is the album where Dave Matthews Band broke into the mainstream, thanks in part to its romantic pseudo–title track, "Crash into Me"—the group's first significant hit on the Adult Alternative airwaves. "So Much to Say" also made waves, earning the band a Grammy for "Best Rock Performance by a Duo or Group with Vocal." Along with industry acclaim and chart hits came sold-out concerts at increasingly larger venues. At this point, the live taping—a practice the band condoned and Capshaw heartily encouraged—started to spill over into unauthorized live bootlegs, so the group combated this practice by launching a series of official live albums, and those too became major hits, starting with 1997's double-disc *Live at Red Rocks 8.15.95*.

Dave Matthews Band seized upon its burgeoning popularity and elevated industry status with 1998's *Before These Crowded Streets*, a lengthy, expansive record that features cameos by fellow adult-alternative rock star Alanis Morissette, progressive bluegrass banjoist Béla Fleck, and the classical group the Kronos Quartet. Such diverse names indicate that DMB wasn't necessarily gunning for the charts with *Before These Crowded Streets*, but the album nevertheless became its first to debut at #1 on *Billboard*'s Top 200, starting a streak of seven chart-topping albums that ran until 2018's *Come Tomorrow*. Touring and a rapid series of live records—including *Live at Luther College*, the first of many concert albums featuring Matthews with his old friend and Miller's cohort, Tim Reynolds—followed, before the band started work on its fourth album in 2000. Building its own recording studio, Haunted Hallow, on a 140-acre estate just outside of Charlottesville, the group reconvened with producer Steve Lillywhite and began a long series of sessions that ultimately wound up collapsing before a new record was ever finished. These sessions were not done in secret. At the turn of the millennium, the internet was thriving; information was disseminated swiftly, so the band's legions of fans knew DMB was holed up working on a new record. When the album failed to materialize, the abandoned sessions quickly attained the

A promo shot of Dave Matthews Band dating from the mid-'90s. *Author's collection*

status of legend; the untitled record, dubbed *The Lillywhite Sessions* by fans—a fitting moniker, but one that rang slightly strange, considering the group's three previous albums were, in fact, sessions produced by Lillywhite—entered the rock lexicon of great lost albums.

Turbulence

Shaking off the failed sessions, Dave Matthews teamed with Glen Ballard, the Hollywood producer who had helped Alanis Morissette shape *Jagged Little Pill* into a juggernaut, to create a brand new group of songs. These tunes formed the core of *Everyday*, which appeared early in 2001. Containing "The Space Between"—a moody, mid-tempo anthem that became one of the group's biggest hits—the slick, precise *Everyday* caused consternation among DMB's core fans, which may be part of the reason those same fans so fervently embraced the bootlegged *The Lillywhite Sessions* when it leaked onto the internet a month after the release of the Ballard-produced album. To fans who believed the shiny *Everyday* represented a sellout, this bootleg was a tonic.

Dave Matthews Band responded quickly to the release of *The Lillywhite Sessions* by returning to the studio to create *Busted Stuff*, an album largely comprised of newly recorded versions of the shelved material. Appearing in 2002, the album served as a punctuation mark to this turbulent period in the band's life; after this, the group went on hiatus. Each member pursued a new creative outlet during this downtime. As the band's namesake and biggest star, Dave Matthews made the biggest waves. *Some Devil*, his first solo album, appeared in September 2003, and although Dave Matthews Band gave a free show in Central Park in the week of its release, he supported the record with a tour billed as Dave Matthews and Friends. *Some Devil* was successful enough to suggest a solo career was viable; it debuted high on the charts, and its first single, "Gravedigger," brought Matthews a Grammy for "Best Rock Performance Solo." Such accolades overshadowed Boyd Tinsley's *True Reflections*, which was released two months before *Some Devil*.

These solo ventures weren't the beginning of a breakup but a restorative hibernation presaging DMB's regrouping in 2004. The group toured the US throughout that year, then, as '04 drew to a close, returned to the studio to cut a new record with Mark Batson, a producer best known for making modern R&B hits with Alicia Keys and Seal. Released early in the summer of 2005, *Stand Up* did have a pair of big singles in "Dreamgirl"

A promotional postcard from 2003, depicting the DMB discography to date.
Author's collection

and "American Baby," but its glossy sound seemed like a continuation of *Everyday*; and, like that album, *Stand Up* wound up alienating segments of the group's hardcore, the fans who always longed for Dave Matthews Band albums to sound as loose and lively as the group's concerts.

Over the next few years, DMB relied on those very concerts as its primary work. Occasionally, Matthews would perform intimate duet shows with Tim Reynolds, but the group would spend the summer touring stadiums and amphitheaters throughout the US, slowly testing out new material. The group brought some of these tunes into the studio for another session with Batson, but they parted ways when the recordings sounded unsatisfactory to the band. Although it wasn't much commented upon at the time, this signaled larger problems within the band, whose members were having difficulty communicating with each other. Matthews told Charlie Rose in 2009 that Moore had told him, "You know, you have to lead this band, unless we're not going anywhere. I said, 'It's impossible to lead this group of people.' I sent everybody a letter, which is the opposite of being a leader, and said, 'I just can't handle it anymore.'"

Instead, the band reconvened at Haunted Hallow and began working with Rob Cavallo, a producer best known for his work with the neo-punk band Green Day. This was in the spring of 2008, when Tim Reynolds officially became a member of the band. The sessions got off to a good start but were derailed when LeRoi Moore suffered an ATV accident on June 30, 2008. Initially, Moore's prognosis suggested a full recovery was likely, but on August 19 he died from complications resulting from the accident. The surviving band members went ahead with a scheduled Los Angeles show that night and continued with the tour, stating that there was no better way to pay tribute to their departed friend. Moore's spirit flows through *Big Whiskey and the GrooGrux King*, the 2009 album named after their departed colleague.

Regrouping

Following *Big Whiskey and the GrooGrux King*, Dave Matthews Band eased into a period where it became an elder statesman of sorts—a group that could rest on its laurels. When the band's twentieth anniversary arrived in 2011, its members decided to pay respects by not staging a blowout. Rather, they decided to *not* tour for the first time in two decades, instead returning to action in a big way in 2012 with *Away from the World*, an album that reunited them with their initial producer, Steve Lillywhite. Released in the autumn of 2012, *Away from the World* became the group's sixth straight studio album to debut at #1 at the *Billboard* charts—a record no other American rock band can claim. But perhaps the truer testament to the group's enduring popularity is how, in the four years that followed—a timespan that brought it right up to its twenty-fifth anniversary in 2016—Dave Matthews Band could continue to sell out concerts throughout the US, all without a lick of new material. DMB would extend its streak of #1 albums with the 2018 release of *Come Tomorrow*, but these steady ticket sales prove that the group had become what it always wanted to be: a band that achieved and sustained success by its own rules.

2

Why I Am

Who Are the Members of Dave Matthews Band?

Like all rock groups, Dave Matthews Band is more than the sum of its parts—and certainly more than a singer/songwriter supported by anonymous backing musicians. Dave Matthews Band has a particular, idiosyncratic chemistry—a truism that holds for most great bands—but where many of these bands share a similar background—think of the Beatles and U2 growing up as childhood friends, or Pink Floyd and Radiohead meeting at school, not to mention the brotherly bonds of the Kinks and Oasis—Dave Matthews Band is comprised of members with wildly divergent backgrounds who all happened to converge in the college town of Charlottesville, Virginia, in the late '80s.

Of the five original members—guitarist/singer Dave Matthews, drummer Carter Beauford, bassist Stefan Lessard, saxophonist LeRoi Moore, and violinist Boyd Tinsley—only Beauford and Moore had a long history together. Both were fixtures in Charlottesville's jazz-fusion scene, playing together for many years before Matthews approached them to support him on a songwriting demo. Once this demo morphed into a full-time project, the trio brought in teen bass prodigy Stefan Lessard and violinist Boyd Tinsley—additions that broadened the group's appeal and musical range.

Lessard told David Fricke in 2002 that "we didn't grow up playing in the mud together," which is true. They didn't slog it out in garages; they were highly skilled musicians playing to receptive audiences. This odd dynamic is key to understanding Dave Matthews Band: this is a racially, demographically, and creatively diverse unit united by music. These are five distinct personalities that combine into a distinctive, unique joint personality—one where the different roots and sensibilities are all felt, but no one member is stronger than another.

At several points in its career, Dave Matthews Band has consisted of more than five members. A keyboardist called Peter Griesar played with the band in its early days, long before the band signed to a major label; and after Moore died in 2008 and was replaced by Jeff Coffin, the band expanded further to encompass longtime associate Tim Reynolds and trumpeter Rashawn Ross. Although these musicians were all official members of Dave Matthews Band, it's hard not to think of DMB as the five men who held tight during the tough times and found success against all odds. Because of this—a feeling that derives from the heart, not head—this section focuses on the core five, with the rest of the members chronicled later.

Another early publicity picture of Dave Matthews Band. *Author's collection*

Dave Matthews—guitar, vocals

As its singer, songwriter, and guitarist, Dave Matthews would've been the center of attention of Dave Matthews Band even if the band weren't named after him. Call it front-man syndrome: whoever stands in front of the microphone gets an inordinate share of attention. Still, the very presence of Matthews's name in the group's moniker suggests that DMB is a one-man show—a band created as mere support for the singer. There is a small grain of truth in this assumption. Matthews recruited musicians for the group that wound up being called Dave Matthews Band, drafting local players to help him commit his original songs to tape. But by the time this fledgling band adopted the appellation, the group had turned into a genuine collective—a loose-limbed, egalitarian organization where each member had an equal voice onstage.

This sensibility speaks volumes for the personality—musical or otherwise—of the group's front man. Dave Matthews doesn't seem like a natural-born leader. Quiet and casually handsome, he's happy to cede the spotlight to whichever of his bandmates is ready to take it. Early on, he didn't even play lead guitar on his own records, choosing instead to have Tim Reynolds—a local institution in the band's native Charlottesville, Virginia, and somebody who taught Dave a great deal about music—be the band's soloist. This reticence didn't go unnoticed. In a 1998 *Washington Post* profile, Richard Harrington wrote, "Matthews is so normal and down-to-earth, at times he seems almost bland. That's how he comes across in the band's videos, where he often appears laid-back, passive and somewhat indifferent." Harrington immediately acknowledged that behind that placid surface, something changes. "In concert, Matthews is famous for the crowd-pleasing patter known as "Davespeak." Offstage, he's known for his wacky humor, skillful impersonations and character bits served up in a smorgasbord of accents."

With these two observations, Harrington captured a key to Dave Matthews's appeal: behind a seemingly normal surface lies a complex character, one who is prone to both silliness and seriousness; a musician whose concerts extol joyous life, yet his compositions contain a dark undercurrent that suggests it all could slip away at a moment's notice. His music shifts along this spectrum, easing from celebration to meditation, sometimes sounding as fluid as water and sometimes as sculpted as carved wood. He's at ease with folk, rock, pop, and fusion—a hybrid that hints at his own backstory as a South African expatriate who might appreciate the American melting pot more than some of that country's native citizens.

Certainly, the racial divisions and legacy of apartheid of his homeland have deeply affected Dave Matthews. Dave told NPR's *All Things Considered* in 2012, "Being a white South African, I enjoyed the better things that that country gave to a small percentage of its population—but still having a mother who was so devoted for making sure that we knew that to be credited or discredited for something that you were born with, that you had the inability to change—whether it's the color of your skin or, you know, anything about you—was just the worst kind of crime."

This was a lesson he'd learn a little later, when he returned with his mother to his homeland. He was born there in Johannesburg, on January 9, 1967, to John and Valerie Matthews. Dave was the family's third child—there'd eventually be four siblings—and he spent his first two years in Johannesburg before his family immigrated to Yorktown Heights in New York's Westchester County. John, a research physicist by training, landed a job at IBM, and he worked there for five years before taking his family to Cambridge, England, when Dave was just seven years old. While at Cambridge, John continued to do pioneering work on the superconductor; his son would brag later that his father was "one of the granddaddies of the superconductor." Within a year, however, the family had returned to New York.

Hopscotching across the globe exposed Dave Matthews to a great variety of cultures at a formative age. He absorbed the music of the US and the UK, falling in love with the Jackson 5 and the Beatles before eventually gravitating to Bob Dylan when he was quite young. Apart from music, he also immersed himself in local culture, with the Quakers of upstate New York providing a profound spiritual education.

In Yorktown Heights, John Matthews was diagnosed with lung cancer; some have speculated that he contracted the disease through his handling of radioactive material. He died of the disease in 1977, and Valerie decided to bring her family back to their native Johannesburg. She made this move to be closer to a support system, but Dave Matthews already felt a deep connection to the United States of America, and in 1980, while still residing in South Africa, he became a US citizen. This didn't prevent him from bonding with South Africa, however, or from developing sharply critical views of a country still operating under the tenants of apartheid. As a teen, he rebelled against this system and also loved the country's indigenous music. He recalled those teenage years to NPR in 2012. "The guys who worked at my uncle's dairy, I'd sneak over there and drink with them and play music—and more than play, I'd listen to these guys play music. But that felt almost like a revolutionary act."

Such questioning of authority is the reason why Matthews once again departed South Africa upon his graduation from St. Stithians College in 1985. He had occasionally run afoul of the administration in this private school, but he bristled against the divisive South African government. Matthews's mother worked as an anti-apartheid activist and instilled a deep belief of pacifism in her children, so when Dave was obliged under South African law to join the military, he chose to leave the country instead.

Leaving South Africa at the age of nineteen, Dave returned to his adopted home of New York. He took a job in the same IBM research facility where his father once worked, and, after a short spell, he headed down to Charlottesville, Virginia—a city that became his home base, thanks to his family relocating from South Africa to the American South in 1986.

Dave enrolled at a community college and immersed himself in Charlottesville's vast creative scene, acting in plays while also reviving his interesting in performing music. Initially, he channeled his energies toward the stage. He appeared in productions at the Offstage Theatre and Live Arts Theater, receiving good notices for his costarring role in the September 1990 production of *Just Say No* at the former. When he wasn't acting, he played music. He had learned to play guitar at the age of nine, but he hadn't attempted performing until he started living in Charlottesville and began trying his hand at the city's many open-mic shows.

Matthews started a bartending job at Miller's, one of downtown Charlottesville's prime venues. There, he earned a reputation as a very generous pourer, but the lasting impact of his time at Miller's was how he ingratiated himself into the local music scene. He befriended Tim

Reynolds, a guitarist with a sizable following, and started sitting in with Tim's band TR3 in 1987. Dave played Tim some of his original tunes, and Reynolds encouraged Matthews to pursue songwriting. Dave seized on other musical opportunities as they arose, the biggest coming when local trumpeter John D'Earth composed a song called "Meaningful Love" for Dave and Dawn Thompson to sing at a 1989 production by the Miki Liszt Dance Company. Also in 1989, Matthews teamed up with fellow Miller's bartender Mark Roebuck to record the album that became known as Tribe of Heaven's *Imagine We Were*. An early version of the Matthews staple "The Song That Jane Likes" sat alongside five of Roebuck's originals, along with a cover of U2's "In God's Country"—an early indication of Matthews's affinity for emotional, arena-filling rock.

Tribe of Heaven, along with his other musical activities, lit a fire under Matthews. He spent the bulk of 1990 working on original material, encouraged by a new friend, Ross Hoffman. A lawyer with musical aspirations—he wrote songs himself and owned a recording studio—Hoffman pushed Dave to take his own music seriously. Dave would head over to Ross's warehouse apartment to test out tunes—Matthews would romanticize the pink building on South Street in a song called "Warehouse"—and soon Hoffman was encouraging the fledgling singer/songwriter to commit these songs to tape . . . and not just as homemade demos, but as full-bloodied recordings with a band. Around this time, Hoffman became Matthews's "personal manager"—a role he'd hold until the band's quick rise to fame in the mid-'90s.

Hoffman encouraged Matthews to go pro. He bankrolled the singer/songwriter's initial demos and provided editorial feedback on the tunes, helping to get Matthews's original songbook in place. Dave had quit his job at Miller's by the end of 1990, and early in 1991 he recruited players for his demo, setting his sights on drummer Carter Beauford and saxophonist LeRoi Moore. He had seen both play regularly at Miller's, usually with John D'Earth—he also remembered getting into drunken conversations with LeRoi—and he worked up the courage to ask the two accomplished players to accompany him. The initial sessions were rocky, but the musicians sensed a chemistry, so they jammed again, soon recruiting additional players. Stefan Lessard provided a needed anchor on bass, then violinist Boyd Tinsley was brought into the group to play on "Tripping Billies"; he'd become a full-time member in 1992.

During these early days of Dave Matthews Band—the days when the group had yet to earn a name—Dave continued to act, performing in local productions into the summer of 1991, including the musical *Speakeasy: The Rags of Ragtime*. Soon, though, the music started to overshadow the theater. The group made its debut performance in March 1991, and eventually earned the name Dave Matthews Band—some say it was LeRoi Moore's doing, some say it was the work of an unnamed club worker—and the group's star started to rise within the busy college town of Charlottesville.

At the Flood Zone, Dave Matthews Band earned the attention of the club's owner, Coran Capshaw, who soon took the group under his wing. The band signed with RCA/BMG on November 1, 1993. Before the group could record its major-label debut with Steve Lillywhite, however, personal tragedy struck Matthews. On January 27, 1994, his older sister, Anne, was murdered by her husband, who then committed suicide. Matthews performed with Tim Reynolds two days later, dedicating the concert at the Wetlands to her memory, and the group's major-label debut, *Under the Table and Dreaming*, was also dedicated to her. Dave and his sister Jane took responsibility for the raising of Anne's two children. It was a major trauma that was overshadowed by the success that came soon afterward. Years later, on a 2009 episode of *CBS Sunday Morning*, he admitted, "I don't know if I've dealt with my father's death. I should probably talk to an analyst. Or my sister's death, probably."

In the wake of this loss, Matthews dedicated himself to the creation of *Under the Table and Dreaming*, which saw release in September of 1994. RCA put a lot of money into the record, and Dave Matthews Band worked the album hard, touring regularly, appearing on TV, and generally accepting any promotional appearance that came its way. The next few years were heady: *Under the Table and Dreaming* turned into a steady seller; its 1996 sequel, *Crash*, performed even better on the charts; and, as the band's profile rose, Matthews's star shone brighter than the rest.

During these hectic years of the late '90s, Dave Matthews Band occupied much of Dave Matthews's time, but he maintained his steady relationship with his longtime girlfriend, Jennifer Ashley Harper. The pair married in 2000 and had twin daughters in 2001, followed by a son in 2007, and wound up raising their family in Seattle, Washington. Around this time, Matthews started to branch away from DMB. Like so many of its jam band peers, Dave Matthews Band thrived on collaboration, letting musicians share its stage and often returning the favor. Dave started moonlighting on record in 1998, appearing on Béla Fleck's 1998 album *Left of Cool*, then Santana's 1999 blockbuster *Supernatural*, on which he sings "Love of My Life." Over the next few years, such cameos became a regular thing: he duetted with Emmylou Harris on 2000's *Red Dirt Girl*, and fronted the Blue Man Group for "Sing Along" on *The Complex* in 2003. The latter arrived during a turbulent time for Dave Matthews Band, during which the group started to pursue solo projects following the bumpy birth of its own studio—an occasion commemorated by the scrapping of *The Lillywhite Sessions*.

Matthews didn't limit his extracurricular explorations of the early 2000s to music. In conjunction with craftsman William Johnson, he opened the Blenheim Vineyards in Charlottesville in 2000. Over the next decade and a half, the Vineyards earned a reputation as an eco-friendly sustainable winery, hosting events on its grounds and operating "Wine of the Month" clubs; Matthews would later expand the winery through a series of wines called the Dreaming Tree. Dave himself also contributed original artwork to the labels of Dreaming Tree wines, the first public flowering of his flair for illustration; later on, he'd draw the artwork for the DMB albums *Big Whiskey and the GrooGrux King* and *Away from the World*.

Charity, always an important element for Dave, started to take an increasingly large part of his time, too, and he'd return to it frequently, earning a role on the board of directors for Farm Aid, along with working with organizations promoting gay rights, voter registration, and environmental concerns. He also returned to acting in the early years of the 2000s, playing Will Coleman in a 2003 feature-film adaptation of *Where the Red Fern Grows*. As Dave Matthews Band ramped up to regular tours and records, Matthews didn't leave acting behind. Throughout the 2000s, he acted with some regularity, appearing often in Adam Sandler movies—he has bit parts in 2007's *I Now Pronounce You Chuck and Larry* and 2008's *You Don't Mess with the Zohan*; later, he had a larger role in 2011's

Just Go With It—and a lead in 2005's *Because of Winn-Dixie*. Even as the band returned to regular work, he continued to moonlight as an actor, co-starring with Sissy Spacek in 2008's *Lake City*, appearing in an acclaimed 2007 episode of the medical drama *House M.D.* called "Half Wit."

Despite all this activity, the biggest solo project Matthews undertook during Dave Matthews Band's informal hiatus was a solo album called *Some Devil*, which saw release in the autumn of 2003. Supported by "Gravedigger" and an accompanying tour billed as Dave Matthews and Friends—one of those friends was Phish guitarist Trey Anastasio—*Some Devil* was a considerable success, highlighted by "Gravedigger" winning a Grammy for "Best Rock Performance." Nevertheless, the album didn't prove to be the opening of a solo career: it was a one-shot, and although Dave would continue to jam with other musicians over the years—he, Jakob Dylan, Charlie Sexton, and Brady Blade formed a busman's holiday group call the Nauts in 2013, which didn't amount to

A postcard promoting the 2003 release of Dave Matthews' first solo album, *Some Devil*.
Author's collection

much of anything—he returned to DMB shortly afterward, and the group remained his main creative outlet, in addition to being one of the most popular bands in the United States.

Carter Beauford—drums

"I'm the principal songwriter, I'm singing things I came up with. But Carter was the one who spoke out that summer of *The Lillywhite Sessions* and said, 'We need to change.' I often choose not to speak my mind. I do that in every part of my life. That's my shortcoming. But if Carter says we need to talk, we talk." Dave Matthews said this to *Rolling Stone*'s David Fricke in 2002, just as Dave Matthews Band was attempting to right itself following the tumultuous *Lillywhite Sessions.* Matthews's comment reveals two important things: that drummer Carter Beauford isn't merely the musical anchor of the band, he's its creative lodestar; and that, just as importantly, the group's singer/songwriter is happy to publicly acknowledge him as such.

In a sense, this power differential is essential to the inherent structure of Dave Matthews Band. Matthews certainly provided the impetus to start the band: he had the songs, and he, encouraged by Ross Hoffman, recruited the players, choosing Beauford and LeRoi Moore because he was dazzled by their regular performances at Miller's, where he tended bar. At that point, *they* were the stars in Charlottesville, not he, and he always treated the two musicians with a sense of deference, as if he considered himself lucky to be sharing a stage with them.

Even more than Moore, Beauford was a fixture in his native Charlottesville, a drummer who left the local scene and came back, not with stardom or fortune but with an experience that was evident in his slyly versatile playing. When Dave Matthews sought out players to flesh out his quirky, original songs, Beauford provided a necessary anchor due to his fluid technique. Naturally ambidextrous, Beauford developed an idiosyncratic yet free-flowing style, rooted partially in his childhood misunderstanding of how his idol, Buddy Rich, arranged his drum kit. Watching Rich play on television, Beauford set up his kit to mirror

Buddy's, so wound up with the standard set reversed—an accident that helped develop his signature style.

Buddy Rich looms large in the life of Carter Beauford. According to family lore, he first fell in love with the drums at the age of three, when

Carter Beauford selling Pro-Mark drumsticks in a magazine advertisement from 2008.
Author's collection

his father dragged him to a Rich concert in lieu of leaving the child home with a babysitter. Rich's explosive style resonated with the toddler—not for nothing did the Muppets pattern Animal after Rich; he had an explosive, vigorous style that feels primal—and soon Carter was banging on everything, leading his father to purchase him a toy drum set.

Jazz never was far from Beauford's heart, which perhaps is appropriate, considering how his father was a jazz trumpeter. Roland and Anne Beauford had Carter Beauford on November 2, 1957, and throughout his childhood he was surrounded by music. Carter heard R&B and rock and roll on the radio, while his father tipped him to jazz greats, taking him to concerts and playing him old records. Around the age of three, Beauford started playing drums, which he taught himself. When he was nine, he played his first gig with musicians two and three times his age. Throughout his adolescence, he'd play with this local jazz combo while continuing to devo ur music, gaining an understanding of jazz drumming from several different angles. Upon graduating high school, he went on to enroll at Shenandoah Conservatory in Winchester, Virginia, where he chose to pursue a degree in occupational therapy.

Upon graduating from college, Beauford taught school, flitting between elementary and high schools in Winchester and Winston-Salem. As he taught, he continued to perform music, playing wherever he could. He didn't limit himself to jazz; if there were a disco band in need of a drummer, he'd sit in with the group. After logging twelve years as a teacher, Beauford decided it was time to attempt a career as a professional musician, eventually gaining traction with Secrets, a fusion band based in Richmond, Virginia.

Within its nine-piece lineup were saxophonist LeRoi Moore and guitarist Tim Reynolds—both to become full-time members of Dave Matthews Band—along with DMB auxiliary keyboardist Butch Taylor and trumpeter John D'Earth, a fixture in the Virginia scene. Between 1984 and 1990, Secrets played up and down the eastern Seaboard, sometimes stopping in at Miller's in Charlottesville, releasing an eponymous album along the way. When they had time, Beauford and Moore moonlighted in a smaller combo called Blue Indigo, but Carter scored a coup by earning a supporting slot on the television show *BET on Jazz*, a show starring Ramsey Lewis that filmed in Washington, D.C. This gig allowed Beauford to play with a variety of major jazz stars, including Roy Hargrove and Larry Coryell, but after four years, the show ground to a halt. Beauford then headed out to Los Angeles, where he unsuccessfully auditioned for a spot in the band on *The Arsenio Hall Show*. In January 1991, after he didn't get that gig, he went back to Charlottesville, where he began playing in pickup groups and eventually supporting Matthews on his original songwriting demo.

At this point, Beauford's history becomes intertwined with that of Dave Matthews Band. Carter continued to play with other acts—over the years, he'd show up on recordings by such friends of the band as Carlos Santana, John Popper, and Victor Wooten, not to mention future DMB trumpeter Rashawn Ross; he'd also appear on a Vertical Horizon session—but the popularity of DMB saw his drumming star rise. By the 2000s, Carter Beauford began to appear regularly in the pages of the percussion industry trade magazine *Modern Drummer*. He placed at the top of its Readers Poll in 2003—a move that coincided with the peak of the group's popularity—but his popularity wasn't limited to fellow drummers: in 2010, a *Rolling Stone* reader poll placed him tenth on a list of greatest drummers of all time. Such fame allowed him to release his own instructional video—cleverly titled *Under the Table and Drumming*—and, at one point, plans were in place for a Yamaha Signature snare drum; he performed with a prototype, but the drum never materialized, nor did much come of his expressed interest, in 2002, in scoring films. Instead, Beauford concentrated on Dave Matthews Band. He settled down with his second wife—he had two children in this marriage and a child from a previous one—and devoted himself to Dave Matthews Band, a group that allowed him to show the full range of his multifaceted talents.

LeRoi Moore—saxophone

In some ways, saxophonist LeRoi Moore could be considered the soul of Dave Matthews Band. When Matthews was seeking musicians to expand his fledgling songs, saxophonist Moore was first on his list due to his work in Secrets with drummer Carter Beauford. At that point, Moore was something of a Charlottesville lifer, seizing any opportunity to play in any number of jazz combos in Virginia. Once Moore joined the group that became Dave Matthews Band, he formed a deep, lasting bond with Dave. The two became close collaborators. They'd write together, and Moore would arrange Dave's tunes, making an indelible mark on Matthews's music—one that would be felt long after LeRoi's tragic death following an AVT accident in 2008. Moore may have passed, but his absence only underscored how much he had given to the world and to the band that made him famous.

One thing that all his friends and colleagues would agree upon is that LeRoi Moore never enjoyed the attention that came with fame. He was in it for the music, not the publicity—he even suffered from stage fright, which was one of the reasons he always wore sunglasses while performing onstage—and his love of music stretched back to his childhood. Born on September 7, 1961, in Durham, North Carolina, LeRoi Moore was raised in Virginia. He remembered music filling his household, and he picked up saxophone when he was thirteen, playing alto in his junior-high school band. Soon, he'd work his way through tenor and settle on baritone saxophone, around the time he struck up a friendship with his neighbor, Carter Beauford.

At this point, Moore primarily enjoyed soul and rock, but an instructor turned him on to jazz. After graduation, he attended James Madison

LeRoi Moore, as depicted in the liner notes to the 2006 compilation *The Best of What's Around*.
Author's collection

University, where he studied tenor saxophone—he also began playing soprano sax—but the clarion call of a professional career proved irresistible, so he dropped out of college and began playing with various combos in Virginia, ranging from the more traditional Charlottesville Swing Orchestra to the fusion of the John D'Earth Quintet. D'Earth's band, which also featured Beauford on drums and played Miller's every Thursday night in the late 1980s—which is why Moore was on Dave Matthews's radar when he looked to find instrumental support to flesh out his fledgling demos.

Matthews first got to know Moore at Miller's. The saxophonist would frequent the establishment, and the pair would sit at the bar and get into arguments—ones that often involved race and Dave's heritage as a white South African. Yet their friendship blossomed into a deep collaboration, and the open-ended nature of Dave Matthews Band also gave LeRoi the ability to play not just every variety of saxophone but also other reed instruments ranging from flutes to pennywhistles. In fact, Moore generally seemed creatively satiated by Dave Matthews Band. Where his bandmates often appeared on albums by other artists, he pretty much kept to himself. In 1996, just as DMB's star started to rise, he appeared on Soko's *In November Sunlight* and the eponymous record by Code Magenta—both local Virginia friends—and he later showed up on Hootie and the Blowfish's third album, 1998's *Musical Chairs*, but when everybody pursued their own projects in the early 2000s, Moore didn't. He only popped up on *Superfastgo*, the 2003 album by Peter Griesar, Dave Matthews Band's early keyboardist. Apart from that, the only other moonlighting he did was on Samantha Farrell's 2008 album *Luminous*, which he produced.

Instead of pursuing other creative avenues, Moore poured himself into Dave Matthews Band. He had found his creative home, so he wound up settling down in Charlottesville, purchasing a farm in the area. He had recently become engaged to Lisa Beane when tragedy struck. On June 30, 2008, Moore was riding in an ATV on his farm, checking the fence along the perimeter of his property. He accidentally steered into a ditch camouflaged by grass, sending his ATV upside down. It landed on Moore. A lung was punctured, several ribs were broken, and he was hospitalized. After a spell at University of Virginia, he relocated to his home in Los

Angeles to recuperate, but on August 19 he suffered a setback. He was rushed to the hospital but died that day; an autopsy later revealed the cause to be pneumonia.

Dave Matthews Band paid tribute to the saxophonist at a concert at Los Angeles's Staples Center that night. He was buried at Holly Memorial Gardens on August 27. His last show with the band, a concert given in Bristow, Virginia, on June 28, 2008, was released as *Live Trax, Vol. 14*.

Stefan Lessard—bass

The youngest member of Dave Matthews Band—there's a seventeen-year gap between him and drummer Carter Beauford—Stefan Lessard is a preternaturally gifted bassist who quickly learned the instrument he picked up for the first time at fourteen years old. Lessard had music in his blood. Both his parents were professional musicians. Ron, his father, earned a BA in music composition from Boston's Berklee College of Music and made a living playing bass. His mother, Janaki, scored a hit single in Spain when she was a teenager. The pair had Stefan in Anaheim, California, on June 4, 1974, and during the first two years of his life, the family ping-ponged between the East and West Coasts, alternating between California and Rhode Island. Ron graduating from Berklee in 1976, and the family continued its nomadic ways even after the birth of two sisters. His parents were attracted to holistic ways of life, which led to their eventually settling in Yogaville, an ashram located an hour away from Charlottesville, in 1984. Stefan was ten years old.

Through this all, Lessard absorbed all kinds of music, developing a taste for adventurous jazz-fusion and new wave alike. The family continued to bounce around the country, due largely to Ron's work; his contracts with various musical instrument companies pushed him to different markets. Three years in Richmond, Virginia, led to two years in Madison, Wisconsin, but in 1989 the family went back to Virginia, this time setting up shop in a mobile home in Charlottesville. Stefan enrolled in the private Tandem Friends School, where he studied jazz with bassist Peter Spaar and John D'Earth, the trumpeter who played with Carter Beauford and LeRoi Moore in Secrets. D'Earth was impressed by Lessard's talent and temperament: "Stefan is the youngest but he acts like a wise old man, an Obi Wan Kenobi," he recalls in Morgan Delancey's biography, *Step into the Light*. These two skills were what led D'Earth to recommend Lessard to Beauford, Moore, and Matthews—it probably also led to him getting the nickname "Fonzie" in the group, since he had an inherent sense of cool,

Stefan Lessard on the cover of the September 2005 issue of *Bass Player* magazine.
Author's collection

just like Henry Winkler's *Happy Days* character—knowing that the trio were seeking a sympathetic bassist.

The band recognized a kindred spirit but also realized that making Lessard a member of the group wouldn't necessarily be easy due to his young age. At the time he joined, Stefan Lessard was still in high school. The bassist was a mere sixteen years old, so the group often had to sneak him into clubs prior to gigs. As the band started to take off, Lessard dropped out of school following his junior year—he'd earn his GED in the summer of 1991—and although he attended the jazz studies program at Richmond's Virginia Commonwealth University, he dropped out after six weeks when Dave Matthews Band's popularity hit overdrive. Lessard recalled, "I remember I put a note on the head of the jazz department's door: 'I'm sorry I won't be able to go to school anymore here. I've decided to go play with the Dave Matthews Band. Thank you for everything you've done.' Tacked on the door. He was *furious*."

Although Lessard threw himself into a career with Dave Matthews Band, he also seized the opportunities that came his way as a member of an exceptionally popular rock-and-roll band. He frequently accepted offers to jam, both onstage and in the studio, appearing on Gov't Mule's 2001 album *The Deep End, Vol. 1* and Pete Kilpatrick Band's 2012 set *Heavy Fire*; he also made a heavy contribution to Devon Sproule's 2001 album *Long Sleeve Story*, and played bass on its 2000 predecessor, *Devon*. Onstage, he's sat in with several groups, but one of his most noteworthy excursions was playing with vocalist/guitarist Adam Gardner from Guster, vocalist/guitarist Ed Robertson of Barenaked Ladies, and drummer Eric Fawcett from Spymob under the name Yukon Kornelius, at a benefit concert at Vermont ski resort in January 2008; the band would occasionally reunite for similar gigs. Also in 2008, he composed original music for the 2008 IMAX movie *Grand Canyon Adventure: River at Risk*, a side project that arrived during a time when Lessard also had a significant internet presence. He cultivated a MySpace page called LowenDude and ran a blog at www.izstyle.com, and he also took the time to create video blogs for YouTube during Dave Matthews Band's 2007 tour of Europe.

Lessard's personal life saw its share of tragedy. He married girlfriend Josie Baucom in 1997; they had two children—including an infant daughter who died of SIDS in 1996—prior to divorcing in 2004. He married

Jaclyn Burton in 2005, and had three daughters with her. On November 29, 2007, his home in Albemarle County, Virginia, was burned down, with the bassist losing over two million dollars in property; he and his son from his first marriage, who were the only people at the house when the fire struck, both survived.

Following all the upheaval of the late 2000s, Lessard wound up concentrating primary on Dave Matthews Band in the 2010s, with the band touring on a regular basis throughout the decade.

Boyd Tinsley—violin

"A lot people thought Boyd Tinsley was Dave Matthews, because he was talking all the time," Carter Beauford told David Fricke in 2002, long after Dave Matthews Band had found success and its front man had learned how to front a group. Such effervescence came naturally to violinist Boyd Tinsley, the last of the core five to join Dave Matthews Band.

Like so many members of Dave Matthews Band, Boyd Tinsley came from a musical background. Born on May 16, 1964, in Charlottesville, Tinsley was raised in the same neighborhood as Carter Beauford and LeRoi Moore. Unlike the others, however, Tinsley, the son of a choir director, didn't spend much of his childhood enthralled with music, and he stumbled upon his instrument: when he signed up for an orchestra class in middle school, he thought he was going to learn guitar, but he was instead given a violin. The twelve-year-old stuck with the unexpected instrument, eventually developing his signature languid style.

Tinsley never was drawn toward fiddle, choosing instead to study classical violin while attending Charlottesville High School. He formed the Charlottesville–Albemarle Youth Orchestra as a teenager, and then moved over to studio classical music under the tutelage of conductor Isidor Saslav of the Baltimore Symphony Orchestra. Saslav suggested he move to Baltimore to pursue classical music, but the teenage Tinsley was struck by the fusion of jazz, rock, and blues, so he decided to pursue popular music.

Enrolling at the University of Virginia in 1982, Tinsley rushed Sigma Nu and then started to play in various jams and groups. This wasn't necessarily an easy transition. As a classical player, he didn't know how to improvise, so it took him time to develop his own signature style, which was based partially on listening to a lot of Jean-Luc Ponty and Papa Jon Creach—the two main rock violinists of the classic rock era—and also the legendary French jazz violinist Stéphane Grappelli.

Tinsley graduated from University of Virginia with a degree in history, but he continued to play music, eventually teaming with guitarist Harry Faulkner to form Down Boy Down, which expanded to feature bassist Brian Wagoner; by that point, Down Boy Down became the Boyd Tinsley Band, with the addition of drummer Andrew "Drex" Weaver. Matthews remembered seeing the Boyd Tinsley Band at a frat party and being blown away. Similarly, Tinsley remembers seeing the singer/songwriter tending bar at Miller's. "I remember playing with Down Boy Down at Miller's," he recalled to Delancey. "Dave was the bartender there, and he would serve me Cokes."

Boyd Tinsley as depicted in the liner notes to the 2006 compilation *The Best of What's Around.* *Author's collection*

Early in 1991, Matthews extended an invitation for Boyd to play on the Dave Matthews Band demo of "Tripping Billies." At this point, Tinsley had no intention of joining the band because the Boyd Tinsley Trio was doing quite well along the Eastern shoreline. He intended to simply add color to the demo. "Right away, I was blown away by the sound of the band, Dave's singing—because I'd never heard anybody sing like that—and also just the songs," Tinsley told *Billboard* in 2007. He began playing regularly with DMB, but he had yet to disband his own group. It wasn't until mid-1992 that he decided to abandon his own band and continue to play with Dave Matthews Band, sensing the latter act's star was on the rise.

Boyd Tinsley became an integral member of Dave Matthews Band, but he didn't abandon his own projects. He was the first of the group to put out a solo album, releasing *True Reflections* in 2003. Through a matter of timing and circumstance, Boyd Tinsley wound up being the first member of Dave Matthews Band to release a solo album, beating Dave's *Some Devil* by a matter of months. Released on RCA on June 17, 2003, *True Reflections* is anchored on its title song, a composition that dates back to the dawn of the '90s. In 1991, he brought the song to the band, which kept it in circulation throughout that decade, pushing it to the back bench around the time of *Before These Crowded Streets* but playing it often between 2000 and 2001. The song has some resonance for fans—a collection of fan fiction was titled after it—but the striking thing about this album is how it's steeped in the thick, ragged rhythms of Neil Young and Crazy Horse, who are even covered here in the form of a nice version of "Cinnamon Girl."

The rest of the record is rather ramshackle—it ambles, it doesn't vamp or groove—and that alone is enough of a suggestion that Tinsley put his signature violin aside here, which he does. This gives *True Reflections* a distinct feel, quite separate from Dave Matthews Band. Its title track winds up being a funky and dramatic, gaining strength as it rolls along, and a muscularity can be heard throughout the album, even when it descends into swirling psychedelia and shaggy jangle-pop. All of this, too, is quite different from Dave Matthews Band—it's subdued, and very much indebted to Neil Young—but that's its charm: it's a vibe album, not a groove record, and its lackadaisical and ragged spirit is alluring.

Apart from this solo album, Tinsley regularly guested on albums by other musicians, playing on 1994 albums by both the Samples and

Allgood—he'd play on another Samples album, *Return to Earth*, in 2001—and on Hootie and the Blowfish's 1998 album *Musical Chairs*; he'd also play on Third Day's 2004 album *Wire*.

Boyd and his wife Emily had children in the late '90s—a daughter in 1996, a son in 1999—and they share a love of tennis, a sport he celebrated in a song called "The Ghosts of Wimbledon" for ESPN's 2006 broadcast of the annual sporting event. Tinsley also scored an endorsement deal with JanSport—additionally, he had deals with Tommy Hilfiger and Twix. Another notable side project of Tinsley's was *Faces in the Mirror*, a short film based upon an idea of the violinist; the movie debuted at the Woodstock Film Festival in 2012.

Tinsley remained in Dave Matthews Band until February 2, 2018, when the violinist announced via Twitter that he was taking a break to focus on his family and health. Three months later, James Frost-Winn—a trumpet player for Crystal Garden, a Seattle-based band Tinsley produced in 2017—filed a lawsuit against the violinist, accusing him of sexual misconduct. In wake of the lawsuit, Dave Matthews Band fired Boyd Tinsley on May 18, 2018.

3

I'll Back You Up

Latter-Day Members and Auxiliary Players

From its inception, Dave Matthews Band prized collaboration. Indeed, what drew Matthews to drummer Carter Beauford and saxophonist LeRoi Moore was their improvisatory skills—how the two bounced ideas off of each other—and that core trio not only created an open-ended, flexible sound, they were attracted to other players who shared their sensibility. Soon, they'd flesh out their group with bassist Stefan Lessard, and, eventually, violinist Boyd Tinsley, but before the latter joined DMB on a permanent basis, a few other players would cycle through the ranks. Peter Griesar played keyboards early on but dropped out just as the group was poised to go national. Guitarist Tim Reynolds, a fixture of the Charlottesville musical scene, played with Matthews and the band from the beginning, and he'd always be in the wings, playing lead guitar on its studio albums, teaming with Matthews for acoustic concerts, and, eventually, becoming an official member in the late 2000s.

Around the time Reynolds became a full-fledged member of Dave Matthews Band, the group expanded in several directions. In one sense, its hand was forced: Moore died in 2008, and the group needed a replacement, so hired Jeff Coffin. However tragic LeRoi's death may have been, it also allowed for the group to officially add trumpeter Rashawn Ross and keyboardist Butch Taylor to the lineup, the two musicians having touring regularly with the band for years.

Not every auxiliary musician wound up as part of DMB—the backing vocalists the Lovely Ladies only toured with the group during the '90s—but each played a significant role in helping Dave Matthews Band expand and grow.

Tim Reynolds—guitar

Tim Reynolds was not an original member of Dave Matthews Band, but he was there at the beginning, before there even *was* a Dave Matthews in Charlottesville. He was one of the regular musicians playing Miller's, the C'ville venue where Dave tended bar, and that is where the multi-instrumentalist—Reynolds's main instrument may be guitar, but he plays a variety of stringed instruments, percussion, and keyboards, too—met the fledgling songwriter and encouraged Dave to set out on his own as a performer.

While Reynolds declined an offer to join Dave Matthews Band at its inception, he nevertheless continued to play with Matthews. After DMB became a national act, Dave would often play acoustic concerts with Tim. And when Dave Matthews Band reconstituted itself in the wake of LeRoi Moore's death, Reynolds moved from the role of cherished associate to full-time band member—a position he always seemed destined to hold.

Reynolds was a military brat, born on December 15, 1957, on a base in Wiesbaden, Germany. He relocated frequently as a child, with his family moving first to Alaska, then Kansas, before settling in St. Louis, Missouri. Raised as a Christian, he first fell in love with inspirational music, and began taking piano lessons at the age of eight. The first secular music he heard and loved was the Beatles, the group providing an inspiration for him to gravitate toward guitar. He also learned bass, and played the instrument in a church band, but the pull of rock proved overwhelming. In 1981, once he'd finished high school, he relocated to Charlottesville, Virginia, and established himself as a formidable guitarist, gigging constantly in a variety of styles. He formed his own band, the Tim Reynolds Three—a moniker that was quickly shortened to TR3—in the mid-'80s, and that was his regular outfit when he first crossed paths with Dave Matthews at Miller's. At that point, he was a longtime associate of both Carter Beauford and LeRoi Moore—the childhood friends were a cornerstone of the Charlottesville community, beloved for their fluid, improvisatory style—and he encouraged Matthews to set out on his own.

Once Dave Matthews Band was established, Reynolds and Matthews began playing acoustic duet shows in 1993, sneaking a few of Tim's songs into the sets. These shows became a regular satellite venture for

Matthews; the pair launched their first full-scale tour in 1996, and, within three years, *Live at Luther College*—an album recorded at a concert in Iowa on February 6, 1996—became the second official Matthews-related live record. Its release elevated Reynolds's profile, and, appropriately, the guitarist now began to pursue a number of newly opened options. He disbanded the TR3 and headed out to Santa Fe, New Mexico, to try his luck as an acoustic guitarist. Between 1993 and 2010, he recorded nine full-length studio albums—many of which were available as downloads on his official website—and released two live albums. Throughout this time, he continued to play acoustic concerts with Matthews, and he'd also appear on studio albums by Dave Matthews Band.

A handbill designed by Mark Arminiski for a concert by Dave Matthews and Tim Reynolds in East Lansing, Michigan, in 1996. *Author's collection*

During DMB's rough patch at the start of the new millennium, Matthews and Reynolds's collaborations waned, but when Matthews released the solo *Some Devil* in 2003, he supported it with a tour called "Dave Matthews and Friends," where his duet set with Tim Reynolds was the opening act. Further joint tours followed in America and Europe, along with 2007's *Live at Radio City*.

Changes were afoot for Reynolds during the last few years of the 2000s. He moved back east, settling in North Carolina in 2007. There, he met bassist Mick Vaughn and drummer Dan Martier, hiring them to anchor a new incarnation of TR3. Over the next decade, this group would be an active performing and recording outfit, but Reynolds didn't limit himself to his trio. He participated in the recording of 2008's *Big Whiskey and the GrooGrux King*, marking his first time in the studio with Dave Matthews Band since 1998's *Before These Crowded Streets*. His role soon expanded onto the stage, too: he played with the band during the *Big Whiskey* tour, and then became an official member of Dave Matthews Band. It had taken him nearly twenty years to accept a full-time position.

Throughout the 2010s, Reynolds would split his time between DMB and TR3. Maintaining his residency in North Carolina, he also raised his daughter, Eura, born to his girlfriend, Diane Thomas, in 1995; he also has a son, Josef, born in 1982 to his first wife, Linna.

Peter Griesar—keyboards

In a sense, Peter Griesar could be called the Pete Best of Dave Matthews Band: a pivotal member from the early years who left just before the group hit the big time. But where Best was fired from the Beatles, Griesar decided to leave DMB voluntarily in 1993, preferring to operate on a much smaller scale than the rest of the band.

A native of Westchester County, New York, Griesar sang with his siblings in a musical group as a child. Eventually, he wound up taking piano lessons, and keyboards became his main instrument. During high school, he played keys in a band called the Yodells; then, after graduating, he enrolled in Charlottesville's University of Virginia. College didn't agree with him. After eighteen months, he dropped out. He took a job at Club Med—a gig that only lasted a few months—then returned to Charlottesville, where he promptly got a job as a waiter at Miller's. The two became friends, each pursuing music in their own fashion. Griesar used to host jam sessions at his apartment, and that was his avenue into playing music professionally. In 1990, he played in the Basics, a group that also featured saxophonist LeRoi Moore and guitarist Tim Reynolds, and he'd also step out with Matthews to perform duo sets at open-mic nights.

When Moore began playing alongside Matthews, Carter Beauford, and Stefan Lessard in the summer of 1990, Griesar started to sit in with the group. Over the next year, the group's local popularity started to rise—aided partially by the addition of violinist Boyd Tinsley—and, by 1992, it was clear that the group was poised for greater things. In 1993, the group was on the verge of recording its debut album, but Griesar chose to leave the band after a gig on March 23, 1993.

Why did Griesar leave? He's cited a couple reasons over the years, including an ailing mother and his general unease with the band's increasing popularity; he also claimed there was a "breakdown in communication" between himself and Matthews. He said he preferred the smaller stages—a claim that gained some credibility when he returned to music in 1995, playing in local outfits, including a collaboration with Lauren Hoffman, and, then, the Ninth, a group that also featured a moonlighting Lessard. Next up was Supertanker, a band formed in 1998, along with a solo album called *Disposable Love Songs*. Griesar ditched Supertanker at the turn of the millennium, although he wound up titling a solo EP *From the Supertanker Dude with the Zero Obsession*. Clearly, he had problem leaving the band behind, because he then formed a second incarnation, which fell apart quickly.

In 2002, Griesar released a solo album called *Superfastgo*, which featured cameos by Moore and Reynolds. As it arrived at the peak of Dave Matthews Band's popularity, it received a review in *Rolling Stone*, opening the door for a second album called *Candyshop* in 2003. In 2013, he was part of a team led by geneticist Dr. Spencer Wells attempting to purchase the brand of Antone's—the famed blues club in Austin, Texas—but the deal fell apart before they had a chance to establish a new residence. Griesar next moved into the restaurant business with Charles Newman, Dave Matthews Band's first manager, opening Brazos Tacos—an Austin-style taco emporium—in the downtown Charlottesville location known as IX in 2015.

Rashawn Ross—trumpet

The trumpeter Rashawn Ross joined Dave Matthews Band late—in 2006, to be precise, just after the release of *Stand Up*. He appeared on "Louisiana

Bayou," an album cut, and that opened the door to a fruitful collaboration that has lasted over a decade and counting.

Born January 16, 1979, in St. Thomas, US Virgin Islands, Rashawn Ross enrolled in Boston's Berklee College of Music in 1996, graduating from the school in 2000. He began inching his way into professional musicianship in 2003, sitting in on Ron Blake's *Lest We Forget* and joining Yerba Buena on that year's *President Alien*; he also appeared on the Beatnik's 2004 set *Milk Me*. In 2004, he joined the neo-soul/jazz trio Soulive as a supporting horn player, touring with the group steadily. This opened the door to other high-profile gigs, including an appearance on Talib Kweli's 2005 LP *Right About Now*, and guesting with Dave Matthews Band that same year. During the course of 2006, he continued to play with both Soulive and DMB, while taking other gigs such as guesting on Robert Randolph's *Colorblind*. Once he became a full-time touring member of Dave Matthews Band, his session work never stopped: in 2009 alone, he showed up on Uncle Kracker's *Happy Hour*, Chris Cornell's *Scream*, and Rick Ross's *Deeper Than Rap*. Whenever the band wasn't touring, Ross would go back to the studio, playing on trumpet on Robin Thicke's *Blurred Lines* album and Booker T. Jones's *Sound the Alarm* in 2013, and writing horn arrangements for Josh Groban's *All That Echoes* that same year. In 2015, he played flugelhorn on Lee Ritenour's *A Twist of Rit*.

Ross was billed as a touring member of Dave Matthews Band through 2009, but it appears he became a full-time member of the group in 2010. On DMB's next album, 2012's *Away from the World*, he is credited as a band member.

Butch Taylor—trumpet

Butch Taylor was never a formal member of Dave Matthews Band, but, in some circles, he functioned almost as the group's sixth member, touring and recording with DMB during the decade between 1998 and 2008.

Born April 13, 1961, in Shawsville, Virginia, Taylor went to college at James Madison University, which is where he first crossed paths with LeRoi Moore. The two were in the JMU Jazz Ensemble—Moore on sax, Taylor on trumpet. Taylor stayed in college, earning bachelors in English and a master's in music. He also gigged on the side, playing in a band called Secrets with Carter Beaufort and Tim Reynolds, and this background led to him entering DMB's orbit for 1998's *Before These Crowded Streets*. He stayed with the band until May 27, 2008, when he decided to leave the group and return to Charlottesville. There, he gigs on his own and with the Robert Jospé Trio, often playing at Miller's—sometimes with John D'Earth—bringing him back to the ground zero of Dave Matthews Band.

Jeff Coffin—saxophone

Saxophonist Jeff Coffin first came to national prominence as a member of Béla Fleck and the Flecktones, playing with the band from 1997 to 2010. He began playing with Dave Matthews Band in 2008, becoming a full-time member following the death of LeRoi Moore in 2009.

Born August 5, 1965, in Massachusetts, Coffin started playing the saxophone in fifth grade, beginning with the alto. He was living in Dexter, Maine—the band director was Arthur Lagassee—and he took quickly to the instrument, attending the University of New Hampshire's Summer Youth Music School for two summer terms in the '80s. He graduated from Spaulding High School in Rochester, New Hampshire, in 1983, and then spent two years at the University of New Hampshire before relocating to the University of North Texas, where he earned his BA in music education in 1990. Next, he earned a "Jazz Studies" grant from the National Endowment for the Arts. As part of his grant, he studied with saxophonist Joe Lovano.

Steady work and gigging followed—along with the 1997 album *Outside the Lines*, credited to the Jeff Coffin Ensemble—eventually leading to his spot in Béla Fleck and the Flecktones. He joined the band in March of 1997, first appearing on the 1998 album *Left of Cool*, and he stayed on for fourteen years, during which time the band won three Grammys: "Best Contemporary Jazz Album" for 2001's *Outbound* and 2007's *The Hidden Land*, and "Best Pop Instrumental Album" for 2009's *Jingle All the Way*.

During his downtime in the Flecktones, Coffin pursued his own projects. He made a solo album called *Commonality* in 1999, and in 2001 he formed the fusion group the Mu'tet—a band that he kept going while he was also part of DMB. The band's lineup mutated frequently, but in its various incarnations the Mu'tet released six albums between 2001 and 2012. Two of these, *Into the Air* and *Live!*, appeared on Ear Up, a label Coffin founded. He also played sessions with a variety of jazz and jam bands, and he's spent time teaching, appearing in colleges and universities around the world. Additionally, he authored an instructional book called *The Articulate Jazz Musician* with Caleb Chapman in 2013.

Coffin maintained this hectic pace as he joined Dave Matthews Band. He stepped in for LeRoi Moore after his 2008 ATV accident, and, once the saxophonist passed, Coffin became a full-time member. He finished the recording of *Big Whiskey and the GrooGrux King* in 2009. Following the release of *Big Whiskey*, Coffin became an official member of DMB; the first album to feature him in its entirety was 2012's *Away from the World*.

The Lovely Ladies

A trio of backing vocalists introduced on record on *Before These Crowded Streets* and a staple of tours in the late '90s and early 2000s—the tours before the slick sonic revision of *Everyday*—the Lovely Ladies were Tawatha Agee, Chinah Bess, and Brenda White King.

You and Me

Collaborators and Coconspirators

No band—no artist—gets to the top of the heap on its own. That's certainly the case with Dave Matthews Band. Throughout its career, Dave Matthews Band has had a series of significant behind-the-scene collaborators whose contributions helped turn DMB first into an experience and then into an institution.

Like all bands, DMB was helped considerably by the presence of savvy managers—first Ross Hoffman, who signed Dave Matthews to a personal contract, and then Coran Capshaw, who spearheaded Dave Matthews Band to superstardom. Although the two managers wound up having a series of serious conflicts, culminating in a contentious lawsuit, both were essential to the band's progress.

They were two of many crucial associates. Dave Matthews Band cultivated a loyal crew that stayed with the group throughout the years, helping to keep the DMB train rolling while also making their own mark on the group. Chief among them is Fenton Williams, the band's production and lighting designer who eventually graduated to video director; Jeff "Bagby" Thomas, who ran the band's sound and helped facilitate audience taping during the band's early years, was also pivotal. Outside of the road, there's Steve Lillywhite, the producer of the band's first three albums, and the man who probably had the largest impact on how the band sounded to a general audience and, therefore, had the greatest impact on the trajectory of its career.

All of these men occupied a different place in the DMB universe, but they shared one thing: without them, the trajectory of Dave Matthews Band would be quite different.

Ross Hoffman

It is arguable that without Ross Hoffman, there never would've been a Dave Matthews Band. Hoffman existed on the fringes of Charlottesville's musical scene, practicing law and encouraging local musicians, often setting up shop at Miller's, where he'd shoot the breeze with a bartender called Dave Matthews. Eventually, he learned that Matthews was a songwriter, and he pressed Matthews to pursue his dreams—and, more importantly, pushed him to join forces with Carter Beauford and LeRoi Moore.

To an extent, this qualifies Hoffman as the man who organized Dave Matthews Band, or at least the one whop provided the impetus toward Dave going pro. Matthews would later recall, "He was the guy who pushed me. He was the one who'd say, 'No, don't smoke that pot. Finish that verse. Finish that song.' He was my musical mentor, the guy who said, 'You should do this.'" Certainly, Hoffman recognized the musical talent within Matthews, but he also sensed an opportunity: there was a good possibility that Matthews might have the goods to make it beyond Charlottesville.

"Before then, I had only doodled around on the guitar and never finished a song until Ross encouraged me, steered me towards writing," Matthews is quoted as saying in Delancey's biography. Hoffman would bring Matthews over to his apartment in downtown Charlottesville's pink warehouse—Dave would later write a song about it, fittingly called "Warehouse"—and, after the songs took shape, Ross encouraged Dave to approach Carter Beauford and LeRoi Moore to make the demo. He also arranged the recording sessions and footed the bill.

Hoffman would continue to offer feedback and input on Dave's original songs, and he'd also seek out places for the fledgling group to play, effectively acting as the band's manager. However, technically he was Matthews's personal manager, a distinction that set him apart from the rest of Dave Matthews Band; he had Dave's interests in mind, not the group's. He also had his own interests in mind. With Dave as the principal songwriter and leader, he'd bring in more cash, and Hoffman would continue to take points on the group for a long, long time.

As Dave Matthews Band hit its popular stride in 1996, Matthews reflected upon this situation. "I was thinking about where I come from, and why I wrote songs and what was my inspiration. And how I was now in this situation where things that I'd done, I so loved, had now suddenly become a source of incredible pain for me. Suddenly there's all this money and people pulling, asking, 'Where's *mine*?' The wild dogs come out. The innocence of just wanting to make music was kinda overshadowed by the dark things that come along with money and success."

This statement from Matthews is somewhat disingenuous, because Hoffman was there from the beginning, helping to form Matthews's rough talents into something recognizable and sellable. Hoffman wasn't the one who got Dave Matthews Band to the big time, though. It was Coran Capshaw who truly knew how to market the group: how to adapt a grass-roots sensibility to the band's fluid fusion, and how to turn this college band from Virginia into a worldwide sensation. Once that major success came down the pike, there were long, intense arguments about how the money would be divided, and Hoffman came out on the losing end.

Things started to come to a head in 1992, just as the group's following was beginning to crest outside of its native Virginia. According to Delancey, there was some internal pressure within Dave Matthews Band regarding the fact that the group simply didn't have enough songs to fill a set list. There were two solutions to the problem: either the group would play more cover songs, or Matthews had to write more originals. Sensing that the latter option was the way to proceed, Matthews and Hoffman went on a retreat in the spring of 1992, coming back with several new songs. Relations between the two men quickly soured. Early in May 1992, Hoffman and Matthews agreed to sever their business alliance and, on May 13, 1992, Dave signed an agreement that gave Ross 7.5 percent of Matthews's songwriting earnings. This was deemed to be appropriate, considering that Hoffman was often functioning as a co-writer, or at least an editor, plus he was filing the copyrights on Matthews's songs.

Caught Between Two Managers

By this point, Coran Capshaw had taken on the role of being Dave Matthews's main manager, channeling his efforts toward finding live gigs for Dave Matthews Band and finessing the group's schedule. This agreement was formalized on February 3, 1993, when Matthews signed a deal with Capshaw that was negotiated by lawyer Chris Sabec. Hoffman remained onboard as Dave's "personal manager"; Hoffman was given 25 percent of Capshaw's gross, while the pair of managers began working together as Red Light Management. Later that year, Hoffman and Sabec would negotiate the contract Dave Matthews Band signed with BMG in October 1993.

Not long afterward, Hoffman encouraged Dave Matthews to start his own publishing company, instead of signing with an existing outfit. The two formed Colden Grey Ltd. on November 17, 1993, with Matthews serving as the president and lone shareholder of the company and Hoffman as its secretary/treasurer. Colden Grey Ltd. was designed to publish the first twenty-nine songs written by Matthews. On May 2, 1994—only a few months after its inception—Hoffman, Sabec, and businessman Stirling McIlwaine formed an additional company called Triune, which was to perform three distinct services. First, Triune was to collect worldwide royalties for Matthews songs; second, it was to administer copyrights for new Matthews songs; and, finally, it was to discover new outlets for Matthews music.

Triune claimed that it served Matthews free of charge between May 2, 1994, and January 10, 1995, "in order to demonstrate to Dave Matthews that it was fully capable of being his sole and exclusive administrator of music publishing worldwide." In effect, this period served as a transition time between Colden Grey and Triune, where the administration of copyrights moved from one company to another, but the sticking point was that there was no legal connection between the two companies, so Triune could not actually collect the money generated in overseas markets. Sabec claimed he had secured Matthews's approval during a two-day trip down the West Coast in December 1994, during which time he claimed Dave said not only that the deal was "jammin'" but also that Hoffman would always be the key man in regard to publishing.

The deal was made official late in January 1995, when Matthews signed an agreement formalizing the connection between Colden Grey and Triune during a dinner at McIlwaine's house that also was attended by Hoffman and Sabec. Additionally, Matthews signed a conflict-of-interest waiver, allowing Sabec to both function as his personal attorney and be a partner in Triune—a setup that would be deemed a conflict of interest if this waiver were not signed. Matthews allegedly claimed that Coran Capshaw need not be privy to these negotiations because he only managed the band's career and had no say in publishing.

Matthews changed his mind about Capshaw's involvement fairly swiftly after signing this deal. During the spring of 1995, Capshaw discovered the new deal instituting the connection between Colden Grey and Triune, and, within a few months, Matthews signed a further agreement demanding that all operations by Colden Grey/Triune be immediately transferred to Capshaw. Additionally, Sabec was released as attorney. That July, Capshaw hired a new set of attorneys to take over Colden Grey; Hoffman, Sabec, and McIlwaine all left the company.

On September 12, 1995, Hoffman filed a suit against Capshaw at Richmond Circuit Court. The suit claimed Capshaw had tried "to squeeze Hoffman's company out of a management and publishing deal," both of which were made with Matthews alone, not Dave Matthews Band. Hoffman and Triune were seeking "compensatory damages on account of Capshaw's conspiracy to injure Triune in its reputation, trade, business, or profession in an amount not less than $2,100,112.80," along with an additional two million for defamation of reputation, plus $2,100,000 in punitive damages. On October 6, 1995, Capshaw requested that Colden Grey and Matthews be named as codefendants in the case; the judge agreed on November 16, stating that the entire lawsuit hinged on a document Matthews had signed.

Not long after Matthews officially became part of the suit, he and Capshaw released a statement regarding the case. "Mr. Matthews acknowledges the valuable assistance that Ross Hoffman gave to his career. In return for this assistance, Mr. Hoffman has been paid handsomely and continues to receive ongoing compensation. Mr. Matthews regrets that Mr. Hoffman has chosen to bring this suit, as it is damaging to their friendship."

During November, Capshaw filed a request that Matthews's contracts with Triune be voided due to conflicts of interest. Triune responded with a countersuit, claiming a breach of contract on Capshaw's part. These two suits were part of the lead-up to a trial set for February 1996, just as Dave

Matthews was finishing up DMB's second album, *Crash*; before it could get that far, the two parties settled out of court in January 1996. Questions lingered about how much compensation Hoffman received. *Step into the Light* cites the "Matthews in the Middle" article by Fox: "By persuading Matthews to write songs and by helping line up members for the Band in 1991, Hoffman is widely considered to be the Band's creator. He is still receiving the 7.5 percent cut of publishing royalties that Matthews deeded to him in 1992."

Sabec headed to Los Angeles, as did Hoffman. The pair would later represent teen-pop sensation Hanson. Meanwhile, Matthews wrote the song "#41," which, by most accounts, is about the lawsuit filed by Ross Hoffman.

Coran Capshaw

If, as has been argued—vociferously by himself, among others—there would have been no Dave Matthews Band without the influence of Ross Hoffman, the group may never have been a success without the contributions of Coran Capshaw, the most pivotal member of the DMB organization who never set foot onstage. When Capshaw discovered Dave Matthews Band, he was an established figure in Charlottesville, Virginia, as the owner of Trax, one of the biggest nightclubs in the city. More than that, though, he had the business connections, plus he had the vision. As a Deadhead of long standing, he understood how his favorite band had built and maintained a following throughout the country: through long, hard touring, and live audience tapes traded back and forth by hardcore fans.

Capshaw used this model to help develop a dedicated fan base for Dave Matthews Band, but he was also uniquely positioned to help push the band toward the forefront. He had previously managed other bands from Charlottesville, including a group called Paris Match, which featured Shannon Worrell. He owned not just Trax but a venue in nearby Richmond called the Flood Zone, giving him two places to push his acts. Crucially, he was looking for a new band to manage, so when Dave Matthews Band crossed his radar, he was ready to strike.

Not that Capshaw was bowled over by Dave Matthews Band the first time he heard the group. "Not everybody gets this band when they first hear it," he told *C-Ville Weekly* in 1993. "I always thought it was good, and then at one show, I was just suddenly like, 'Hold on a second. This is important.'"

So important, Capshaw managed to set into motion a series of events that would soon find him replacing Charles Newman as Dave Matthews Band's main manager, and, ultimately, getting Matthews's patron and personal manager, Ross Hoffman, out of the picture as well. First off, Capshaw put DMB to work between his two main venues. The group played Trax on Tuesdays, then the Flood Zone on Wednesdays, building a sizable following within the two biggest cities in Virginia. The band would open for other acts on its way to establishing itself as a main draw, which was all according to Capshaw's plan. By early 1992, Dave Matthews Band was popular enough in Richmond to headline a regular gig at the Flood Zone—the first step toward establishing a larger regional foothold.

By this point, Capshaw started the next phase of his management plan: to capitalize on the taper culture instituted by Grateful Dead fans in order to spread the word of Dave Matthews Band beyond the East Coast. Tape trading began in the '70s as an outgrowth of the counterculture that arose around the Dead—the band somewhat accidentally fostered a whole separate economic ecosystem on the Shakedown Street that popped up in the parking lots before their gigs—but as the Dead turned into stadium-filling rock stars in the '80s, the band's appeal started to bleed into the frat houses that never would've bothered with hippies back in the '70s. This was Capshaw's target for Dave Matthews Band: he wanted to get DMB into frat houses, and then have the brothers spread the word far and wide.

Remarkably, Capshaw's plan worked almost precisely as envisioned. His past experience as a promoter and booking agent meant that he had an idea how the live music circuit worked, so he was able to take Dave Matthews Band further into the South, letting the band cut its teeth at frat houses before graduating to local theaters. Capshaw did all this prior to officially signing on as the band's manager. That milestone arrived on February 3, 1993—the opening salvo in a busy year for Dave Matthews Band. Capshaw signed a deal negotiated by lawyer Chris Sabec; Hoffman remained onboard as Dave's "personal manager," and was given 25 percent of Capshaw's gross, while the two began working together in a management company called Red Light Management.

That year, Capshaw hired Mindy Peskin—a longtime fan of Dave Matthews Band who went so far as to have DMB play her high-school graduation party at Trax—to help promote and organize events. Soon, this division became Bama Rags, which would in turn be DMB's merchandizing branch. Bama Rags became a powerful aspect of the Dave Matthews Band organization, responsible for the ongoing merchandizing operation and, later, fan-released live albums. From the outset, Bama Rags was designed to move heavy amounts of merchandise. The band issued a newsletter, also called Bama Rags, that updated fans about touring schedules and pushed merchandise; within the CD package for *Under the Table and Dreaming*, the group's major-label debut, there was an insert selling official DMB caps and T-shirts.

By the time Dave Matthews Band—through Hoffman and lawyer Chris Sabec—negotiated a deal with BMG/RCA in the fall of 1993, Capshaw had helped prove that the band was a low-risk gamble for the label, since the group was bringing a wide, dedicated fan base to the table. This was partially by Capshaw's design. He wasn't ready to have DMB beholden to any label; he wanted the group to succeed on its own terms. Perhaps this is the reason why a few deals fell through prior to the band's signing with BMG/RCA: he wanted to take the group to a label that considered it a valuable resource. BMG/RCA did, and the band inked a deal with the label on November 1, 1993. Capshaw smartly timed the announcement of the deal to coincide with the November 9 release of the independent *Remember Two Things*. to the outside observer, the long lines at Plan Nine Record Store appeared to play a role in securing the deal, when it was all a publicity stunt.

Early on, Capshaw stated, "This is an independent, self-running machine. If for some reason the record company falls off the earth tomorrow, this band will keep going without losing ground." He had some help in this regard, though. As DMB started to take off, he sold Trax and the Flood Zone, choosing instead to dedicate himself to managing the band. Early in 1994, he brought in Ambrosia Healy as Dave Matthews Band's publicist, a position she retains to this day. Later that year, he brought in a booking agency, Monterey Peninsula, so he could focus on the day-to-day management of DMB.

During 1995, a good portion of Capshaw's energy involved untangling the management lawsuits between Matthews and Hoffman's Triune company. Once everything was settled out of court, Capshaw became the sole manager of both Dave Matthews and Dave Matthews Band, not to mention the lone proprietor of Red Light Management. He quickly helped the band grow into one of the most popular concert attractions in the United States.

During the back half of the '90s, Capshaw also instigated action against the bootleg live CDs that were cluttering independent records stores at the time. He helped support legal action against the bootleggers, and he also decided to have DMB follow the Grateful Dead's model of regularly releasing official live albums, thereby undercutting the market for bootleg DMB CDs. Capshaw also expanded Red Light Management beyond Dave Matthews Band. One of his first signings was Agents of Good Roots; the organization would go on to manage Phish, Alabama Shake, Luke Bryan, and Chris Stapleton, among other acts.

In 2000, Capshaw and Matthews launched ATO Records—which stood for According to our Records—and made singer/songwriter David Gray their first signing. ATO Records proved to be another enduring success, boasting a diverse roster featuring such acclaimed acts as Drive-By Truckers, Brandi Carlile, Hurray for the Riff Raff, Okkervil River, Rhett Miller, Primus, Old Crow Medicine Show, and Dean Ween.

Steve Lillywhite

Steve Lillywhite is the most important musician involved with Dave Matthews Band who has never been a full-fledged member of Dave Matthews Band.

Lillywhite was born on March 15, 1955, in Surrey, England. He started as a tape operator at Polygram in 1972, recording demos during his off hours. One of these was a demo for the new-wave act Ultravox, which got the group signed to Island; Lillywhite, in turn, wound up with a role at the label as well. Working as Island's staff producer, he cut several pivotal punk and new-wave albums. One of his early successes was Johnny Thunders's 1978 solo debut, *So Alone*, but his first chart hit was Siouxsie and the Banshees' "Hong Kong Garden," which opened up the artier aspects of post-punk.

He further showcased this aural trickery on the eponymous 1980 debut by the Psychedelic Furs. That year was pivotal for Lillywhite, bringing the third eponymous album by Peter Gabriel—a lacerating, inventive work—and *Boy*, the bracing first album by U2. Lillywhite also produced *October* and *War*—records that established U2 as a major force in rock and roll.

Lillywhite continued to work with new wavers and practitioners of what the Brits called "new music"—he was instrumental in creating the full-throated roar of Big Country's 1983 debut, *The Crossing*—and all this led to him getting a plum gig with the giants of classic rock, the Rolling Stones. He helmed their much-misunderstood 1986 album *Dirty Work*, then pivoted back to his comfort zone of college-rock specialist. He worked with the Pogues on 1988's *If I Should Fall from Grace with God*, as well as *Naked*, the last album by Talking Heads; other notable productions included records by XTC and his then wife, Kirsty MacColl.

One of his key albums of this period was the lone album by the La's, a chiming, infectious collection of classic British guitar pop. The La's suggested Lillywhite was thoroughly British and, apart from Thunders and Talking Heads, he generally avoided working with American artists—and those that he did work with were rooted in either punk or art-rock. This meant that Dave Matthews Band—a group grounded in a distinctly American sensibility that underscored the country's "melting pot" ideals—was quite unusual for Lillywhite, but his keen artistic ear zeroed in on the elements that separated the group from its jam-band peers, particularly the elastic compositions and flexible interplay.

Lillywhite didn't abandon British music—in 1994, the same year he produced *Under the Table and Dreaming*, he worked with Morrissey on the very British *Vauxhall and I*—but he slowly incorporated American jam bands as part of his wheelhouse. He brought techniques he learned with DMB to his albums with Phish—the granddaddy of all jam bands—but his work with Dave Matthews Band represented a breakthrough in his music; plus it opened the gateway to working with other major commercial American artists, including Jason Mraz.

During the 2000s, Lillywhite split his time between producing and A&R. In 2002, he signed with Universal Music Group as a managing director; he stayed there for a few years, before moving to Columbia as Senior Vice President of A&R in September 2005, a role he held for a year. Some of his signings were hits—he brought Razorlight to Universal and MGMT to Columbia—but most of his noteworthy work was as a producer. During this period, he scored hits with U2—he did "Beautiful Day" from *All That You Can't Leave Behind*—and worked with Chris Cornell and Switchfoot. The 2010s brought records by Liam Gallagher's post-Oasis band Beady Eye, the Killers, a Grammy-winning set by Juanes, and, once again, Dave Matthews Band, with Lillywhite producing 2012's *Away from the World*.

Bruce Flohr

Bruce Flohr was the senior A&R development director for the California division of RCA who discovered and signed Dave Matthews Band in 1993. His process of discovery was a little streamlined. He found Dave Matthews Band through an intern named John Brody, who had brought a live tape of DMB into work. Flohr immediately contacted Peter Robinson, his East Coast equivalent, to rave about the band and discovered Robinson was planning to see Dave Matthews Band that night. These two developments helped usher DMB into a speedy signing with RCA.

Fenton Williams

Fenton Williams started out as the Dave Matthews Band's lighting designer, joining the organization in 1992. At that point, he doubled as the road manager, but it was through his lighting work that he became well known enough of a figure among DMB fans that the band could sell bumper stickers emblazoned with "Do It for Fenton" in 1999. Nobody can agree upon the precise origins of the phrase, but it's acknowledged to be some kind of inside joke.

In 2000, Williams began coordinating the group's video productions, in addition to designing the stage lighting, which paved the way for him directing videos, including collaborating with Matthews on Dave's 2007 solo single "Eh Hee." Around that time, he started to branch out from Dave Matthews Band, first working on Tim McGraw's 2011 tour and then joining with the Zac Brown Band for its 2011 and 2012 tours, plus directing the 2011 video for "Keep Me in Mind."

Jeff "Bagby" Thomas

Jeff "Bagby" Thomas was Dave Matthews Band's soundman from the start, operating the boards at Trax and then going on to work with the band for years. At the outset, he was better known among fans than Fenton Williams for one simple reason: he allowed fans to plug their recorders into the soundboard to get tapes of the show. Indeed, among tape traders, the term "Bagby" carried some weight, because a direct-from-the-board recording endorsed by Thomas superseded the recordings passed along as live bootlegs. The use of such phrases peaked at the end of the '90s; though taping still existed afterward, its role was diminished by the official live releases from DMB. But Bagby remained at the boards as the band's soundman.

Warehouse

The People and Places of Charlottesville and Richmond, Virginia

Without a doubt, the members of Dave Matthews Band are creatures of their surroundings. They absorbed all of the different sounds and styles of Charlottesville, building upon the musical legacy of the '80s and creating deep roots in the community—something that sustained the group throughout the years. Even though Matthews would later move to Seattle, and other members would have homes scattered across the country, they planted roots in Charlottesville early on, and they never left it: when they had a chance to build a studio, they chose a spot just outside of Charlottesville.

So what kept Dave Matthews Band tied to C'ville (and, to a lesser extent, Richmond)? Three of the band members are natives—Carter Beauford, LeRoi Moore, and Boyd Tinsley all grew up in the town—and that certainly had something to do with it, but Matthews and Stefan Lessard both claimed the city as their own, largely due to the vibrant artistic community that embraced them in the early '90s. This community encompassed Miller's, the downtown bar where Matthews worked, and Trax, where the group established a residency. Both venues would regularly feature performances by local musicians—Matthews first heard Beauford and Moore at Miller's—and that also encompassed jazz musician John D'Earth, a trumpeter who played with Carter and LeRoi and helped introduce DMB to Lessard.

Both the people and the places are what tie Dave Matthews Band to Charlottesville. It's possible to imagine the group existing at a different time at a different place, but, really, Charlottesville is in its blood and soul—something that's evident not just in DMB's music but in everything the band has done since.

Miller's

The epicenter of Dave Matthews Band is Miller's, a downtown bar where Dave used to serve as a bartender. It was here that he got to hear Beauford and Moore, which in itself is enough to push the bar into DMB lore. This means Miller's is often a destination for Dave Matthews Band fans, and they're invariably disappointed to discover that Miller's isn't a shrine to DMB. It's precisely what it claims it is: a simple, hometown bar, perhaps with a couple of mementos to Matthews—and John D'Earth still returns for the occasional set—but it hasn't been turned into a Matthews museum. It is what it should be: a basic bar with strong drinks and good burgers—the kind of thing that brings in both townies and college kids.

Trax

Trax is a pivotal place in the history of Dave Matthews Band, even if wasn't necessarily pivotal in the history of Charlottesville, Virginia. But it was something that every college town needed: a college bar to host local acts and touring bands.

Trax—so named because it was located close to the railroad tracks—sat close to the University of Virginia, on a property first built in the early 1930s on West Main Street. Between its construction then and the early '80s, it served several roles, as a National Guard armory, a boxing ring, and—fittingly enough for Dave Matthews Band—a warehouse.

Even though its roots as a warehouse didn't give the venue sterling acoustics, the property became a rock club with a capacity of nine hundred in the 1980s; the same building hosted a country club, too, with the nicely alliterative name of Max. By the end of the decade, a lot of college-rock bands came through Trax, including They Might Be Giants, Ziggy Marley, and Sonic Youth.

In the early '90s, Coran Capshaw was the venue's owner and manager—a role he served when Dave Matthews Band made its debut live appearance at Trax on March 14, 1991. Over the next three years, the band became a regular fixture, playing 123 gigs, almost all of them arriving on a Tuesday, culminating on April 29, 1996. This was the last time Dave Matthews Band played Trax, at a show celebrating the release of *Crash*.

By that point, Capshaw had left the running of the club to concentrate on managing Dave Matthews Band. The bar was called Crossroads for a spell—a reflection of how the place lost some direction in the years following Capshaw's departure. Even if it wasn't quite what it was in the early '90s, Trax nevertheless hosted a number of local bands—a few of which had ties to future *American Idol* star Chris Daughtry, who reportedly learned how to play guitar from Trax cook Matt Jagger—but the venue started to slide into hosting amateur wrestling by the end of the decade, and was eventually shuttered in 2001, when then-owner Dana Murphy sold it to Michael Duchesneau, who intended to re-open Trax but never did. On July 1, 2002, the University of Virginia purchased the property for $1.2 million, and in December of that year started to raze the

Dave Matthews Band as depicted in an early publicity photo from RCA. *Author's collection*

property with the intention of using the location for the expansion of the UVA hospital.

Warehouse

Located at the corner of South Street and 1st Street, the Pink Warehouse was where early Dave Matthews manager Ross Hoffman lived, not far away from Miller's. By the time Hoffman started renting a room in Warehouse, it had only recently opened for public use, and Matthews would often come by to hang and write. Later, Dave would immortalize the venue in the song "Warehouse," while the building became the location of the Dave Matthews Band's first paying concert, which was staged on the roof.

Today, the building is home to the South Street Brewery.

Flood Zone

What Trax was to Dave Matthews Band in Charlottesville, Virginia, so Flood Zone was in Richmond. Located on 18th Street in the Shock Bottom area of the city, Flood Zone first was constructed as a tobacco warehouse back in 1898, and it went through several incarnations before it turned into a multipurpose audio/visual space in 1986. In addition to recording and video studios, there was a performing space, which is where Dave Matthews Band performed regularly from 1992 until 1994, when it made the leap to majors.

Flood Zone stayed active a few years, until a concert by GWAR, during the course of which the costume front man Dave Brockie was wearing fell off; he didn't bother to cover up, so he ended up performing semi-naked. This was enough to cause Flood Zone to lose its liquor license—a death knell for any rock club. In the 2000s, the venue became a dance club called the Have a Nice Day Cafe. In this incarnation, it earned a reputation as a trouble spot, with at least one documented shooting at the location, which was generally seen as cultivating a clientele that was all too eager for trouble. Community pressure led to its closing early in the

2010s. It was put up on the market in 2013, finally earning the attention of developers in 2014.

Bizarrely enough, several years after the GWAR incident, a GWAR themed bar—appropriately called GWARBAR—opened near the Flood Zone location.

John D'Earth

A pivotal member of the Charlottesville jazz and fusion scene, trumpeter John D'Earth functioned as a fulcrum for many future members of Dave Matthews Band. He regularly played with drummer Carter Beauford and saxophonist LeRoi Moore, often at Miller's. Once Dave Matthews Band struck gold, D'Earth was brought back into the loop, playing on several recordings by the group.

Born in Holliston, Massachusetts, on March 30, 1950, D'Earth briefly attended Harvard but dropped out so he could eke out a living as a working musician. After playing with Bob Moses, he, drummer Robert Jospé, and singer Dawn Thompson formed Cosmology, and soon he settled in the Charlottesville area, taking a job as an instructor at the Tandem school. He stayed there between 1982 and 1985; he'd eventually become the Director of Jazz Performance at the University of Virginia. As well as teaching, he was regularly performing, usually at Miller's, sometimes with the band Secrets, and helping to lay the groundwork for the fluid, exploratory fusion of Dave Matthews Band.

Over the years, D'Earth has appeared on over one hundred albums, including records by Bruce Hornsby, Miles Davis and Quincy Jones, Buddy Rich, Pat Metheny, Joe Henderson, and Lionel Hampton. He's also arranged for DMB, Hornsby, and the Kronos Quartet.

The Deal

Every college town has its own flagship pop band. Charlottesville, Virginia, had the Deal, a group fronted by Mark Roebuck and Haines Fullerton and featuring Hugh Patton, Jim Jones, and Eric Schwartz. The

Deal was quintessentially of its time—a guitar group walking the fine line that separated the skinny ties of new wave and the underground jangle of power pop. This was Big Star by way of the Knack, combing the raw, nervy, Southern guitar grind of Alex Chilton's legendary unsung outfit with the big hooks and melodies that could've brought them into the charts.

The Deal never got anywhere close to the charts, however. The group stayed on the East Coast, playing the seaboard college circuit, but attracted positive noises, including being named as one of the "20 Best Unsigned Bands" by *Musician*, which was enough to earn the attention of Albert Grossman, a former manager of Bob Dylan who had his own Warner-distributed label called Bearsville—the label's biggest act was power pop prankster Todd Rundgren—and who seemed poised to bring the Deal to a larger audience. Before the Deal could make any major-label recordings, though, Grossman died of a heart attack on a transatlantic flight, which meant the group's entire recorded legacy amounted to sessions in local studios, from which enough material was amassed to be compiled onto a CD called *Goodbye September*, released in 2003 by the stalwart power-pop imprint Not Lame. *Goodbye September* is good power-pop, trebly and nervy, the fidelity betraying its local origins, but the songs are tight and urgent, the music seeming to point toward R.E.M. at its most garage.

It does not, however, much suggest Dave Matthews Band. Nevertheless, the Deal wound up being an important predecessor to DMB, because Mark Roebuck and Haines Fullerton stayed in Charlottesville after the Deal's split. Roebuck worked at a bar called the Eastern Standard—a place where several future members of Pavement, a '90s indie-rock band that was the musical and temperamental opposite of Dave Matthews Band, also worked—and he instituted an open-mic night there in hopes of drumming up local business. Matthews often played these gigs with keyboardist Peter Griesar.

Roebuck continued to offer encouragement to Matthews, and eventually the friendship turned into a collaboration. Mark had been working on some new songs and decided to invite Dave to help him flesh out these originals, but in an ironic turn of events, they wound up completing one of Matthews's unfinished songs instead. Together, they polished the words for the song that wound up as "The Song That Jane Likes"—the first composition that Matthews finished, and a song destined to become one of his most enduring tunes.

The collaboration between Roebuck and Matthews wasn't limited to these songwriting sessions. The pair attempted to work as a duo called Tribe of Heaven, recording a demo in 1989 that wound up as the album *Imagine We Were*. Although the record sat on the shelf for a decade and a half, it's a pivotal part in Matthews's legacy: this is where he started to learn how to write and record music.

Despite all this, Haines Fullerton may have been an even bigger influence on Dave Matthews than Roebuck. Fullerton also collaborated with Matthews—the pair wrote "#34," a tune included on 1994's *Under the Table and Dreaming*, together—but Fullerton also functioned as a cheerleader and champion, encouraging Matthews to pursue music and helping to sharpen his skills.

Fullerton did receive a boost from *Under the Table and Dreaming*, from which he pocketed some royalties, but by that point Haines had started to go down the path of a Christian cult. He went deep into the philosophy taught in *A Course of Miracles*, proselytizing his own skewed interpretation of the text. He attracted some followers but he alienated more friends; toward the end of his life, he told his old friend Roebuck that God was talking through him. On September 20, 1996, he purchased a handgun and shot himself at Ivy Gardens Apartments in Charlottesville.

Houston Ross

Ross is a bassist who played with Tim Reynolds, LeRoi Moore, and Peter Griesar in an early '90s band called the Basics. It was through this band that Griesar entered the circle that would eventually conjoin with Dave Matthews. Eventually, Ross joined forces with Michael Sokolowski as Soko, which initially featured LeRoi Moore before it became a duo. The pair later re-named themselves as Sokoband.

What You Are

DMB's Influences

Every band is, in some sense, the sum of its influences, but that axiom seems to ring truer in the case of Dave Matthews Band. Each member has different influences—something that's apparent in their own personal styles and collective sound—but DMB shares a few common influences that helped create the group's shared language. Much of the band's twisty, open-ended sound is due to how those different influences combine.

Some of the acts that made an impression are quite well known—it's hard to deny that Sting hiring Branford Marsalis paved the way for LeRoi Moore, or that Paul Simon's world-beat explorations first suggested the cultural crosspollination that is the DMB signature. Others are relatively obscure—the moodiness of Daniel Lanois, for example, is a clear antecedent to *Before These Crowded Streets.*

Looking at these influences as a group is revealing: adding them up, it's possible to get a sense of what matters most to Dave Matthews Band, and what made the group into what it is.

The Beatles

Any biography of Dave Matthews, no matter how small, mentions that, in his earliest years, he was a considerable fan of the Beatles. This is hardly unusual. Many millions of Gen-X'ers grew up with the Beatles as a fixture in their lives. The albums were in their parents' libraries, the music was heard on the radio, the songs were simply in the air—part of the fabric of life that never goes noticed but is only felt. Matthews also did something so many fledgling musicians do: he learned how to play by singing the Beatles' songs. By doing this, he started to intuit what made for a good song.

The Beatles themselves did this, too. One of the keys to their success was their omnivorous taste and ferocious thirst to be the first band in Liverpool to cover the new American rock-and-roll hits, so they bought stacks of 45s and learned how to play them all, absorbing the chord structures and melodic phrases. Matthews did this with the Fabs. He wound up covering a fair amount of Beatles tunes over the years, and would sometimes pick songs that were slightly left of center: "You Won't See Me," a track from 1965's *Rubber Soul*, popped up in set lists, and the hard-rocking "Hey Bulldog" was covered by Dave Matthews and Friends on the tour supporting *Some Devil*.

Bob Dylan

The fact of the matter is this: whether they like it or not, all modern singer/songwriters are influenced by Bob Dylan. Matthews's songs rarely bear the imprint of the Bard, but DMB turned "All Along the Watchtower" into a concert staple, basing its version on Jimi Hendrix's radical reworking. This is how Dylan worked his way into the Dave Matthews Band world, but Matthews has also found space for other Bob songs in his concerts, such as when he covered "Oh Sister" with Emmylou Harris in concert in 2003. "Oh Sister" dates from Dylan's mid-'70s, when Bob immersed himself in the carnival-esque Rolling Thunder Revue—a large, multi-piece group that extended his songs onstage. It was the closest that Dylan ever got to a jam band, and the songs he wrote for *Desire* are also big, winding, and open-ended—an ideal touchstone for the kind of song Dave Matthews Band plays in concert.

Sting

The clearest antecedent to Dave Matthews Band is Sting. Not that DMB ever sounded like the Police—perhaps there was a similar pop instinct and a fondness for reggae, but Dave Matthews Band had no apparent punk influences, nor any of the Police's overarching literary pretension. Yet the group certainly was influenced by Sting's solo work, which pairs moody original tunes with the limber, in-the-pocket funk of fusion professionals. This is the very template that Matthews would follow when he assembled his band, choosing jazz players to support his songs. While Dave's originals were considerably folkier than Sting's—even when armed with just an acoustic guitar or lute, Sting never trades upon confessional singer/songwriting, nor the impressionistic work of Dylan—his instincts were honed by *The Dream of the Blue Turtles* and *Nothing Like the Sun*, on which the British rock star expanded his worldview greatly, giving Branford Marsalis a space normally occupied by hot-shot guitar slingers and letting his band ride a slick groove to its limits.

Peter Gabriel

Whenever Dave Matthews murmurs over arid landscapes, he owes some kind of debt to Peter Gabriel. Once he left Genesis, Gabriel carved a niche that few other musicians could match: he was adventurous, embracing the music of different cultures but also the arty reserve of prog-rock, marrying this to heartfelt confessions that were nevertheless somewhat obtuse. Never the most direct of lyricists, Matthews picked up on this trend and also carried through on Gabriel's world-beat explorations: "Spoon," from *Before These Crowded Streets*, bears the influence of Gabriel's *Passion*. Strangely, this is not the sound that Dave Matthews Band chose to replicate when covering Gabriel in concert. Instead, the band chose his smash 1986 hit "Sledgehammer," a salute to Stax soul that seems like a party tune, but in its roundabout carnality also points toward Matthews's own sex songs.

Grateful Dead

Any group that could conceivably be called a jam band owes some debt to the Grateful Dead. Not only did the Dead create the sound that is often identified as "jam band"—a loose, improvisatory exploration of American roots music wherein the borders between folk, blues, country, and rock disintegrate—it accidentally created the career path for jam bands to

A badge promoting the Grateful Dead's three-night stand at the Sam Boyd Stadium in Whitney, Nevada, in May 1995, where the opening act was Dave Matthews Band.
Author's collection

follow, where records weren't as important to lasting success as marathon tours and the fan-created tapes that document these shows.

Contrary to popular belief, the Dead did have hit albums in the '70s—*Workingman's Dead*, *American Beauty*, and *Europe '72* all charted and sold well—but to the Jam Band Nation at large, these records were almost incidental to the community that formed around the band, the dedicated Deadheads that followed it from town to town, and the hardcore fans who taped concerts and then traded cassettes with other fanatics across the country. Such stuff seems standard now that it's so deeply ingrained into the DNA of jam bands, but back in the '70s, the Dead simply stumbled into this brave new world through its signature blend of nonchalance and passive aggression.

Dave Matthews himself never claimed the Dead as a primary influence, nor did anybody else in the band, and the music proves this point. Very little in the DMB catalogue owes any debt to the Dead's free-flowing, weird Americana. Despite the group's frequent collaborations with Béla Fleck, there is no discernible trace of a bluegrass influence. There is no country and little blues. Psychedelia is an afterthought—something learned secondhand and diluted, so it always feels earthbound, never a voyage out to a dark star. What folk lies in Dave Matthews Band—and there is quite a bit; this is a band led by a singer/songwriter who primarily plays an acoustic guitar—has its roots not in tradition but in post-Dylan explorations: the stuff that makes up the coffeehouse confessional and dorm-room strum-along.

The only tenuous musical connection comes via jazz and a sideways glance toward groove. The Dead hinted at jazz—bassist Phil Lesh embraced contemporary classical and always pushed the band toward the avant-garde—and the rhythm section of Bill Kreutzmann and Mickey Hart not only favored world-beat polyrhythms but also could adapt New Orleans funk into slick, slinky jams. Some of this latter tendency can be heard on "Eyes of the World," the only Dead tune Dave Matthews Band ever covered. With its heavy, neo-disco swing, it's a good fit for DMB, but its inclusion on a 1995 set list speaks not to any great love for the band but rather to a tip of the hat to Jerry Garcia, who left this earth on August 9 of that year, just two days before Dave Matthews Band played the song at the Greek Theater in Berkeley, California.

Despite this musical disconnect, it's impossible to imagine Dave Matthews Band's success without the precedent of the Grateful Dead for one simple reason: DMB manager Coran Capshaw was a huge Deadhead who spotted an opportunity to transfer the Dead's business structure over to an emerging band. Capshaw is the person in the DMB organization who realized how fan taping would spread the word of Dave Matthews Band far and wide; the person who realized constant gigging would help build the fan base; the person who wanted to make fans not of one album or song but of a band at large. Without these elements, Dave Matthews Band may not have risen as high or as quickly as it did. This wasn't a mere serendipity, either, where the group benefitted from a scene created by the Dead years ago: other bands in the '90s certainly did amble their way into a circuit that was already established, but Capshaw courted this market, not simply letting DMB fill the gaps but translating the Dead's business to a baby band—something that paid off not only in the early years, when word of mouth was at a premium, but also after the hits came. Capshaw helped DMB retain the rights to its merchandise, which brought in considerable income for the band, and he also helped transfer the fan tapes into a series of official bootlegs that mirrored the Dead's *Dick's Picks* archival series. Where the Dead dug deep into the vaults, Dave Matthews Band relied on the relatively recent past and wound up establishing a series called *Live Trax* that was nearly as comprehensive as the Dead's.

Phish also managed to adapt the Dead's infrastructure but wound up essentially following the blueprint closely, appealing primarily to the freaks who were already in the fold. Capshaw and Dave Matthews Band's innovation was to take this idea to the mainstream, bringing in people who never would've been caught dead—or in a tie-dye—at a Dead show.

Bruce Hornsby

Perhaps the biggest rock star to emerge from Virginia in the '80s, Bruce Hornsby straddled a line between heartland rock and jazz. His songs, particularly on his first two albums—both hits—were about the plight of the working class, but he didn't bother with simple, three-chord rock and roll. He was a lithe, fluid pianist, classically trained but molded by the weird Americana of the Grateful Dead. Recognizing a fellow traveler, the Dead hired Hornsby as a touring replacement for Brent Myland after he passed in 1990, and Bruce was one of the few outside members who ever stood up to that legendarily passive-aggressive unit; he had his own reputation at stake, after all.

So, Hornsby set something of a precedent for Dave Matthews Band, but their circles joined elsewhere. Hornsby hired John D'Earth for a spell in the 2000s, making the DMB connection plain, and they often toured in the same circuits, sometimes showing up on the same bills. In 1995, Bruce sat in with Dave Matthews Band for a performance of "All Along the Watchtower."

Daniel Lanois

Perhaps the most obscure act among Dave Matthews Band's influences, Daniel Lanois nevertheless is one of the biggest influences on Matthews—and not just for his celebrated productions for U2 and Bob Dylan. Instead, Matthews found sustenance in Lanois's 1989 debut, *Acadie*, cherry-picking "Still Water" and "The Maker" to cover—they showed up early in the band's career and were revisited frequently—and extrapolating its gorgeous, moody churn for *Before These Crowded Streets* and *Some Devil*. Whenever Matthews decides to get somber and serious, the specter of Daniel Lanois isn't far behind.

Little Feat

The Grateful Dead and the Allman Brothers may be the cornerstones of modern jam bands, but with its deft, dexterous rhythms, carefully sculpted songs, jazz bent, and integrated lineup, Little Feat is a closer antecedent to Dave Matthews Band than either. Dave Matthews underscored this point by singing the group's classic "Fat Man in the Bathtub" on 2008's star-studded *Join the Band*, and the song can't help but feel like a template for DMB: rhythm is at its core, and the song builds up around it. Often, the band interpolated "Dixie Chicken" at the tail end of "Crash," turning that bit of Southern-fried funk into something sweeter.

Bob Marley

For a long time, a Bob Marley poster was an obligatory dorm-room decoration, almost as if they were handed out upon the first day of registration. Marley, who never really had hits in the US, became an icon after his death—or a *Legend*, as the 1984 compilation called him. Curated by Dave Robinson, the maverick head of Stiff Records who helmed Island in the mid-'80s, *Legend* turned Marley from a rebel into a love-and-peace icon, singing songs about harmony and universality—ideas that flowed throughout his work but now turned him into a Rastafarian hippie.

This is the Bob Marley that influenced Dave Matthews. Reggae as a rhythm doesn't precisely pulse within his music—there are asides and breakdowns, but they're almost used as coloring—but the message that courses through *Legend* can be felt throughout Dave's work, whenever he's preaching for love, peace, and unity.

R.E.M.

R.E.M. was the greatest band to come out of the South in the '80s, so it's little surprise that the group had an impact on Dave Matthews Band, which at its core was a college band from the South. Usually, R.E.M.'s influence is seen in terms of indie-rock, but its jangle-pop—partially folk, partially garage—also made an impact on Dave Matthews the songwriter, especially lead singer Michael Stipe's airy, winding melodies. This can be heard clearly in the early track "The Song That Jane Likes."

Paul Simon

Perhaps it's a bit glib, or at least easy, to draw a direct line from the South Africa–born Dave Matthews to Paul Simon's landmark 1986 record *Graceland*, an album largely recorded in South Africa with South African musicians. To Charlie Rose in 1999, Matthews said that he thought *Graceland* was great, and that in the South Africa he knew, "The overwhelming consensus there among musicians that I met and that I've known was that he really opened the door to them, because there are these different styles of music that couldn't get across the ocean, there wasn't a chance."

Despite South Africa being his home country, Matthews isn't particularly musically influenced by Soweto rhythms: they can occasionally be heard on the fringes, but they never occupy center stage. Certainly, his home country shaped his politics and worldview—it's unavoidable, even when his exile to avoid armed service isn't taken into equation—but Paul Simon helped shape his music in a different way. Matthews wasn't attracted to the globetrotting, world-beat explorations—he was attracted to the songs.

Talking Heads

During the '80s, Talking Heads may have been the greatest example of how arty college kids could get funky. The group's nervy, herky-jerky dance-rock was introduced on their fourth album, *Remain in Light*, but was popularized on its 1983 sequel, *Speaking in Tongues*, which featured the hit single "Burning Down the House." Dave Matthews Band wound up covering "Burning Down the House" many years later—it entered live rotation in 2008—but even before that, DMB showed a debt to the Heads:

listen to the tight, nervous energy of "Too Much" and the connection becomes clear.

U2

U2 specialize in sonic soundscapes—the kind of music designed to fill an arena. Some of these sonics informed Dave Matthews Band, but so did the yearning spiritual quest that underpins many of U2's best songs. Early on, Matthews sang "In God's Country"—a pivotal track from 1987's *The Joshua Tree*—on the Tribe of Heaven record, a clear sign that U2's music provided a touchstone for the group.

Perhaps a bigger sign of Dave Matthews Band's debt to U2 is its collaboration with producer Steve Lillywhite. Lillywhite, the producer who would later become a pivotal collaborator with Dave Matthews Band, produced U2's first three albums. When he got to DMB, Lillywhite pursued a different sound, but he retained some of the widescreen spectacle he honed while working with U2.

Yellowjackets

When pressed about the connection to the Grateful Dead, Dave Matthews responded that he saw the band more like the Yellowjackets. It was not a hip reference by any means—the Yellowjackets were long seen as something of a joke by true jazzbos—but a revelatory one, because so much of DMB's sense of groove and improvisation does derive from the slick, accomplished fusion of the '80s—the kind of music the Yellowjackets so thoroughly embodied.

Neil Young

Another one of the classic '70s singer/songwriters, Neil Young wielded power and influence on the rock and roll of the '90s. On one hand, noise pioneers Sonic Youth found inspiration in his feedback-drenched solos—sensing a kindred spirit, he brought the group out as support on his *Ragged Glory* tour—and Pearl Jam adopted him as a godfather, cherishing his obstinate quirkiness, and even recording a full album (1995's *Mirror Ball*) with him. Dave Matthews, however, was generally drawn to the gentler side of Neil Young—not the country corn of *Harvest*, but the Laurel Canyon hippie who made *Everybody Knows This Is Nowhere*, or the rebel who found shelter on Zuma beach.

Early on, Matthews covered Neil songs—they're excellent choices for fledgling performers, as they're usually built around a G-C-D progression—and these simple songs provided the basis of Dave's early songwriting. Once DMB achieved success, the group would often choose Neil songs for live improv showcases, but the greater connection came when Neil Young brought the band at to play his annual Bridge School Benefit concerts. Soon, a connection was established, and Young sometimes sat in with the band, jamming on his originals "Down by the River" and "Cortez the Killer"—open-ended rockers designed for exploration, or at least epic guitar solos. In 2001, the bond between Young and Matthews was strengthened when Dave joined the Board of Directors for Farm Aid, the charity organization Young co-founded in 1985.

Dancing Nancies

What Is a Jam Band?

In a certain sense, the term "jam band" seems self-explanatory: simply put, it's a band that jams. Plenty of bands have improvised and grooved over the years, but a jam band has come to mean a band that emphasizes long, live improvisations over tight, controlled songs. It's a term that came into vogue in the early '90s, just around the time Dave Matthews Band came out of Virginia, but the aesthetic stretches back into the '60s and '70s, when the Grateful Dead turned bluegrass psychedelic.

While Dave Matthews Band didn't strictly sound like the Grateful Dead, it's nevertheless impossible to imagine DMB without the precedent of the Dead and the entire jam band scene that grew up around the group. That's what established the community that wound up supporting Dave Matthews Band through traded tapes and fans that thrived on hand-to-hand communication. After a certain point, Dave Matthews Band became so big that it didn't seem that it had any kind of grassroots support, but that scene remains at the foundation of its success, so it needs to be examined if we're to understand Dave Matthews Band.

Defining "Jam Band"

To an extent, every band jams. They spend time circling through chords and churning out solos, all in an attempt to figure out where to take their music. This isn't unusual. Long, improvised, rock-and-roll jam sessions date back to the late '60s, when a variety of blues- and jazz-inspired bands started to stretch out their songs, giving plenty of space for their members to play winding, intricate solos. Although certain British blues bands made a specialty of these jams—in particular, the Eric Clapton, Jack Bruce, and Ginger Baker supergroup, Cream, was known for long improvs onstage, stretching out some songs past ten minutes—this overdriven sound didn't provide a template for jam bands. Instead, the loose-limbed, spaced-out Americana of the Grateful Dead and the earthy boogie of the Allman Brothers Band proved pivotal for the sound and aesthetic of jam bands.

Formed by a pack of renegade Bay Area folk and blues musicians, the Dead wasn't a conventional rock-and-roll band: its members didn't hammer out three chords in a garage, they preferred picking bluegrass changes and old folk tunes. When they started ingesting psychedelics, their desire to experiment increased. Although these mind-warping expansions certainly were *fueled* by jams, these early explorations were grounded in the avant-garde; *Aoxomoxoa*, the group's third album, was constructed on electronic trickery. These late-'60s excursions were groundbreaking, but they didn't have much to do with the aesthetic that came to categorize jam bands. The actual *sound* that's come to be identified with jam bands coalesced in the early '70s, when the Dead returned to its roots for a pair of acoustic-anchored albums, *Workingman's Dead* and *American Beauty*. While the Dead didn't stick in this vein for long, this reconnection to Americana provided a sensibility from which the band could riff, opening songs up so they either soared or grooved.

Over on the other side of America, the Allman Brothers Band operated from a different vantage, rooting itself in jazz, country, and electric blues but cherishing the wide-open vistas of half-hour improvisations. Where the Dead's jazz inflections tended toward the cerebral, the Allmans aimed at the gut, riding the grooves so the soloists could find new territory.

The Dead and the Allmans were popular draws in the '70s, but the depth of their influence started to surface toward the end of the '80s, when a new generation of bands appeared. Raised on the Dead, these groups belonged to the generation that followed the band as it crisscrossed the country. They'd trade tapes of the experience, using these recordings as a template for their own wide-ranging, improvisatory rock and roll, emphasizing live experience over studio recordings. Bands like this could be found throughout the country, but they flourished along the East Coast, with the likes of Phish, Blues Traveler, and Dave Matthews Band all coming to prominence at the start of the '90s.

Birth of a Name

The term *jam band* didn't come into vogue until the late '90s, when the phrase entered the popular parlance and its use grew so widespread that its origins became obscured. The name had been kicking around for a while—it was an easy way to characterize a group of bands whose shared trait was a love of live improvisation—but Dean Rudnick codified it when he published *Jam Bands* in 1998. This was Rudnick's second book, following *The Phishing Manual*—a self-explanatory and early exploration of the roots and lore of Phish—by just two years, and this tome is a turning point in the genre, partially because the author accompanied the launch of the book with a website called www.jambands.com. Budnick led a drive to standardize "jam bands" as a single word—a phrase that was neatly tied into his website—but even if his 2003 edition of *Jambands* wound up eclipsing his 1998 volume, most publications continued to separate "jam" and "band" with a space.

Rudnick may have popularized the term—he has never claimed he invented it, and said as much in Peter Conners's 2013 *JAMerica*—but he was instrumental in having a scene coalesce around this name and sound, offering support through the website and accompanying tours, beginning with a 1999 jaunt featuring such third-wave jam outfits as the Disco Biscuits and the Slip. A year later, Rudnick and Peter Shapiro—the owner of the pivotal New York club Wetlands—launched the Jammys, an awards organization dedicated to spotlighting the very best bands in the scene.

Whenever there are awards involved—even self-aware, vaguely tongue-in-cheek awards like the Jammys—it's a signal that a counterculture has turned into an institution, and now has the desire not to only define but to enshrine itself. Such is the case with the Jammys, through which the jam-band community wound up naming leaders and gobbling up history, retroactively claiming earlier superstars as their own and gobbling up any music that entered their ever-expanding orbit. On www.jambands.com, Sister Mary Carmen published an essay claiming that any artist a jam band covers is, in effect, a jam band—an overreach that diminishes the eclecticism at the core of the best jam bands, while also misreading the source material. A jam band may draw from many sources—several of those sources are familiar within their own specific circle, such as country, funk, bluegrass, and blues; several might be slightly surprising—but what makes a jam band a jam band is how it stitches together these influences and ideas. It's not merely about improvisation. There is an elasticity to the performances of jam bands—

A handbill promoting Dave Matthews Band's August 23, 2004 show at Albuquerque, New Mexico's Journal Pavilion. *Author's collection*

something that stretches at the ideas of genres or styles, and sometimes pushes at the notion of what constitutes a song—and the end result is music that exists within the moment, while also transcending it. It is about a perpetual now.

This may be the shared vernacular of jam bands, but they, as a group, learned how to speak and how to act by listening to the Grateful Dead. Other rock bands of the '70s would stretch out and jam, taking cues from the heavy blues improv of Cream, but it's hard to call a twenty-minute "Dazed and Confused" by Led Zeppelin a root in jam band; it is too heavy, too solipsistic to look outside of itself. The Allman Brothers Band certainly are an important part of jam band heritage—illustrating how barriers between blues, jazz, rock, country, and soul could be blurred or broken—but never created their own roving counterculture in the form of legions of disciples who roamed the great wilderness of America with nothing in mind but getting to the next gig.

The Grateful Dead, however, did.

The Dead stumbled through its own eccentricities, arriving at a passive-aggressive onstage truce where each member got to follow their own whim to create a sound greater than the whole. Generations of bands followed this lead—sometimes replicating the Dead's arrangements, sometimes taking cues from an individual era, performance, or even song—but the bigger influence is how the Dead created the jam-band counterculture out of nothing. Prior to the Dead, there was no nation of freaks hanging on every guitar note or polyrhythm, expecting transcendence from a three-hour concert. There were no regular summer tours of outdoor amphitheaters, no taper culture where hardcore fans traded homemade cassettes of local concerts. Fans didn't hang out in the parking lot for hours before the show, reveling in a shared love of music that spilled out into a shared love of a softer, gentler life—the mellowing of hippie culture into something sustainable.

The Dead created all of this, and, while actively touring through the '70s and into the mid-'80s, the group sustained the culture while remaining essentially self-sufficient. When the Dead rolled into town, that's all that the local freaks needed: they lived for that show, or perhaps packed up their things and followed the band around town. All this countercultural popularity peaked in 1987, goosed along by the Dead releasing the slick *In the Dark*, a record so accomplished and shiny it achieved what was previously unthinkable: a Top 10 hit for the Grateful Dead, in the form of "Touch of Grey." Soon, Dead shows were overrun by newcomers—a situation the organization had difficulty navigating—but this new popularity also meant there were new ears ready for new bands playing in a similar aesthetic.

None of these bands were hopping onto a trend unleashed by "Touch of Grey." These were groups that were already jamming on songs by the Dead, Neil Young, Bob Marley, and Dylan around their own college campuses—musicians who already pledged allegiance to the ever-expanding notion of what it meant to jam.

These are the groups that formed the first wave of jam bands: Phish, Blues Traveler, Widespread Panic, the Spin Doctors; all groups that popped up on the first H.O.R.D.E. tour. Dave Matthews Band came later. DMB started playing in Charlottesville around 1990, just as the jam band movement began to gain momentum, and surfaced in the mainstream in 1994, two years after the Spin Doctors had already hit the Top 10 twice. In essence, DMB was part of the second wave of jam bands—bands that knew how to either sculpt their sound to appeal to a wider audience or played directly toward the cult. Despite their considerable jazz chops—Beauford and Moore both were essentially jazz players before teaming up with Matthews—its members could channel their proficiency into pop songs, and that's what made them stand apart from the crowd.

The Riff

Is Dave Matthews Band a Jam Band?

To most outside observers, the answer is clear: if Dave Matthews Band could be called any one thing, it's a jam band. If the group is known for anything, it's long live performances—the kind of shows that endeared DMB to millions of fans.

Any band that relies on concerts to build a fan base could reasonably be called a jam band, but Dave Matthews Band also had many other qualities that tagged it as a jam band, even if the term doesn't fit perfectly. There are many ways DMB departed from jam-band traditions, but these are the undeniable traits that forever identify the group as a jam band, so the answer to the question, "Is Dave Matthews Band a jam band?" is yes . . . and no.

How Is Dave Matthews Band a Jam Band?

Jam bands are united by a few commonalities. Usually, these are reduced to a desire to stretch out and play, resulting in long, winding performances onstage and on record, but this definition is a little too pat. Jam bands are united not by mere improvisation but by an attitude that stretches through their repertoire and outlook—an aesthetic that Dave Matthews Band adapted to its own ends.

Improvisation

In the common musician parlance, to improvise is to "jam." Even though the term "jamming" often brings to mind noodly guitar solos, not all jamming is the same. Certainly, a lot of jam bands favor lengthy solos, but jamming can also cover rhythmic vamping—grooves designed to get the audience jumping.

Although Dave Matthews Band is comprised of players who can take intricate, winding solos—this isn't merely reserved to violinist Boyd Tinsley or saxophonist LeRoi Moore; Tim Reynolds, the guitarist who became a full-time member in 2008, specializes in free-flowing six-string showcases—they often are drawn to jamming as a collective, to ride a groove for as long as twenty minutes. This bends the standard definition of what a jam band is, but how Dave Matthews Band embraces the adventure of rhythm is every bit as exploratory as the guitar-driven excursions of Phish.

Ever-Changing Repertoire

Any band that concentrates on live performance will find the need to change up its repertoire, and so is the case with Dave Matthews Band. There may be certain songs that remain staples in its set lists—it's difficult to imagine a summer going by without "Ants Marching," "Tripping Billies," or "All Along the Watchtower"—but part of the appeal of the group's concerts is how the order shifts, and how certain songs are retired, only to be brought back years later. Dave Matthews Band also isn't above teasing its audience by playing snippets of songs, getting fans revved up only to switch direction.

Most jam bands operate in a similar fashion because, for fans, part of the fun is listening for the unexpected twists and turns. That's especially true with DMB fans; some of the truly dedicated on www.dmbalmanac.com keep a "liberation list," noting the songs that haven't been played in years and then crossing them off the list once the band finally deigns to put them back in rotation.

Close-Knit Colleagues

Jam bands often form a community, and did so especially in the late '80s and early '90s, when the whole scene began to gel. These bands supported each other, placing their peers on a bill as an opening act, taking them out on tour, and often inviting other musicians to jam onstage. Dave

Matthews Band benefitted from this community from the very start, with acts like Phish, the Samples, and Blue Traveler hiring the group as an opener. Then, having earned some measure of success, DMB paid it forward, supporting new bands and bringing old friends onto stage.

DMB continued doing this even as its members became stars, supporting newer acts via the mini-festival Dave Matthews Band Caravan and always finding space for guest musicians, whether superstars like Neil Young or such fellow travelers as Warren Haynes.

Dedicated Fans

Where the Grateful Dead had Deadheads, Dave Matthews Band has a whole army of ants marching. The group's early fans in Charlottesville and Richmond helped spread the word of DMB in those formative days by getting in on the waning years of tape-to-tape trading. Dave Matthews Band, however, was fortunate enough to come of age during the rise of the internet. Its first fans may have traded tapes through the mail, but by the time *Under the Table and Dreaming* appeared in 1994, the internet had started to permeate college campuses, which is where many of DMB's fans resided. Soon, the fans ho had been trading tapes over the mail started e-mail groups and listservs dedicated to the band, helping to spread the word and also forming a tight-knit community from coast to coast. Dave Matthews Band wound up starting its own official website, too, but these message boards and fan communities arose out of the passion of the fans—a passion that has endured over the years.

Live Taping

The Grateful Dead pioneered the practice of audience members taping concerts. The Dead did so out of a combination of laziness and savvy, not wanting to deter the passion of fans who wanted a record of the event but also eventually realizing that a community of tape-traders did not slow the sales of either concert tickets or records. Slowly, a sea of amateur microphones plugged into the soundboard became a standard practice for jam bands. By the time Dave Matthews Band started to garner an audience in the early '90s, its newfound fans were eager to get shows down on tape, so DMB manager Coran Capshaw—himself a major Deadhead—opened up dedicated spaces for tapers. Although this practice would change over the years—particularly after the rise of CD bootlegs, which cut into the revenue of DMB while also diluting the market—live taping helped Dave Matthews Band build an audience in these crucial years, and has remained one of the group's strongest connections to the jam-band scene.

How Is Dave Matthews Band *Not* a Jam Band?

If Dave Matthews Band is a jam band in a number of important ways, there's also a reason why the group transcended that category and became one of the few jam bands to ever cross over. Chalk that up to sharp management, at least to an extent—Coran Capshaw understood how to build a grassroots following so big, it'd tip over into the mainstream—but it's also true that Dave Matthews Band had a quite different feel from its peers. The band's music was sunnier, hookier, and altogether brighter, offering good vibrations that would appeal to the less dedicated fan.

There are several reasons why the group had this feel—one that separated the band from the rest of its jam band brethren.

Instrumentation

Most jam bands boast a traditional rock-and-roll lineup: guitar, bass, voice, and drums, sometimes augmented by a keyboard player. Dave Matthews Band blows this convention out of the water. The band's lead singer/songwriter usually plays an acoustic guitar, not an electric—a move that automatically cuts down on the number of showboating solos—but his main melodic support arrives via saxophonist LeRoi Moore and violinist Boyd Tinsley, both of whom play instruments that are usually not heard in a conventional rock setting. When the band had to replace Moore following his tragic death, the remaining members didn't use the opportunity to revise their unusual dynamic. Instead, they hired saxophonist Jeff Coffin, then brought in trumpeter Rashawn Ross—moves that further underscored how Dave Matthews Band owed as much to jazz as it did rock. Even when bands raised on DMB started to appear in the new millennium, very few copied the group's instrumentation—which is odd, because the open-ended sonic vistas the unique combination of guitar, bass, drum, violin, saxophone, and trumpet offers remain bracingly original.

Focus on Singer/Songwriter

A few jam bands have been named after their lead singer, but by being fronted by a vocalist armed with an acoustic guitar, Dave Matthews Band gives the impression that it's led by a singer/songwriter. And, to an extent, this is true. Matthews will collaborate with the band at large, but he also is firmly within the vein of his idols Neil Young, Bob Dylan, and Paul Simon, sculpting songs that speak to both personal and political concerns. By being led by such a singer/songwriter, Dave Matthews Band is fundamentally different than Phish or even the Grateful Dead: no matter how much DMB may groove and jam, the song remains at the center of its music.

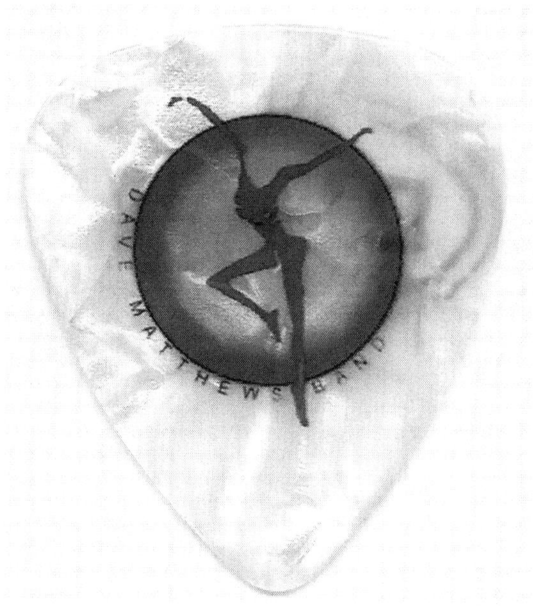

A guitar pick featuring Dave Matthews's illustration of the "Fire Dancer" that turned into the DMB logo.
Author's collection

Strict Arrangements

Related to the above point, Dave Matthews Band keeps the focus on the song. This doesn't mean that the band doesn't jam—its members rely on extended vamping, and will spin out lengthy solos, but they never turn the basic song inside out. Once they have a live arrangement, they stick with it, choosing to find variations within its existing contours. This means that DMB can tease songs at will because the entire audience understands what the songs sound like, but it also opens the band up to the criticism lodged by Dean Budnick in his scene bible, *Jambands*: "Nonetheless, any given DMB show most often retains a reasonably tight focus on the songs themselves, as presented by the euphonious voices of the five band members . . . . The DMB is not a jamband but a pop-rock band, and a fine one at that."

Such sentiment suggests that there isn't much love for Dave Matthews Band among the jam-band cognoscenti, and, to an extent, they're correct: Dave Matthews Band doesn't offer the same charms as a traditional jam band, eschewing such wildly exploratory improvisations because the members prefer to keep their concentration on the composition. This is neither bad nor good; it's just something that differentiates Dave Matthews Band from its peers.

Ease in the Studio

The old canard regarding the Grateful Dead was how the band never figured out how to feel as comfortable in the recording studio as it did onstage. This wasn't strictly true—apart from the big three of *Workingman's Dead*, *American Beauty*, and *In the Dark*, the Dead did indeed make other satisfying studio albums—but it was repeated often and then passed down to next-generation jam bands like Phish, who also were said not to be as good on record as they were onstage.

This maxim was never uttered about Dave Matthews Band, however. From the start, the band members were at ease in the studio, establishing a pattern that carried through their careers. Perhaps they simply had the good fortune of working with an excellent producer at the outset—Steve Lillywhite, the British producer responsible for classic '80s college-rock albums by U2, XTC, the Psychedelic Furs, and the La's—thereby making the group feel engaged in the studio, not alienated, but DMB embraced the possibilities of the studio more than any of its jam band contemporaries. Where many of its peers kept things relatively simple, Dave Matthews Band experimented with different textures, layered in sly studio effects, and would bring in guests to help broaden its sound. At times, this willingness to experiment brought the group onto rocky territory—when the group teamed with Alanis Morissette producer Glen Ballard for 2001's *Everyday*, the results were off-putting to longtime fans—but generally, this eagerness has been an asset to DMB, helping to differentiate between albums and concerts. Dave Matthews is on record as saying that he intended the albums to offer something different than the live shows—a canny attitude that also helps illustrate how this band never was afraid of the studio.

Hit Singles

Most jam bands eke out a living on the live circuit, playing clubs or theaters across the United States. Their fans know that the live experience is where it's at, and while that sentiment also certainly applies to Dave Matthews Band, the band's facility in the recording studio, along with Matthews's melodic sense, meant DMB scored something few Jam bands ever did: genuine crossover hits.

It took the Grateful Dead twenty years to climb the upper reaches of the *Billboard* charts, while just a few years prior to DMB's emergence, the Spin Doctors had a pair of fluke hits that almost seemed like novelties; by comparison, Dave Matthews Band wound up as a fixture on the pop charts throughout the '90s and into the 2000s. Where other jam bands had a hit or two, Dave Matthews Band became reliable hit-makers on the adult alternative radio charts—the place where "Crash into Me" reached the Top 10. The band would later cross over into the Top 40 with "The Space Between," which peaked at #22 in 2001, and "American Baby," which went to #16 in 2005, but by that point there was little doubt that the DMB was an adult-alternative rock fixture, with several recurrent hit singles to its name.

9

What Would You Say

Was Dave Matthews Band Ever "Alternative Rock"?

Dave Matthews Band released its first recordings—the independent *Remember Two Things* and the major-label 1994 album *Under the Table and Dreaming*—right in the thick of the alternative-rock boom of the '90s. Alternative rock was big on US college campuses, just as DMB was on the East Coast, and the first singles from *Under the Table* showed up on MTV's *Buzz Bin* in 1994. However, DMB wasn't quite part of the underground. The band was a flagship of an *alternative* alternative culture—one that saw the designation of "jam band" coalesce, thanks to labels like Aware and festivals like H.O.R.D.E. DMB was part of this, but there were other groups working in the same vein at the same time.

What Was Alternative Rock?

Every history of rock and roll, whether captured in a textbook or chronicled in an online listicle, agrees on one point regarding the '90s: at the dawn of the decade, a vast, Aqua Net'd wasteland of pop-metal was saved by the fury of Nirvana and grunge, after which alternative rock came crashing into the mainstream. It's a nice, tidy little theory that contains some gems of truth but distorts the picture, overstating the popularity of hair metal—Mötley Crüe may have been riding high with 1989's *Dr. Feelgood*, but the genre as a whole suffered a serious body blow with the rise of Guns N' Roses in 1987, their LA scuzz puncturing the frivolity of the Sunset Strip—and also how alternative rock began to break prior to Nirvana's *Nevermind*, with R.E.M.

reaching #1 in the spring of 1991 with *Out of Time*, and Metallica, a Bay Area outfit and by any measure an underground phenomenon whose aesthetics contradicted the hedonistic brethren in Southern California, also monopolizing the *Billboard* charts—developments that set the stage for Nirvana's crossover.

Once the band became stars, Nirvana attempted to share the wealth with its heroes and peers, riding for the Raincoats and the Melvins while adding underground bands as openers, but record execs also found a way to market this counterculture as mainstream, pushing for other Seattle bands and finding alt-rockers in other locales. Again, there was immediate precedence for this. A&M snatched up Soundgarden back in 1989, when Nirvana remained signed to Sub Pop, and also signed Mother Love Bone, the group that became Pearl Jam after lead singer Andrew Wood died. Also in the mix was Jane's Addiction, the Los Angeles quartet that straddled the line separating metal and punk, and whose leader, Perry Farrell, came up with the idea of the traveling bacchanal of Lollapalooza, partially inspired by the roving merrymakers in the Grateful Dead.

Jane's Addiction may have found inspiration in the Grateful Dead, but, in 1990, when *Ritual de lo habitual* came out, there was a clear line separating the band from Blues Traveler, the jam band that made its major-label debut that same year. They belonged to two different coasts, two different worlds, but neither belonged to the mainstream; these were two separate countercultures that would each wind up benefiting from the other during the course of the '90s.

Nirvana's success was the catalyst for this breakdown of barriers because Nirvana indicated that there was a large appetite for new rock and roll that wasn't based in metal. Spin Doctors lead singer Chris Barron recalls this situation clearly in the 2013 book *JAMerica*: Nirvana opened the doors for new club venues, giving jam bands places to play across America.

Really, the ripple effect spread far beyond venues, with radio, MTV, and the press—any arm of the music business at large, really—grouping any emerging, left-of-center band under the rubric of "alternative rock." Such trend-chasing is a time-honored tradition within rock and roll because it's not just where the money lies: grouping bands together helps everybody; it raises exposure, it gives audiences what they want, and it winds up increasing sales.

Jam Bands and Alternative Rock

So, jam bands began to sneak into the mainstream under the umbrella of alternative rock. But jam bands never showed up on *120 Minutes*, MTV's late-night program dedicated to underground rock; that playlist was indebted to English acts, post-punk, and major-label hard rock. However, there was room for jam bands on *Alternative Nation*, a show that began airing daily on MTV in 1992, just after the success of *Nevermind*, and a show that was designed to soften the rough edges of the underground. Simultaneously, the network began to push rock bands in its *Buzz Bin* clips, choosing acts that were poised to break.

Blues Traveler never made it onto these shows, and nor did the Spin Doctors. Led by the corpulent John Popper, Blues Traveler wasn't especially photogenic, but the Spin Doctors were, and had videos to match: "Little Miss Can't Be Wrong" and "Two Princes" were staples on MTV, carving out a front for jam bands. When Dave Matthews Band came along in 1994, it benefitted from all this groundwork. A system, constructed partially from underground rock and partially from nascent jam bands, had been constructed, and it was dubbed alternative rock—a system that could push bands into the mainstream thanks to radio play, MTV, gigs, festival, and press.

Dave Matthews Band worked both fronts, doing press with the expected college outlets—talking to newspapers in preparation for forthcoming gigs at a local bar—but also seeing "What Would You Say" and "Too Much" placed into MTV's *Buzz Bin*. The band's singles started showing up not on college radio, which still tended to be freeform and adventurous, but on major stations that were cultivating the beginnings of adult alternative rock, a format that developed right along with DMB and often relied on the band's new songs. Dave Matthews showed up on MTV's *Alternative Nation*, enduring the barbs of the show's host, Kennedy, and its records were often placed in alternative-rock bins.

How Dave Matthews Band Fit into Alternative Rock

All this means Dave Matthews Band was undoubtedly marketed as an alternative-rock band: RCA saw an opening for exposure and seized it, bringing the band to as many ears as it could. It's also true that DMB represented a specific kind of counterculture—that of the emerging jam band crossed partially with Southern college rock; it's not entirely a coincidence that early DMB reviews often referenced the enigmatic poetry of

A 1995 handbill that pairs Dave Matthews Band with that summer's Lollapalooza tour, proving that DMB was often seen as alternative rock during the mid-'90s.
Author's collection

A Mark Arminski–illustrated handbill promoting Dave Matthews Band's September 28, 1996 gig at Cleveland's Gund Arena. The opening act was Soul Coughing, who were a minor alt-rock sensation in '96. *Author's collection*

R.E.M.'s Michael Stipe, an inexact comparison that nevertheless is understandable—and the band was certainly part of the college vibe of the '90s. Yet, in retrospect, if Dave Matthews Band was indeed alternative rock, it's only because, for a few years in the mid-'90s, nearly every new American band was called alternative rock. Some of this is marketing, some of it is generational—all these bands had shared points of reference, ranging from influences to in-jokes—and when alternative rock encompasses grunge, post-grunge, jam bands, alt-hip-hop, trip-hop, and Britpop, it feels vibrant and wide, as if it were a true cultural movement. However, looking back, it seems that Dave Matthews Band wasn't precisely alternative rock. Apart from that tenuous R.E.M. connection—a bond reinforced by critics, not the band itself—DMB didn't have much to do with underground rock. DMB's points of reference were classic rockers who experienced a bit of a multicultural renaissance in the late '80s—*Graceland*-era Paul Simon, the expansive jazz-rock of Sting, a revived Neil Young—along with jazz-fusion. It was a sound that was alternative to the mainstream but not rooted in punk, garage, or indie-rock of any sense.

That said, it's easy to tie DMB to the beginnings of *adult* alternative rock. The group marshaled its various mainstream and offbeat influences into something that felt comfortable yet slightly left-of-center—something that could appeal to a wide audience without pandering to it. Certainly, this ability to blend comfort with quirk is one of the reasons Dave Matthews Band found such enormous and lasting popularity—its music seemed like a special secret to millions of fans—but is also why the group can't quite be called alternative rock. From the start, DMB wanted to appeal to as many listeners as possible . . . just as long as everybody rode the wave it created.

10

Tripping Billies

Fellow Travelers on the H.O.R.D.E. Circuit

Something that defines the jam band scene is the fellow travelers—the bands that played the same circuits, often sharing the same stage. These groups were crucial to the development of Dave Matthews Band. Not only would they place DMB on the same bill, they established a series of venues along the Eastern Seaboard, and, beyond that, helped establish that there was an audience for this music, along with venues to play it in. Because of this, it's difficult to appreciate Dave Matthews Band's story without also taking into account all of the bands that belonged to the jam-band community of the '90s.

Blues Traveler

If any one jam band could be said to have opened the doors for Dave Matthews Band, it would be Blues Traveler. As the first of its generation to sign to a major label, Blues Traveler was the driving force of the era-defining H.O.R.D.E. music festival, an event designed to live up to its acronym of "Horizons of Rock Developing Everywhere." Blues Traveler also carved out the jam-band circuit on the East Coast, and its presence on bills or records—such as leader John Popper lending a bit of hyperactive harp to "What Would You Say"—acted as an endorsement. Not that Blues Traveler ever exactly *sounded* like Dave Matthews Band.

While Blues Traveler never was the hard-bitten, rough-and-tumble outfit its name suggested, it did skew closer to barroom rock and roll than Dave Matthews Band did, lacking DMB's jazz foundation or fluid folk and fusion. Part of this reflects the band's very different hometowns. Where DMB is anchored in the free-flowing, experimental college town of Charlottesville, Blues Traveler formed in New York City, its core members, vocalist/harpist Popper and drummer Brendan Hill—both high-school bandmates from New Jersey—reuniting and joining forces with bassist Bobby Sheehan and guitarist Chan Kinchla roughly around 1987. Constant gigging around NYC spawned a second band called the Trucking Company, featuring their old high-school friend Chris Barron—a group that would soon spin off into the Spin Doctors. Once that happened, Popper and Hill—the pair moonlighting in the Trucking Company—rededicated themselves to their main gig, earning the attention of Patrick Clifford, an A&R executive at A&M. A management contract with Bill Graham soon followed, with Blues Traveller poised to become a breakthrough success.

A Bob Masse-designed handbill for Blues Traveler's concert at Commodore Ballroom, Vancouver, Canada, on December 2, 1995. *Author's collection*

The only thing is, it didn't happen. The band did well but did not have hits right out of the gate, and it's a testament not just to A&M but to the era that the group was given time to develop, to grow an audience and also a scene. *Travelers and Thieves*, the 1991 album that followed the eponymous debut by just over a year, opened up the band's audience, leading to a first spot on *The Late Show with David Letterman*, and, more importantly, establishing the group as popular enough that it could found its own alternative to the alternative festival juggernaut Lollapalooza. H.O.R.D.E. launched in 1992, and proved instrumental in defining the jam-band scene in America: it created the circuit and fostered a sense of brotherhood among the bands. A year later, H.O.R.D.E. provided Dave Matthews Band with a national forum for the first time, and John Popper soon would be playing on DMB's debut, *Under the Table and Dreaming*.

Blues Traveler may have opened up the door for DMB, but it can also be argued that the Virginia quintet returned the favor for the NYC group. *Under the Table and Dreaming* nudged open the pathway to mainstream radio success for jam bands, and Blues Traveler's *Four* followed right through, with its single, "Run-Around," turning into a smash in the spring of 1995.

Ties between the two camps remained strong over the next few years. At the tail end of the '90s, John Popper released a solo album called *Zygote*, which featured Carter Beauford on drums.

Spin Doctors

As cohorts of Blues Traveler—the band's lead singer, Chris Barron, was a high-school friend of John Popper from back in Princeton, New Jersey—the Spin Doctors were the first '90s jam band to show that there was a wide audience in America ready for fluid rhythms and bent, bluesy chords. Where Blues Traveler steadily grew a following the old fashioned way—through records and tours—Spin Doctors wound up taking off like a rocket when their 1991 debut, *A Pocket Full of Kryptonite*, spawned two huge hits in "Little Miss Can't Be Wrong" and "Two Princes." Such success wound up obscuring how deeply the band was rooted in jam-band culture, and that also proved to be the group's savior, once the records started to slide down the charts.

The roots of the Spin Doctors lay in the Trucking Company, a side gig for John Popper and guitarist Eric Schenkman. Barron joined the duo, and he stayed once Popper dedicated himself to Blues Traveler, leaving

Schenkman and Barron to recruit Mark White and Aaron Comess. This lineup was in place by the spring of 1989, when the group set out for constant gigging, often supporting Blues Traveler, eventually earning the attention of Epic Records in 1990. The label released a debut EP, *Up for Grabs . . . Live*, but this was a mere teaser for *Pocket Full of Kryptonite*, the full-length studio debut that arrived in August 1991. It didn't do much upon its initial release, but it received a significant boost after the Spin Doctors featured on the inaugural 1992 H.O.R.D.E. festival—a tour that set the stage for the album's commercial breakthrough, with "Little Miss Can't Be Wrong" turning into a crossover hit, earning play on MTV and college rock stations, then Top 40 radio, before being eclipsed by "Two Princes."

These hits opened the door for the commercial success of jam bands. The Grateful Dead waited twenty years to score its first Top 10 hit. The Spin Doctors not only had one right off the bat, but they showed labels, audiences, and artists alike that it was possible to go from jamming in clubs to the upper echelon of the charts, rubbing shoulders with classic rockers and grunge. The Spin Doctors didn't maintain that success. They slipped off the charts with their sophomore set, *Turn it Upside Down*, which appeared in the summer of 1994, just after *Under the Table and Dreaming* began its climb. It's too tidy to say Dave Matthews Band benefitted from the commercial underperformance of the Spin Doctors, because their appeal doesn't quite overlap. Where the Spin Doctors were essentially a party band—a group that picked up a torch from Steve Miller Band, playing to college crowds ready for a beer bash—Dave Matthews Band cuts a little deeper, musically and emotionally. Nevertheless, it's hard not to see the Spin Doctors as an important precedent for DMB: they showed that jam bands could be commercially viable.

Phish

In many ways, Phish could be seen as the opposite of the Spin Doctors. Hits were never in the cards for the Vermont quartet. Instead, Phish was in some respects the Grateful Dead of the '90s—a group so comfortable onstage that it struggled to translate its specific charms to the studio, while also cultivating a rabid fan base that would follow the band to every end of the country. In that respect, Phish was an important predecessor to Dave Matthews Band because it carved out a viable route for jam bands to follow. Hits were incidental to popularity; what counted was the freeform live show—something captured and traded on live tapes.

Of course, the Grateful Dead pioneered the field of tape trading, so it's fitting that in Phish's early incarnation, at the University of Vermont, the band specialized in covering the Dead. Trey Anastasio, Jeff Holdsworth, Mike Gordon, and Jon Fishman played their first gig on December 2, 1983. Percussionist Marc Daubert floated through the band in 1984, while Page McConnell became full-time member in 1985. Not long afterward, Holdsworth left the band, leaving it as a quartet in 1986, and, in this

A handbill promoting Phish's September 30, 1995 show at Shoreline Amphitheatre in Mountain View, California. *Author's collection*

incarnation, the members began recording tapes of original material, the resulting tapes circulating in Burlington, Vermont, as the group regularly gigged.

A pair of independent albums—*Junta* in 1988, *Lawn Boy* in 1990—appeared as the group's concerts grew steadily more eclectic and whimsical, each show containing a distinctive element that became prized by fans. Soon, these fans began trading live performances on Usenet newsgroups, an early internet service that debuted in 1991. A few years down the road, Dave Matthews Band would prompt similarly rabid trading, but Phish was one of the only new bands to appear on the service, thereby offering the first suggestion that the jam-band scene was about to break.

Elektra signed Phish to a major-label contract in 1991, about two years after Blues Traveler inked with A&M. *A Picture of Nectar* followed in February 1992, and Phish's appearance on the inaugural H.O.R.D.E. tour—where the band appeared alongside Blues Traveler, the Spin Doctors, and Widespread Panic—functioned as a supporting tour for the album. Despite this boost, *A Picture of Nectar* didn't sell much, yet the group graduated to amphitheaters in 1993—a move that coincided with the release of *Hoist*. Elektra poured money into *Hoist*, having the band film its only ever video for "Down with Disease" in 1994—the same year Dave Matthews Band released its debut, *Under the Table and Dreaming*.

Phish appeared poised for a crossover. Band like the Spin Doctors and, soon, Blues Traveler were having hits, and neither group had the kind of devoted fan Phish had, but the Vermont quartet had a selective appeal: you either got the band's wooly humor and free-flowing music or you didn't. There were no grey areas with Phish, whereas Dave Matthews Band could appeal to people in the middle. Some of this derived from Matthews's gifts as a songwriter—he could write love songs and jams that appealed to the masses—but the group as a whole was less eccentric than Phish; there's an open-heartedness to DMB that brought in the unconverted, while Phish celebrated its quirks.

Over the next two decades, the paths of both groups crossed frequently—sometimes they'd appear at the same festival; they'd guest on each other's records; Anastasio played an instrumental role on Matthews's 2003 solo album, *Some Devil*, and the accompanying Dave Matthews and Friends tour; and they shared a producer in Steve Lillywhite—but often it seemed like they were on parallel planes, the two bands illustrating the diversity of jam bands and the power of fans.

Widespread Panic

Of the crew featured on the original H.O.R.D.E. tour, Widespread Panic may have garnered the fewest headlines at the time. Blues Traveler organized the whole thing, Spin Doctors had the hits, and Phish had the cult, but Widespread Panic was a working band from Athens, Georgia—a Southern city whose best-known rock band was R.E.M., the quartet that epitomized the mystery and jangle of '80s college rock. Widespread Panic didn't trade in such enigmas. Inspired, like so many group of its ilk, by the Grateful Dead, Widespread Panic also had an allegiance to fellow Georgians the Allman Brothers Band, and, appropriately, had a stronger blues and rock influence apparent in its rhythms and improvisations. This wasn't a formula that led to big hits on either the singles or albums charts, but it did cultivate a following that stayed with the group for decades.

Such longevity was the furthest thing from the minds of guitarists John Bell and Michael Houser when they first jammed in 1981, as students at the University of Georgia. Their partnership quickly took off; the pair lived together and spent every spare moment writing. The first inklings of Widespread Panic came into view in 1985, when bassist Dave Schools sat in with them; Houser's childhood friend Todd Nance began drumming with the band in 1986. This gig was the first where the band called itself Widespread Panic.

Adding percussionist Domingo S. Ortiz, the group then continued to play through the Athens college circuit, signing with the indie Landslide Records in 1987. That fall, the band recorded its debut, *Space Wrangler*, at John Keane's studio. The album helped expand the band's reach west and attracted the attention of Capricorn Records—home of Widespread Panic's idols, the Allmans—to which the group signed in 1991, before releasing an eponymous album that fall. Adding keyboardist John Hermann, the group joined the H.O.R.D.E. tour in '92, elevating its profile and leading to two fairly heavily promoted records—1993's *Everyday*, 1994's *Ain't Life Grand*—that seemed to promise a crossover that never came.

Instead, the band settled into a hard-working circuit. It could pull enormous crowds in its hometown—some eighty thousand people showed up to a release party for *Light Fuse, Get Away* in 1998—but was also strong enough nationally to be the headliner on the first Bonnaroo. Not everything was easy for the band, however. Houser died of pancreatic cancer in August 2002—he had been diagnosed with the disease earlier that year—and that led the band into a two-year hiatus, during which it released live albums. Widespread Panic returned with George McConnell, a guitarist who stayed with the group for three years, until Jimmy Herring took over in 2006, and this is the incarnation that took the band through the next decade of steadily recording and touring, during which the group took the occasional break—Hermann said there was a hiatus in 2012, but it only lasted a year—but was otherwise as reliable a draw as Dave Matthews Band, but only on a smaller scale.

The paths of DMB and Widespread Panic were concentric but rarely crossed. They sometimes shared bills, and they had plenty of mutual friends, but they rarely played with each other.

Hootie and the Blowfish

Another band from the Eastern Seaboard that had a strong college following, Hootie and the Blowfish crossed over in ways no other jam band could imagine. That may be because they never precisely *were* a jam band. Specializing in tight songs, sing-alongs, and good vibes, Hootie and the Blowfish captured the feeling of a breezy, beery night out with pals. Where Dave Matthews Band always suggested the possibility of transcendence—its improvisations always threatening to slide into the stratosphere—Hootie and the Blowfish were tethered to the earth, grounded by the growl of Darius Rucker and the band's welcoming songs. Those songs are what turned 1994 debut *Cracked Rear View* into a smash hit—one that spawned "Hold My Hand," "Let Her Cry," and "Only Wanna Be With You," Top 10 hits all—a record so massive in its time that it's thoroughly tied to its era.

In that sense, *Cracked Rear View* illustrates how DMB dodged a bit of a bullet: in the same year of *Under the Table and Dreaming*, *Cracked Rear View* became a phenomenon—one that Hootie and the Blowfish could never quite overcome. Hootie became superstars while DMB started on a road to stardom. DMB built fans through steady touring and recording; Hootie's came in a rush, all attracted to radio hits, and many decided not to stick around for the long haul. The path of the two bands sharply diverged in 1996, when they both delivered their sophomore albums. *Fairweather Johnson*, the second Hootie album, opened big and faded fast, the victim of fickle listeners; the band had tipped its hand at an awareness of the situation, partially titling the album after fair-weather fans. DMB, in contrast, steadily climbed the charts with *Crash*, earning not only a bigger hit but also industry respect, when the record wound up taking home a Grammy for "Best Rock Performance."

Col. Bruce Hampton and the Aquarium Rescue Unit

The oddest of the second wave of jam bands, Col. Bruce Hampton and the Aquarium Rescue Unit didn't fit into any particular quadrant of the nascent jam-band scene of the late '80s. Hailing from Atlanta, Georgia, the group—led by noted eccentric Hampton, whose "Colonel" designation is self-applied—might have been neighbors with the Allman Brothers Band but wasn't so steeped in blues and soul. Bluegrass, jazz, and rock all enter the mix, elements the band shared with DMB but took in a distinctly different direction—one that is nearly psychedelic.

Fittingly, Hampton had his own roots in the original psychedelia of the '60s. Born in 1947, he was a boomer through and through, and, like so many of his generation, he felt the pull of rock and roll. He wound up taking up the guitar and formed the Hampton Grease Band, somehow scoring a deal with Columbia Records, which issued HGB's debut, *Music to Eat*, as a double album in 1971. The band would soon regret this move. According to lore, *Music to Eat* sold next-to-nothing, becoming the second-worst-selling album in Columbia Records history—an anecdote that is amusing in hindsight, but was fatal to the band at the time. The Grease

Band fell apart, but Hampton soldiered on, forming the Late Bronze Age, a group that somehow managed to get songs on the soundtrack for the 1983 teen flick *Getting It On*.

Next up for Hampton was a series of jam sessions in Atlanta—a regular event that eventually birthed the Aquarium Rescue Unit—with a host of like-minded Georgians. The Aquarium Rescue Unit happened to emerge in the early '90s, just as the second wave of jam bands began to crest. Hampton and crew signed to Capricorn Records, released an eponymous album in 1992, and set out on the initial H.O.R.D.E. tour that summer, appearing with Blues Traveler, Spin Doctors, Phish, and Widespread Panic. Some of these musicians popped up onstage and on record with the Aquarium Rescue Unit, all helping to raise the profile of the band, but that wasn't enough to keep the group going. *Mirrors of Embarrassment* appeared in 1993, but the band began to fracture right after its release, losing first Matt Mundy and then Hampton himself.

The Aquarium Rescue Unit continued on without the Colonel, riding through two subsequent full-length albums—1994's *In a Perfect World*, 1997's *The Calling*—and then started to splinter, its members spreading out to other groups in the jam band universe. In 2005, roughly eight years after the disbandment, the original lineup reunited for a few shows, and this became a semi-regular occurrence, with the group still often playing a few shows a year.

The Samples

Hailing from Boulder, Colorado, the Samples represent the western quadrant of the jam-band universe. Formed in 1987, the group followed a similar trajectory to many other jam bands: college kids in love with both the Grateful Dead and a modern sound—in this band's case, it was the Police's new-wave spin on reggae—they started gigging at local Boulder bars, cobbling together a demo but earning most of their attention through regular touring. Unlike their East Coast brethren, the Samples received a shot at the big leagues quite early. Arista signed the band in 1989 and re-released the band's independent debut from that year, making them the first jam band to get a major contract. This re-release was no more than a test run, however; Arista pulled the plug after a few A&R conflicts with the band, so the Samples returned to indie status in 1991, just as the H.O.R.D.E. nation started to emerge. A self-released EP called *Underwater People* arrived before the band inked a deal with pioneering jam label What Are Records (W.A.R.) in 1992.

The Samples didn't make the first H.O.R.D.E. tour, but they did show up in 1993, which is when Dave Matthews Band also appeared on the bill. Later that year, the Samples opened for DMB as well as Hootie and the Blowfish—allegiances that suggested they veered slightly toward the popper side of the jam-band equation. The Samples made a second

A pass for the 1994 installment of the H.O.R.D.E. tour, which featured Dave Matthews Band.
Author's collection

sortie into the major-label world in 1996, when they moved to MCA for *Outpost*. Shortly after signing the group, however, MCA restructured, and all the execs behind the Samples left, leaving the band adrift. Soon the group decided to launch a farewell tour—a gambit that didn't stick. Some members left, but Sean Kelly and Andy Sheldon soldiered on, and over the next decade have remained at the helm, with the rest of the lineup cycling through musicians. Eventually, Kelly was the only original member in the band, leading the latter-day incarnation of the Samples through new records. In December 2014, the original lineup reunited to play the entirety of their debut, along with a second set of highlights—a testament to the band's enduring popularity.

Agents of Good Roots

Another Virginian jam band, Agents of Good Roots formed in the wake of Dave Matthews Band's success, coming together in 1995 and releasing a debut, *Where'd You Get That Vibe?*, within a year of forming. Another indie release—*Straight Around*—followed in 1997 before the band signed to RCA—the same label that housed DMB. The connection was strengthened when Agents of Good Roots opened for Dave Matthews Band, which helped push the single "Come On (Let Your Blood Come Alive)" into *Billboard*'s Heatseekers chart, but the accompanying *One by One* gained no traction. Another major-label effort, *Needle and Thread*, followed, before the band petered out.

Big Head Todd and the Monsters

Hailing from Colorado, Big Head and the Monsters also belonged to the Western contingent of jam bands. Colorado turned into an important epicenter of the jam-band revolution, serving as the anchor for Aware Records; of course, it didn't hurt that Denver was home to Red Rocks, one of the nation's premier outdoor venues. Big Head Todd and the Monsters would eventually become regulars at Red Rocks, but they initially carved out a following like any good jam band: one gig at a time on the college circuit.

Essentially, Big Head Todd and the Monsters were long-distance peers of Blues Traveler, forming around the same time and getting their debut out in the same year. They formed in 1986, when guitarist Todd Park Mohr, bassist Rob Squires, and drummer Brian Nerving—all students of Columbine High School—started to play together. They attended different colleges but continued to play together, starting to tour as Big Head Todd and the Monsters in 1987. They continued to tour over the next few years, independently releasing their debut, *Another Maybe*, on their own Big Records in 1989. The next year brought *Midnight Radio*, which bore artwork by Chris Mars, the drummer for the Replacements. Big Head Todd and the Monsters were a far cry from the crazed rough and tumble of the 'Mats: they were a mellow good time.

The band landed a slot on the inaugural H.O.R.D.E. festival in 1993 and cut a live record, aptly called *Big Head Todd and the Monsters Live*, during the tour. This catapulted them to Giant Records, where they recorded their major-label debut *Sister Sweetly* with producer David Z., formerly of Prince's Revolution. *Sister Sweetly* rode the breaking alternative wave and became a hit thanks to the singles "Bittersweet," "Circle," and "Broken Hearted Savior." The Mohr-produced *Strategem* failed to capitalize on the band's momentum in 1994, so they were teamed with Jerry Harrison for 1997's *Beautiful World*. This produced the moderate Mainstream Rock hits "Resignation Superman" and "Boom Boom," which were then followed by 1998's *Live Monsters*. Giant shuttered in 2002, so the band switched to Warner Bros that year for *Riviera*. This was their last major-label effort. From this point on, the group revived its Big imprint to license records to other labels and dabbled with digital releases, too, over the course of the decade.

During the 2000s and 2010s, Big Head Todd and the Monsters were mainstays of the jam-rock scene, touring steadily and alternating between studio and live releases. They slowly moved in a pronounced blues direction—a shift that culminated with 2011's *100 Years of Robert Johnson*, which was released under the name Big Head Blues Club—but perhaps the group's most notable achievement was when 2005's "Blue Sky" was used as Senator Hillary Clinton's campaign song in 2008.

Cowboy Mouth

Cowboy Mouth represented the Southern contingent of the jam-band scene. Based in New Orleans, the band formed in 1990 and belonged to the wave of second-generation bands that also included Dave Matthews Band. The band's lineup shifted over the years, but the core members were lead vocalist Fred Le Blanc and guitarist John Thomas Griffith. After making a few indie records in the early '90s, the group signed with MCA in 1996 for the release that summer of *Are You with Me?* "Jenny Says" earned some radio play and helped boost the band into the middle of the pack on the jam-band circuit. *Mercyland* followed on MCA in 1988; the band then hopped over to Atlantic for 2000's *Easy*, before ending its major-label career and settling into the jam-band circuit, touring constantly and alternating studio albums with live sets.

Rusted Root

Rusted Root was one of the jam bands that benefited from the major-label alt-rock gold rush of the early '90s, signing quickly to a major and then getting a hit in 1994 before settling into the middle pack. The band eventually earned a large, dedicated following through touring, but its chart success was swift and short.

Based in Pittsburgh, Pennsylvania, the group formed in 1990. This initial incarnation featured guitarist/vocalist Michael Glabicki, vocalist/percussionist Liz Berlin, bassist Patrick Norman, drummer Jim Donovan, and percussionists Jim DiSpirito and John Buynak. The group's self-released 1992 album, *Cruel Sun*, set the stage for Mercury/Polygram signing the band. *When I Woke*, its major-label debut, arrived in 1994, and it turned into a word-of-mouth success partially on the back of the single "Send Me on the Way." On its supporting tour, Rusted Root played "Minarets" with DMB in 1994. Jerry Harrison produced the 1996 set *Remember*, which went to #38 on the *Billboard* charts but didn't produce any big hits. An eponymous 1998 set stalled out at #165, and 2002's *Welcome to My Party* closed out the band's time on a major. From that point on, Rusted Root toured steadily and recorded sporadically, earning its keep as a live outfit.

Leftover Salmon

Another one of the Mountain State jam bands, Leftover Salmon never managed to breach the mainstream, yet did what jam bands do: worked at it steadily, eventually accumulating a wide, dedicated following through its live performances, not its records. The band surfaced nationally around the same time as Dave Matthews Band, releasing its major-label debut in 1995. Nevertheless, the group played the same circles and festivals as DMB, their paths crossing often.

Leftover Salmon had its roots in two separate bands from Boulder, Colorado: the Salmon Heads and the Left Hand String Band. Vince Herman came from the former, while Drew Emmitt, Glenn Keefe, and Mark Vann came from the latter. Once the chemistry was evident upon their initial 1989 jams—the blend of rock, Cajun, and bluegrass clicked—the group decided to keep going, expanding its lineup, with many different musicians cycling in and out of the group over the years, and starting to play regularly. The self-released 1993 studio set *Bridges to Bert* was followed by the live *Ask the Fish*, recorded at Boulder's Fox Theatre. Hollywood Records, noting the success of Blues Traveler, Spin Doctors, and Phish, signed the band that year, at which point work began on a major-label debut. Released in 1997, *Euphoria* didn't garner much attention; nor did 1999's *The Nashville Sessions*, which made an appearance on *Billboard*'s Heatseekers chart but not the main albums chart. The group soon parted ways with Hollywood, before releasing a handful of live and studio records over the next few years.

In 2002, Mark Vann died from cancer, and this had a long-lasting impact on the band. Two years later, the group went on hiatus—a break that lasted for three years. Leftover Salmon reemerged with concerts in 2007, which led to the band moving to semi-active status, playing shows with some regularity during the back half of the 2000s. *Aquatic Hitchhiker*, the band's first album in eight years, came out in 2012, while Leftover Salmon also received further exposure with appearances in the *After the Catch* episodes that followed Discovery's hit reality show *The Deadliest Catch*.

So Damn Lucky

Who Has Sat in with Dave Matthews Band?

Like any group tagged with the term "jam band," Dave Matthews Band has always welcomed other musicians onto the stage to jam. This is something DMB did from the start, when inviting local musicians and inspirations to play at its numerous gigs at Trax, and when the group achieved stardom, the pool of available guests expanded dramatically. Not surprisingly, the group took advantage of this, letting idols sit in for covers of fabled songs just as easily as it made space for old friends and other arena-filling stars.

So many musicians have crossed the stage of Dave Matthews Band that it's impossible to list every one. Instead, it's better to look at a cross-section of regular guests and significant one-shot cameos. By combining these two categories, we get a better idea of the breadth and depth of the music of Dave Matthews Band, not to mention a sense of the journey its members have taken over the course of twenty-five years.

Gregg Allman

The longtime leader of the Allman Brothers Band was a semi-regular at Dave Matthews Band shows, appearing at his first concert in August of 1994 and then popping up over an additional five gigs over the years. Usually, his song of choice when playing with DMB was the Allmans staple "Melissa," a version of which showed up on DMB's 2007 album *Live at Piedmont Park*.

Trey Anastasio

The Phish guitarist is an old friend of Dave Matthews Band and a regular collaborator with the band and Dave himself. Anastasio first played with Dave Matthews Band when DMB sat in with Phish at a gig on April 20, 1994, just a few months before the release of *Under the Table and Dreaming*, and over the course of nearly a quarter decade, he has showed up around forty times on Matthews-related stages. A good chunk of these came during the 2003 Dave Matthews and Friends tour, assembled as a way of promoting Dave's solo album *Some Devil*—an album on which Anastasio plays lead guitar—but his wide-ranging tastes and interests have made him a comfortable fit for nearly any Dave Matthews Band song.

Danny Barnes

The progressive bluegrass banjoist is a founding member of the Austin-based outfit Bad Livers. He came to Dave Matthews Band circles late, playing his first show with the band in 2007. Soon afterward, he appeared on *Big Whiskey and the GrooGrux King*, before popping up at assorted shows between 2007 and 2010.

The Black Eyed Peas—Fergie and will.i.am

Perhaps the most controversial of all Dave Matthews Band guests, Fergie and will.i.am of the Black Eyed Peas slid onstage to sing "Jimi Thing" when DMB played San Francisco's Outside Lands festival in 2009. DMB fans were not taken with the idea of a pop group playing with their favorite band, and the resulting performance was a bit of a train wreck.

James Brown

One of the greatest surprise guests in Dave Matthews Band history was James Brown, who joined DMB for a performance of "Get Up (I Feel Like Being a Sex Machine)" at Madison Square Garden on December 21, 2002. He brought members of his band the Soul Generals onto the stage, too, making for a fine, funky performance.

Zac Brown

The Georgia-based leader of the Zac Brown Band is a latecomer to the Dave Matthews Band universe, partially due to the ZBB not gaining considerable popularity until 2010 and the release of its second album, *You Get What You Give*. That's the year Brown played with the DMB, and over the next couple years he'd show up on several different occasions, duetting with Dave on "Funny How Time Slips Away" and playing "All Along the Watchtower" with the full band.

Brandi Carlile

The literate and passionate singer/songwriter had Dave Matthews provide a harmonic foil on her cover of John Prine's "Angel from Montgomery" in 2011 and 2012, then sat in with the full band in 2013 for a version of "Spoon," which she reprised the next year on the Dave Matthews Band Caravan tour.

Gary Clark Jr.

The Austin-based blues guitarist rose to prominence in 2012, when he released his major-label debut, *Blak and Blu*. That was also the year he first sat in with Dave Matthews Band, playing "Can't Stop" and "All Along the Watchtower," and over the next year he returned a couple more times to play "Watchtower."

Mike Doughty

The leader of Soul Coughing has shown up a couple of times on Dave Matthews Band stages. The first found him playing "Anyone Seen the Bridge" when the song was debuted on October 3, 1996; he appeared again in 2005, when he played "Jimi Thing" twice.

Bob Dylan

The greatest rock singer/songwriter of the twentieth century never sat in with Dave Matthews Band. Instead, he brought Dave and Boyd Tinsley to the stage, having them guest on four songs. Tinsley sat in for all four—"Maggie's Farm" and "The Times They Are A-Changin'" were his alone—while Dave sang on "Everything Is Broken" and "Rainy Day Women #12 and 35." LeRoi made a cameo on the latter as well.

The Edge

The Edge, the innovative and echo-laden guitarist for U2, isn't known for his improvisational skills, but he nevertheless braved the jam-heavy waters of a Dave Matthews Band show in 2006, when the two bands' paths intersected at the New Orleans Jazz and Heritage Festival and they played "Smooth Rider" together.

Béla Fleck

Famed jazz/bluegrass banjoist Béla Fleck is a constant in the Dave Matthews Band universe. He first started playing shows with the band in 1996, and from that point on there wasn't a year where he didn't appear at least once. He has since racked up seventy appearances with the band, and also features on the 1998 album *Before These Crowded Streets.*

G. Love

The funky frat-boy bluesman was something of a kindred sprit to Dave Matthews Band—he was not quite part of the jam band scene but still existed on the fringes of H.O.R.D.E. nation. It made sense then that he showed up on DMB stages in 1996. G. Love returned to the DMB orbit in 2006, guesting at a show in Burgettstown, Pennsylvania, that summer.

Herbie Hancock

The great jazz pianist played six shows with Dave Matthews Band in 1998, a point when DMB was at its popular and creative peak. He showed up again in 2015.

Ben Harper

During the 1996 H.O.R.D.E. tour, Ben Harper wound up playing regularly with Dave Matthews Band. Ever since then, he's been on the outside of the orbit, joining the band whenever their paths cross, always sitting in for "All Along the Watchtower."

Emmylou Harris

One of the great harmonizers in country-music history—she first came to prominence as Gram Parsons's foil in the early '70s—Emmylou Harris wound up establishing herself as a prodigious force in her own right. She developed a strong bond with Dave Matthews Band in the late '90s and has been a regular in band circles ever since. During 2003's Dave Matthews and Friends tour, she took the opening spot and would also sing with Matthews. She continued to guest with the band into the 2010s.

A handbill for a concert on May 12, 1995, where Dave Matthews Band and Big Head Todd and the Monsters shared the bill. *Author's collection*

Warren Haynes

Warren Haynes, the prime guitarist in the last incarnation of the Allman Brothers Band, and the leader of Gov't Mule, has been sitting in with Dave Matthews Band since before either act were stars. The first time he ever showed up at a DMB show was in 1993, and over the next two decades, he would become a regular, appearing over fifty times. Like most guitarists, his showcase was "All Along the Watchtower," but he also frequently played on "Cortez the Killer," "#41," and "Jimi Thing."

David Hidalgo

During the summer 1997 tour, the Los Lobos guitarist/singer sat in with Dave Matthews Band, sometimes bringing along his bandmate Steve Berlin as well, often for a cameo on "Lie in Our Graves."

Greg Howard

The Charlottesville-based king of the Chapman Stick played on *Before These Crowded Streets* and appeared at several shows on the supporting tour, having first appeared with the DMB back in 1992.

Lenny Kravitz

Lenny Kravitz often fancied himself an heir to the fiery guitar theatrics of Jimi Hendrix, so it's little surprise that when he sat in with Dave Matthews Band at the New Orleans Jazz and Heritage Festival in 2001, he chose to play "All Along the Watchtower."

Charles Lloyd

The great jazz saxophonist played on *Before These Crowded Streets*, and several years later played three songs at a 2015 concert by DMB.

Vusi Mahlasela

The South African singer/songwriter first appeared in Dave Matthews Band circles in 2001, when he sang on *Everyday*. He appeared relatively frequently at DMB shows between 2006 and 2014.

Branford Marsalis

The jazz saxophonist who came to fame thanks to his prominent position in Sting's mid-'80s touring band and then in the first incarnation of Jay Leno's *Tonight Show* band has played a handful of shows with both Dave Matthews Band and Dave solo in the 2010s.

John Mayer

The guitar heartthrob played three shows with Dave Matthews Band in the fall of 2007, guesting on "#41" twice and "Gravity" once.

Tom Morello

Under his Nightwatchman moniker, the Rage Against the Machine guitarist wound up opening several European shows for Dave Matthews Band in 2007, and he also ended up onstage with DMB on three separate nights, playing acoustic one night, electric the other two.

Alanis Morissette

Dave Matthews Band brought in Alanis Morissette to sing on two songs on *Before These Crowded Streets*, and she also sang "Don't Drink the Water" onstage in 1999.

Willie Nelson

One of the towering figures in twentieth-century American music, Willie Nelson never says no to a stage, so it's not a surprise that he has sat in with Dave Matthews Band on multiple occasions. Nelson also shares a Farm Aid connection with Matthews—Willie is one of the founders of the charity, while Dave joined its board of directors in 2001. When Willie Nelson and Family toured as DMB's opening band in 2009, the country legend sat in with the headliners quite often.

Maceo Parker

The funk/soul saxophonist first made his bones with James Brown—the Godfather of Soul could be heard commanding, "Maceo, blow your horn!"—and, after his time in the J.B.'s, he remained a powerful performer. In 1998, Parker played "What Would You Say" three times with Dave Matthews Band, including the version that features on *Live in Chicago, 12.19.98*.

John Popper

The Blues Traveler leader was a regular with Dave Matthews Band from the start, playing shows in 1993 and 1994 while also providing a harmonica solo on the group's first single, "What Would You Say." Popper popped up regularly at concerts between 1995 and 1997, and showed up frequently throughout the 1996 H.O.R.D.E. tour, where he would usually sit in for a take on "All Along the Watchtower," although he would sometimes play the hit, too. After that, he didn't show up often, fading away in 2001 and only returning to DMB stages in 2015.

Questlove

The anchor of the Roots and perhaps the most prominent pop musicologist in popular culture, Questlove sat in with Dave Matthews Band a handful of times in 2007, when he played a version of "Warehouse" that found space for an interpolation of "Linus and Lucy," thanks to the joint appearance of Butch Taylor.

Robert Randolph

Robert Randolph is a live force—he is not necessarily part of the jamband scene, but his funky soul blues belongs within the same extended universe. Randolph became a regular in Dave Matthews Band circles in the 2000s, appearing at a whopping seventy shows between 2002 and 2009, racking up most of these appearances during the 2005–2006 tour.

Darius Rucker

Darius Rucker and Dave Matthews Band shared similar backgrounds and could often be found on the same bills throughout the '90s, while several members of DMB also found their way onto Hootie and the Blowfish's second album, *Fairweather Johnson*. Given this, it might seem as though Rucker would be a regular at DMB shows, but he's popped up onstage only once, playing "Granny" in 1996.

Carlos Santana

One of the great rock guitarists, Carlos Santana entered the Dave Matthews Band's orbit in 1999, when Dave sang on the guitarist's blockbuster album *Supernatural*. The two acts shared a tour that year, and Santana wound up sitting in with DMB, usually for "All Along the Watchtower." The connection led to Carlos playing on "Mother Father" on 2001's *Everyday*.

Paul Simon

Paul Simon didn't come to Dave Matthews Band—Dave Matthews Band came to him. When they were both playing the New Orleans Jazz Fest in 2001, the great singer/songwriter sat in with the band for his own "Me and Julio Down by the Schoolyard," a polyrhythmic delight that certainly formed a significant part of DMB's DNA.

Bob Weir

Perhaps Dave Matthews Band wasn't greatly influenced by the Grateful Dead, but the Dead always enjoyed jamming. Bob Weir, one of the group's two guitarist/vocalists—the one who always existed in the shadow of Jerry Garcia—sat in to play "All Along the Watchtower" in 1998. Several years later, the guitarist guested on a 2006 cruise-ship jam of "Iko Iko."

Victor Wooten

The fluid, funky fusion bassist has anchored Béla Fleck's Flecktones since its inception in the late '80s, and he's also made his own name as a teacher and solo artist. Additionally, he often plays with other musicians, becoming something of a regular at Dave Matthews Band shows over the years. He first sat in with the group in 1996, and over the next twenty years he would pop up at numerous DMB gigs, usually appearing on either "#41" or "Ants Marching."

Neil Young

The great Canadian singer/songwriter was a prime influence on Dave Matthews, and he became something of a regular in Dave Matthews Band circles once DMB began playing Farm Aid shows in 1997. From that point on, Young would show up relatively frequently on DMB and Dave stages, showing up eighteen times between 1997 and 2011.

12

Remember Two Things and *Recently*

The First Album and EP

Remember Two Things

Remember Two Things is where it all started for Dave Matthews Band, at least as far as recorded music goes. Released on the band's own independent Bama Rags imprint, the LP contains a pair of studio cuts but focuses on the place where DMB feels most comfortable: the stage.

Recording live at a local club was fairly standard procedure for most regionally popular rock bands in the '80s and '90s because it was cheap, easy, and quick. A swiftly recorded live production would come close to capturing how the band sounded for the great majority of its fans, plus it could function as a calling card to curious labels.

It's telling that the first thing you hear on *Remember Two Things* is thirty seconds of a snare drum: at this point, the senior member of Dave Matthews Band was Carter Beauford, and he drives the record. Captured live, without any of the sly polish that would be applied by Steve Lillywhite just a year later, the band feels lean but rangy, united not just by rhythm but by the need to explore. Hence it feels open ended and exploratory, particularly on "Recently," which plays like nothing so much as an open-ended jam—the riffs on the verse tread water, but the chorus is limber, adding a jolt of electricity. It's also clear on this album that many of Matthews's melodies and words are shaped to follow the jam; he's not bringing the song to the band so much as working his way around the band.

There are also distinct traces of Matthews's influences: as "The Song That Jane Likes" unfurls, first R.E.M. and then Sting come to the forefront, with the tune moving in a direction that would turn out to be distinct to DMB: acoustic songs opened up by jazz rhythms. Similarly, "Minarets," in its arid, spacey atmosphere, is indebted to U2—a connection that doesn't feel overly reverent but rather an expansion of what DMB, and particularly Matthews, found appealing in U2.

Occasionally, DMB could be tentative, particularly on the studio cuts: "I'll Back You Up" seems hesitant, treating the studio gingerly. This is in stark contrast to the live material, where the band feels confident, even bold—a boyish arrogance best heard on early versions of the standards "Ants Marching" and "Tripping Billies." These two songs, along with "Recently," "Satellite," and "The Song That Jane Likes," would all become part of the band's standard repertoire, fleshed out on *Under the Table and*

The cover of *Remember Two Things* is an autostereogram which reveals a peace sign.
Author's collection

Dreaming and *Crash*, but the versions here have an open-hearted charm: this is the sound of a band discovering itself.

Recording

Dave Matthews Band recorded *Remember Two Things* in August 1993, choosing to capture performances at the regular haunts of Charlottesville's Trax and Richmond's the Flood Zone, but also incorporating a few studio performances cut at the Muse in Nantucket, Massachusetts, the Muse for good measure. Although it's the band's first record, the album also captures a Dave Matthews Band in transition, partly because it features the recently departed keyboardist Peter Griesar. He left DMB shortly before the August 1993 dates, yet he shows up on the record—in the credits, he is thanked for "all the musical contributions and inspirations."

The band also found room for guest appearances by musicians close to its inner circle. Carter Beauford and LeRoi Moore's old mentor John D'Earth arranged "Recently," and there are also cameos by Greg Howard, master of the Chapman Stick, not to mention guitarist Tim Reynolds, who plays two acoustic songs with Matthews. The album closes with studio versions of "Seek Up" and "Minarets"—the first time the band tested the waters in the controlled climate of a studio.

The Songs

Several of the songs on *Remember Two Things* were re-recorded with Steve Lillywhite for *Under the Table and Dreaming* and *Crash*. These will be discussed within the chapters for those albums.

"Recently"

The first single Dave Matthews Band ever released, "Recently" bears a strong jazz undercurrent: the chorus lifts up on a flood of sevenths and ninths and a light, percolating beat, creating a buoyant feeling that suits a lyric that captures the rush of a new love. Perhaps the words betray how this song was written early in Matthews's development, but the song is clever and elastic, malleable enough to accept all sorts of interpolations. That's how "Recently" developed live: it would often be expanded into a long jam, and it remained a perennial favorite; though it fell out of favor during a six-year stretch between 2006 and 2012—it was played often in 2009, but that was the only year that it was in rotation during that time—it came back strong as the band approached its twenty-fifth anniversary.

"One Sweet World"

One of the first songs Dave ever wrote, "One Sweet World" celebrates—as its title suggests—all that the earth has to offer, warning that there's so much that we take for granted. Appropriately enough, for a song that exhorts the listener to seize the day, the music of "One Sweet World" is cheerful and also consists of conjoining melodic circles, whether it's Moore's saxophone riff or Matthews's swaggering staccato strums. It's a solid song, and one that doesn't lend itself to detours—the biggest differences lay in arrangements of Moore's horn part—but its sturdiness also means that it's endured as the rare song that Dave Matthews Band has played during every year of its life. "One Sweet World" also saw a second life as the title of the DMB-themed ice cream launched by Ben and Jerry's.

"The Song That Jane Likes"

So named because Dave Matthews's sister liked the melody, "The Song That Jane Likes" almost plays like a hybrid of two early Matthews influences—R.E.M. and Sting. As it starts, the atmospheric acoustic guitar and airy harmonies unmistakably evoke R.E.M.'s Southern jangle, but once the verse wraps up, the song opens up and welcomes a saxophone solo from LeRoi Moore that's unmistakably connected to Sting's *The Dream of the Blue Turtles*.

If the idol-worship is apparent, the elements are stitched together in a clever, distinctive way that suggests how Dave Matthews Band would synthesize these sensibilities later in its career. Even as DMB grew more sophisticated, "The Song That Jane Likes" retained its dewy glow, which may be why it remained a staple all the way through 2004, before being added to sets on occasion in the back half of the 2010s before once again becoming a regular as the band approached its twenty-fifth anniversary.

"Minarets"

A swirling, dramatic piece that consciously draws upon Middle-Eastern music—indeed, a minaret is an Arabic word for a tower placed next to a mosque where Muslims would be called to prayer—"Minarets" has an obvious antecedent in Led Zeppelin's "Kashmir," but it also hints at U2's muscular arena rock and sense of social protest. Where much of *Remember Two Things* is ebullient, "Minarets" mines some dark, foreboding territory—an area the band would embrace on *Before These Crowded Streets*. Hence it's perhaps the most distinctive thing here, which may be why an early online fan group named itself after it, but it also is something that seems designed for the stage, which is where it lived throughout the '90s. "Minarets" wasn't heard much in the 2000s, but it did show up on the summer 2003 tour, and then became a favorite again in the mid-2010s.

"Seek Up"

A murmuring, quietly urgent song, "Seek Up" is the darker corollary to "One Sweet World." Where that tune preaches *carpe diem*, this one recognizes that we're often searching for an emotion, too consumed by materialism, too consumed with our own selves to see the world. This is idealism with darker edges, and it ends the album on a somewhat elegiac note. "Seek Up" is a song that survives, too, having been played every year by some incarnation of Dave Matthews and his touring companions.

"I'll Back You Up"

"I'll Back You Up" is considered the first song Dave Matthews wrote, and it's a sweet, delicate number—a love song that feels like it's whispered, not sung. Its earnestness is its attribute; this is open-heartedness flirting with naiveté, but it's still appealing. Matthews played the song often through the '90s, after which it became an occasional highlight, performed most often in 2010 and 2014.

"Christmas Song"

As its title suggests, "Christmas Song" is a song about Jesus Christ—one that's light and jazzy and contains an evident feint toward the Beatles' "All You Need Is Love" in its chorus. Despite its subject, "Christmas Song" doesn't play as particularly religious or seasonal: Matthews may have loaded it up with a lot of words, but it exists on a small scale, and, in many ways, its mellow mood is as appealing as its narrative. "Christmas Song" was played often during the '90s, and then brought out on occasion—usually during the holiday season—in 2002, 2005, 2010, and 2012.

Release

Remember Two Things appeared on November 9, 1993, an independent release on Dave Matthews Band's own label, Bama Rags. It is the only album where the group is credited as "The Dave Matthews Band."

Notably, the album art for *Remember Two Things* is a stereogram—a visual trick wherein a series of dots and lines hide a heartier image. Look closely, and an image of a hand waving two fingers is revealed—not the "V" insult from Britain, but a peace sign from America. This peace sign underscores the theory that the meaning of the title is "remember peace," but there's an alternate fan theory that the two things to remember are "love your mother" and "always leave footprints."

Remember Two Things was reissued by RCA on June 24, 1997, during the downtime between *Crash* and *Before These Crowded Streets* and just after the RIAA certified the album as gold on March 7, 1997—quite an achievement for an independent release. On July 26, 2002, it was certified platinum.

The 2014 reissue adds studio versions of "Pay for What You Get" and "Typical Situation"—both recorded at Flat Five Studios—and also marks the album's first appearance on vinyl. In the studio, these are moody acoustic numbers bearing slight echoes of R.E.M. but relying on space over succinctness.

Reception

At the time, *Remember Two Things* was intended to be sold to fans, and the fans came out nearly four-hundred-strong for a midnight release held at Plan Nine, a record store near the University of Virginia campus. Usually, only superstars could pull a crowd of that size; Dave Matthews Band had certainly become local heroes, but nobody expected quite so many people to show. The group wound up selling more than eight hundred copies at Plan 9 that day, with the band members holding a meet-and-greet at the Main St. Grill, where they signed copies.

Because it was an indie release, *Remember Two Things* wasn't heard much outside of Charlottesville and the surrounding areas during the first few years of its life, but within that community it was quite well received.

Legacy

Although it was self-released, it's a little difficult to separate *Remember Two Things* from DMB's graduation to the major labels. It appeared just eight days after Dave Matthews Band signed a contract with BMG/RCA, one of several majors that had come courting the band. In that light, *Remember Two Things* is something of a calling card: not a fully fledged fruition of the band's talents but rather a suggestion of potential.

Like many so many indie releases from bands with a strong collegiate following, *Remember Two Things* was designed to please fans, offering crisp, clean versions of the songs they knew by heart. By doing this—and by offering so much of DMB's live set—the album also provides a useful document of Dave Matthews Band in its early years, when its reputation was built entirely through live performances, and the group had yet to learn how to use the gloss of a recording studio in its favor. As such, it provides a window into what the band sounded like at the cusp of its success.

For a while, it would be relatively hard for Dave Matthews Band fans to discover *Remember Two Things*. As DMB's popularity skyrocketed in the mid-'90s, it remained an indie release. In 1997, just after *Crash* turned Dave Matthews Band into one of the most popular bands in the United States of America, RCA reissued *Remember Two Things*, but by that point many of its songs were already well-known to DMB fans due to how they circled through live sets. Some of the songs did wind up on *Under the Table and Dreaming*, but pivotal songs like "Recently," "The Song That Jane Likes," "Seek Up," and "Minarets" were only available here, which illustrates how fully formed Dave Matthews Band was at the outset.

Recently

In May of 1994, Dave Matthews Band put out *Recently* on its Bama Rags label. Unlike *Remember Two Things*, which was primarily an independent release, this one was supported by BMG/RCA, which had the full-length debut *Under the Table and Dreaming* in the pipeline for an autumn release. *Recently* was essentially a way to tide over the band's fans until the release of a new full-length record.

Recording

Like *Remember Two Things* before it, *Recently* was co-produced by John Alagía and recorded live. Indeed, the title track is an edit of a song included on *Remember Two Things*—a performance from August 10, 1993, at the Flood Zone—while the rest of the EP was culled from February 1994 shows in Virginia: one at Alexandria's the Birchmere, and another at the band's regular stomping ground, Trax. Two of the songs—"Dancing Nancies" and "Warehouse"—appear as acoustic duets by Matthews and Reynolds.

Release

Recently was sent out to hardcore fans but also college radio and newspapers, all in an attempt to expand the group's base. One of the promotional versions of *Recently* contains a variation on the album art, showing a bare-chested male model holding a pumpkin, and has become one of the more collectable DMB items, primarily for its artwork, but it also because it has different track listing. "Recently," in a different radio edit, is the only holdover; this version also contains radio edits of "Ants Marching"

Recently EP cover. There is an alternate version of the Recently cover which depicts the male model holding a pumpkin. *Author's collection*

and "The Song That Jane Likes," along with the edit of "Tripping Billies" that appears on *Remember Two Things.*

Legacy

Recently features the recorded debut of several key Dave Matthews Band songs, but none of them is necessarily definitive in these versions. Which isn't to say any of these versions are bad. "Dancing Nancies" and "Warehouse" appear here in nice duet versions by Dave Matthews and

Tim Reynolds, but they were executed better later that year on *Under the Table and Dreaming*. Similarly, "Halloween" wound up achieving its full fruition on 1998's *Before These Crowded Streets*, while "All Along the Watchtower" gained more power the longer Dave Matthews Band played it live. So, essentially, *Recently* works as a footnote to *Remember Two Things*: it's cut from the same cloth, in showcasing the band live onstage, tight but lacking the muscle and grace that would come so swiftly afterward.

Under the Table and Dreaming

The Major-Label Debut

The Album

Under the Table and Dreaming is at the foundation of all of Dave Matthews Band's success—it's the place where the band earned an audience and gained a foothold in North America.

Much of the success of *Under the Table and Dreaming* can be chalked up to the band choosing the right producer at the right time. In hiring Steve Lillywhite, a record-maker who had considerable success with U2, DMB found a producer who knew how to give its songs—which were designed for stage, not the studio—definition and muscle.

Naturally, the band turned to its road-tested repertoire to build the album. Occasionally, the group revived songs that showed up on *Remember Two Things*, but this didn't matter much at this point; to the larger audience, all these songs were new. "Warehouse, "Dancing Nancies," and "Ants Marching" had all been recorded before, but they were revived for *Under the Table and Dreaming*, matched with newer songs like the first single, "What Would You Say."

Colorful and slightly cloying, "What Would You Say" helped break the band, and it provided a good entryway to the band and to *Under the Table and Dreaming*. Maybe it isn't indicative of the ambition or the soul-searching heard elsewhere on the album, but it is loose, lively, and fun, replicating the vibe that can be felt at a Dave Matthews Band concert.

The same can be said about *Under the Table and Dreaming* as a whole. It is a bright record, one that gives the appearance of a party, but it doesn't quite feel like a Dave Matthews Band show: it's sculpted and crafted, a studio record through and through. Blame the texture on producer Steve Lillywhite. Upon first listen, it's clear how much Lillywhite lends to the band; he tempers the eccentricities of Matthews's singing and adds depth and dimension to the others' performances but never diminishes either the fluid, hot-water attack of the rhythm section or its need to slide into spacey atmosphere. He manages to stay true to how Dave Matthews Band feels while adding considerable color and shade—the kind of thing that would draw in listeners who may not otherwise be interested in jam bands.

The Songs

Dave Matthews Band drew upon its existing songbook for *Under the Table and Dreaming*, adding a few newly written songs to the mix. The combination of the old and new resulted in a rich major-label debut that showcases the group's range, heart, and ambition.

"The Best of What's Around"

First played live in March of 1991, "The Best of What's Around" is a relatively simple song—a lively little number encouraging listeners to look on the brighter side. It's also a song that doesn't offer a lot of space for the band to stretch out. Perhaps that's why it was sometimes played solo by Dave Matthews, the spare setting letting its themes shine through. When the band's repertoire was rather small, "The Best of What's Around" often worked its way into the set list—it was played often between 1993 and 1996, then frequently between 1996 and 2000. After that point, it was hauled out every year, but not that often: there were times where it was played only once or twice, although it experienced a revival in 2015. Given its title, it's not surprising the song wound up lending its title to the band's first-ever hits compilation in 2006.

"What Would You Say"

For a generation of listeners, "What Would You Say" is the first Dave Matthews Band song they ever heard. As the first single from *Under the Table and Dreaming*, it received a considerable push from MTV and radio, leading to it peaking at #22 on the *Billboard* Hot 100, as well as #11 on the Alternative chart and #5 on the Mainstream Rock chart.

"What Would You Say" is certainly the catchiest song on the album—it has hooks, plus a melody that pulls a listener in, all accentuated by the illusion of a sing-along created by Steve Lillywhite. John Popper plays harp on the song, and, according to lore propagated by Matthews, the Blues Traveler harmonicist played his entire solo while Dave was upstairs sitting on the toilet.

"What Would You Say" may have helped establish the band, but Dave Matthews and band always had mixed feelings about the song. Dave recounted to *Entertainment Weekly* just three years later, "I really didn't like that song. It was a throwaway tune when I wrote it. So we just stopped playing it. One time we played it in L.A. RCA said, 'Please, there's gonna be industry people here, please play that song, please!' As soon as it was over, the whole room emptied. I was like, 'Wow. We're never gonna play that song again.'"

He told a similar tale to *Billboard* in 2007. "We were doing a show in Los Angeles and we played our set, and in the middle or pretty early on, that song was in there," Matthews recalled. "And when we played it the whole crowd left, like it filed out. We stopped playing that song, we stopped playing it completely. I don't think we played it for years after that."

This isn't precisely true. "What Would You Say" remained a reliable staple of sets throughout the early '90s. It was first heard in the fall of 1991 and played throughout 1992, then, once it was the single, it stayed in the set list until January of 1997. Then it was back-benched for a year—played only once in July 1997—before being revived at the end of 1998. From that point on, the song has been either a lynchpin of a set list or an afterthought. It was played a lot in the early years of the 2000s, not played much between 2008 and 2010, then brought back with a vengeance in the 2010s.

"Satellite"

A lovely, lilting ballad, "Satellite" first was heard onstage in November 1991, then played quite a lot in 1992, and, from that point forward, has never gone out of circulation. A few years, it was played only a handful of times—in 2005 and 2011, it was heard just five times each—but there was never a year where it wasn't performed. The reason it endures is that its ambitions are modest: it's a love song as a miniature, with Matthews demonstrating some level of restraint in his lyrics, and the song keeping its focus on the melody, which is as romantic as Dave Matthews has ever been.

Such concentrated power is why this song has had legs outside of Dave Matthews Band. Mika has covered it, assigning it as the B-side of his smash "Grace Kelly," and Josh Groban put it out as a bonus track on *All That Echoes* in 2013. These covers reflect the fact that "Satellite" was an actual hit, reaching #18 on *Billboard*'s Alternative chart and #36 on its Mainstream Rock chart—which is pretty good for the fifth single pulled from an album. It was saved until the end because RCA was concentrating on high-octane party songs—"Jimi Thing" and "Typical Situation" were both serviced to radio, even if they didn't chart—plus "Satellite" had initially appeared on *Remember Two Things*, so it wasn't exactly fresh. Still, this is as enduring as anything Dave Matthews Band ever created; it's been a staple of the band's sets ever since, and it transcends the group's catalogue, too.

"Rhyme and Reason"

A churning, minor-key groove, "Rhyme and Reason" explores an interior existential crisis: the narrator is talking to himself, justifying his excesses and trying to figure out his reasoning, eventually winding up in his grave; in this sense, it's one of the earliest Dave Matthews songs to be obsessed with mortality. It opens with a winding, percolating acoustic-guitar figure, but it builds to a crescendo, the musical power ultimately obscuring the lyrics.

For a while, this was a staple in Dave Matthews Band sets—it was played constantly between 1993 and 1996, then disappeared in 1997, before slipping back into rotation between 1998 and 2005. From that point forward, it was still played, but usually as an occasional nostalgic blast; 2008 and 2009 were the only years where it was heard often.

"Typical Situation"

Although it may be a live staple, "Typical Situation"—the third single pulled from *Under the Table and Dreaming*—didn't go anywhere: it failed to show on any *Billboard* chart, and no video was made for it. Nevertheless, it was something of a pivotal song for Dave Matthews Band—a song that was designed for a singer/songwriter and opened up by the will and skill of the band.

"Typical Situation" was a fully formed song that Dave Matthews brought to the group. He first played it onstage in the spring of 1991, and it was part of the DMB repertoire throughout the 90s, appearing regularly until 2000, when it started to fade away. After two years of hibernation, it was revived in 2003 and 2004, then used as spice between 2005 and 2015, when it suddenly became part of the regular set list again.

"Dancing Nancies"

Another one of Dave Matthews Band's signature songs, "Dancing Nancies" was first heard late in 1991, then played throughout 1992 and 1993, before the band was signed to RCA Records. During the years surrounding the release of *Under the Table and Dreaming*, it was one of the band's main songs, played in almost every set between 1994 and 1999. At the turn of the millennium it was pushed toward the back bench, but there never was a year where it wasn't played, and between 2002 and 2018, it always wound up somewhere in the set list at some point in the tour.

"Dancing Nancies" proved resilient because it offers plenty of space for the band to explore. Once Dave finishes a verse, there is space for LeRoi and Stefan to jam, and for the group to vamp for a considerable stretch of time. Lyrically, it's slightly amorphous, with Matthews questioning his own mortality, so the searching finds a counterpoint in the open-ended instrumentals, which help push the music toward wide-open vistas.

"Ants Marching"

Debuted at the tail end of 1991, "Ants Marching" is possibly the best known of all Dave Matthews Band songs, even if there are songs that did better on the *Billboard* charts. Issued to radio a full year after "What Would You Say," "Ants Marching" essentially marked time while the band began work on its second album, *Crash*, and it wound up peaking in the midrange on *Billboard* charts: #25 on the Adult Contemporary chart, #18 on the Alternative chart, #18 on Mainstream Rock.

The title suggests that we're all ants running around in circles—a metaphor that's extended in the video, which is set in New York City—but what's really important about the song is the herky-jerky rhythm. It's not quite danceable—not in the sense that there's a groove that's laid down throughout the song—but it's bright and chipper, giving plenty of space for LeRoi Moore's Branford Marsalis–style runs and a rhythm that provides the band a place to vamp.

There has never been a year when "Ants Marching" wasn't part of Dave Matthews Band's repertoire. The closest it came to being phased out was in 2011, when it was played just four times, but otherwise it has been played every year, and often.

"Lover Lay Down"

As the title suggests, this is a bit of romantic tune, but the song doesn't follow simple lines. By the time it reaches its conclusion, the sweet folky undercurrents are abandoned in favor of an open-ended jam, which is something that helps bring the song into the realm of early Dave Matthews Band material, as a song that lets the band surge and flaunt its skills.

The song was first aired in November 1992 and played often in 1993, just prior to the band signing to RCA. It was played often through the '90s, somewhat forgotten during the first part of the 2000s, brought out quite a bit in 2002 and 2005, then retired until 2015, when it became a regular part of the repertoire again.

"Jimi Thing"

The second single pulled from *Under the Table and Dreaming* makes no bones about its debt to Jimi Hendrix—something underscored by the appearance of "All Along the Watchtower" as one of its B-sides when it was released as a single—and it didn't chart, but it is one of the major Dave Matthews songs. One of the reasons for its enduring popularity is that the song gives plenty of space for rhythmic improvisations and solos.

Matthews offers a few carefully constructed verses—words that don't have a specific connection with Hendrix, but do have passing references to Hendrix and pot smoke—but the real Jimi in "Jimi Thing" comes from the slightly jazzy vamps at the core of the song, something that is slightly soulful, slightly rocky. In a sense, the song itself isn't an homage to Hendrix so much as to the sensibility of Hendrix: "Sometimes a Jimi Thing slides my way and keeps me swinging."

Boyd Tinsley has a jumping solo on the studio version of "Jimi Thing," but the thing about the song is that it is resilient, letting the band be rhythmic, letting the musicians show off their chops. That's why it's always been part of the band's live repertoire. Since 1991, there's never been a year where DMB hasn't played it. Though 2011 saw a mere six performances, usually this is an anchor in the band's set.

"Warehouse"

Atmospheric and epic, "Warehouse" is at the core of Dave Matthews Band mythology, probably because it's a song about the group's origins. The Warehouse is where Dave used to write songs and rehearse, and he immortalized it in this song, which was first played onstage in March of 1991.

"Warehouse" is a complicated piece, shifting in time signature and mood, trading on polyrhythms and jazz solos, grounded in a skittish acoustic guitar line from Matthews, all building to a majestic close. The song has a specific structure, but it allows for several interpolations, not to mention places for crowd participation. Lillywhite's production of "Warehouse" on *Under the Table and Dreaming* is measured, assured, and colorful, but "Warehouse" truly comes alive onstage, where the band can play off the energy of the audience and expand the song.

Since its debut in 1991, there never was a year where the song wasn't played. Usually, it was a staple of set lists: only in 2011, when the group was laying low, and 2009, when it was played seven times, was it not a regular part of the repertoire.

"Pay for What You Get"

One of the songs on *Under the Table and Dreaming* that has essentially been forgotten, "Pay for What You Get" is a light, mellow, jazzy number, one that's all about the ramifications of a departed lover. The slight swing is appealing, but the group didn't spend much time with it. It was debuted in September of 1992, then played often throughout 1993 and 1994, then slowly retired in the '90s before being played a lot in 2003. From that point on, it was usually shelved, but showed up as a dose of nostalgia in 2008, 2014, and 2015.

"#34"

The first time that Dave Matthews Band's habit of numbering songs in the order of their composition showed up on record, "#34" is indeed the thirty-fourth song the band attempted. Co-written with Haines Fullerton—the co-leader of the Deal who would commit suicide in 1996—the song is a gentle instrumental, sometimes sung with a chorus, but usually a tonal piece. The band played it a lot in 1993, then never again until 2005, when it became a familiar part of the summer set list. It was subsequently played once in 2007 and twice in 2013, but it's generally a forgotten number.

Recording

Dave Matthews Band signed with RCA on November 9, 1993, but didn't enter the studio to record its debut album until May of 1994. A lot of work goes into the preparation of a major-label debut—particularly one from a band poised to break into the big time—so RCA let DMB plan things out, giving the band members time to find the right producer and put themselves in the right settings.

Dave Matthews Band eventually settled on Steve Lillywhite, a British producer who was best known for helming hits by U2, Morrissey, and XTC. Despite his success, Lillywhite didn't make a lot of music that suggested he'd feel comfortable with Dave Matthews Band's loose-limbed fusion. The exceptions were two: Joan Armatrading, a singer/songwriter who often dabbled in jazz; and the Pogues, a gang of Irish ruffians who sounded vibrant and precise in the hands of Lillywhite.

Dave Matthews Band auditioned plenty of potential producers—T-Bone Burnett came to a show on February 2, 1994, to scope out the band, while according to Lillywhite, Hugh Padgham "turned them down because he said the drummer was too jazzy"—but Lillywhite earned the job by claiming, "I don't want to change you. I don't think you need to be changed. I just want what you do to become cleaner and clearer on an album." According to lore, he also guaranteed the band that the record would go platinum, although he refuted that in an interview with Matt Norlander of *Relix* in 2014: "I don't even know what platinum is. Is it a million? That's the sort of thing the sort of producer I hate will say."

"I produced Rolling Stones and didn't do my homework with them," Lillywhite added. "I wasn't going to do my homework with Dave Matthews Band." This wasn't arrogance so much as confidence, combined with a positive feeling about the band. Recalling the indie debut that was sent his way, he continued, "I don't really so much remember about [the beginnings of] U2, but I really remember *Remember Two Things*."

Lillywhite made a case to RCA that he really wanted to produce the band, only to be told that the group had decided upon using Jerry Harrison, the Talking Heads guitarist/keyboardist who had begun earning a reputation as a producer after his own band fell apart. Undaunted, Lillywhite headed to New York, because, "A lot of producers did not, would not, put their money on Dave Matthews because they did not see a history of music like that being successful." He attended a show at New York's Irving Plaza on November 10, 1993, and soon persuaded the group he was the man of the job.

Lillywhite took the band, plus guitarist Tim Reynolds, up to Bearsville Studios, a New York State recording emporium founded by Albert Grossman where some of the greatest albums of the '70s were recorded, including several Todd Rundgren productions (notably his own *Something/Anything* and the Band's *Stage Fright*). Lillywhite had Matthews and Reynolds play acoustic guitar parts together, cutting upward of four guitar tracks; then, in the mix, the producer would swap between the two parts. Often, he relied on Reynolds, and he also had the guitarist do a fair share of overdubs, including some electric parts. For the rest of the band, meanwhile, the time spent holed up in the studio was the longest they had ever spent without gigging, so they wound up blowing off steam by playing shows at the Tinker Street Cafe in Bearsville.

"Granny," a staple in the band's live set, was cut during the sessions but left off the final record. For years, fans speculated that Dave Matthews Band intended "Granny" to be released as a single, something that Lillywhite debunked in 2014, admitting that he wasn't enthusiastic about the song, thinking that the "love, baby" lyric didn't make for a good chorus. That version of "Granny" can be heard on the twentieth-anniversary reissue of the album, along with acoustic versions of "Dancing Nancies" (a song that did make the final album) and "The Song That Jane Likes" (which did not). "Say Goodbye" and "Let You Down" were both initially recorded during these sessions, too, but not released until 1996's *Crash*.

The one guest that was flown in was John Popper, the vocalist/harpist from Blues Traveler. Popper played his solo on "What Would You Say" quickly. Legend has it that Popper played his showcase while Matthews was in the bathroom, which is true, but he was also pressed for time. To Norlander, he said, "I did only take one pass because the Gremlin they had rented to pick me up broke down not he New York Thruway. I had to hurry so I could catch a plane to England for Blues Traveler's first tour there."

Lillywhite was in the midst of a divorce, so he did not supervise the final mix—Tom Lord-Alge finished it, sanding down some of the eccentricities in the process, including the sound of Boyd Tinsley taking a hit off a joint.

Release

The band poached the title of *Under the Table and Dreaming* from a line in "Ants Marching," then prepared the record for an autumn release. The album itself was dedicated to Anne Matthews, Dave's older sister—who was tragically killed by her husband in a murder/suicide in January of 1994—but in a way that didn't call attention to itself: underneath the jewel case in the CD tray are the words, "In memory of Anne."

As this was an era when albums were not usually released in variants, there were no alternate edition until *Under the Table and Dreaming* was reissued in 2014 by RCA/Legacy in a Twentieth Anniversary Edition that added the shelved "Granny" along with the aforementioned acoustic

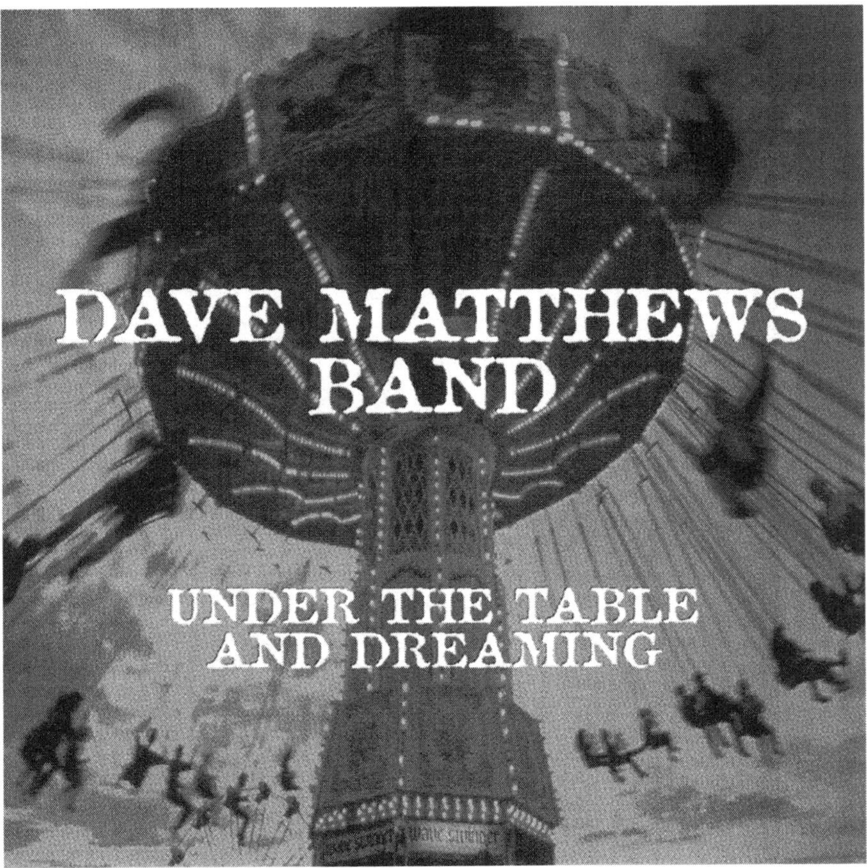

The carnival depicted on the cover of *Under the Table and Dreaming* hinted at the circus to come for DMB. *Author's collection*

versions of "Dancing Nancies" and "The Song That Jane Likes." The album also received its first vinyl pressing with this anniversary edition.

Reception

Fans embraced *Under the Table and Dreaming* quickly: on March 7, 1995, about six months after its release, it earned a gold certification from the RIAA, with its first platinum certification following in May. During its rise, the album climbed to #11 on the *Billboard* Top 200, and it remained a fixture there for a while. By August 1995, it had gone double platinum; it sold steadily through the fall of 1997, when it earned its fifth platinum certification. Three years later, it went platinum for the sixth time.

Critics weren't necessarily as enthusiastic about the album. The *Village Voice*'s Robert Christgau dismissed Matthews by saying "he's as bland as a tofu sandwich," but Paul Evans in *Rolling Stone* countered that "Dave Matthews Band sound like four or five groups in one," before claiming that *Under the Table and Dreaming* "is one of the most ambitious releases of '94."

Legacy

It's very hard to imagine Dave Matthews Band without *Under the Table and Dreaming*. Other albums were bigger hits right out of the gate, and some sold more, but this record is at the foundation of all of DMB's success. A lot of this is due to the fact that it introduced Dave Matthews Band to the world at large, but the record also benefits from the group's deep early songbook—so many of DMB's standards are here, from "Ants Marching" and "Dancing Nancies" to "Satellite" and "Warehouse"—and Lillywhite's nimble production. That combination of song and sound is why it endures: it's clean and colorful, optimistic and open, an album that suggests new beginnings every time it's played.

14

Crash

The Breakthrough

The Album

By every measure, *Crash* was the breakthrough album for Dave Matthews Band. Certainly, *Under the Table and Dreaming* established the band as a potential commercial force, but *Crash* consolidated that success, thanks to the inclusion of several major hits that helped establish the band as a force in the industry. Consider this: *Crash* contains the adult-alternative rock staple "Crash into Me"—the first genuine crossover in the band's catalogue—and also has "So Much to Say," a song that won a Grammy for "Best Rock Performance." That was enough to push Dave Matthews Band from the college circuit and into mass consciousness.

It was a hit, to be sure, which is one of the reasons why *Crash* went so far in fomenting the fame of Dave Matthews Band, but it also was an improvement on *Under the Table and Dreaming*, showcasing a band sowing its oats and testing out how much it could do in the studio. Part of that comfort undoubtedly derives from the band re-teaming with Steve Lillywhite, the producer who helped shape its loose-limbed improvisatory sound for the studio. Where *Under the Table*'s groove seemed to rely very much on atmosphere to create a mood, *Crash* pushes the rhythms to the forefront, letting the record bend and mutate. Much of its accessibility is due to Lillywhite's bright, slick gloss, but that isn't to say there aren't songs here: certainly, "Crash" arrived fully formed, the best of Matthews's romantic ballads, and "Too Much" winds up as less of a vamp than it appears. There's the feeling here that the band is coming to the song, instead of Matthews finding the song within the jam.

Lillywhite knew how to make the band sound sharp and clean, but crucially, he also didn't force the band members to write new songs. Consequently, they cherry-picked tunes from the past and combined these with newly-written compositions—a fairly standard operating procedure for most bands, who tend to stockpile songs prior to the recording of a second album. As the old joke goes, you have your life to write your first album, then six months to write your second, but Dave Matthews Band didn't rush back into the studio to record *Crash*. RCA and DMB invested considerable time in building 1994's *Under the Table and Dreaming*, supporting the record with considerable tours and releasing no less than five singles from it. Outside of certain segments of rock radio and MTV, none of these singles were significant hits, but they, along with those regular concerts, did something that may have been a bit better: they created awareness, helping to build a platform to launch Dave Matthews Band into actual stardom.

That's precisely what happened with *Crash*. The album remains the touchstone in the Dave Matthews Band catalogue—it's not the band's highest charting album, not necessarily its best, but it's certainly the best-selling, and the album that wound up turning the band into stars.

The Songs

Some of the songs on *Crash* date from the earliest days of Dave Matthews Band; some were newly written in the wake of *Under the Table and Dreaming*. Combined, the songs on *Crash* suggest a band that's restless and eager to explore the territory uncovered on its major-label debut.

"So Much to Say"

One of the few Dave Matthews Band songs to bear a co-writing credit for Peter Griesar, the keyboardist who departed before the group signed to RCA, "So Much to Say" is, at its core, something of a psychodrama. The narrator struggles between his own personal heaven and hell, eventually finding a bit of redemption in his lover. In some ways, "So Much to Say" is the ideal Dave Matthews Band song: the message is vaguely inspirational, yet the message is overshadowed by its hooky verse and chorus, which nevertheless give plenty of space for the band to stretch its legs.

The song was first aired early in 1992 and stayed in the band's repertoire from that point forward, dropping out of sight in 1994 as work began on *Under the Table and Dreaming* but becoming a set-list staple again in 1996, just as *Crash* was getting ready for release. "So Much to Say" wound up being the second single pulled from *Crash*, and it did well, peaking at #19 on *Billboard*'s Alternative Songs, #31 on Pop Songs, and #38 on Adult Pop Songs.

"Two Step"

"Two Step" debuted in April of 1992, which means it's one of the group's earliest songs, and one that was played while Peter Griesar was still in the group. From that point on, "Two Step" has never been out of rotation; it was played a mere six times in 2004, but that was an anomaly. "Two Step" is a Dave Matthews Band perennial because it is open-ended, rangy, and lively—it's begins with a minor-key vamp, floats from verse to chorus, picks up speed in the bridge, and has plenty of places where the musicians can indulge in either solos or endless vamps—as they often did. Sometimes, Dave Matthews Band could stretch "Two Step" out to as long as twenty-seven minutes, as it did in 2000. By then, "Two Step" had come to full fruition; most of its evolution occurred during the recording of *Crash* with Steve Lillywhite, who helped the band turn it into a complete circle.

"Crash into Me"

In some regards, "Crash into Me" is the biggest song Dave Matthews Band has ever had. "American Baby" wound up reaching #16 in 2005, but that was a different era in the *Billboard* charts, one that was goosed along by digital downloads. In 1996, "Crash into Me" climbed to #19 through slow, steady radio play, winding up at #9 on the Adult chart and #7 on the

Alternative chart, a crossover that shows that the melodic ballad could draw in a large crowd but was still anchored in alternative rock.

Prior to this, "What Would You Say" was the band's biggest hit, but "Crash into Me" stayed in the charts longer, and it also wound up becoming the kind of song that would be covered in coffeehouses and heard in movies and TV throughout the '90s; the Alicia Silverstone/Benicio Del Toro film *Excess Baggage* played it straight in 1997, but the 2001 film *Joe Dirt* included it with a smirk. Furthermore, Stevie Nicks covered the song for *Soundstage* in 2008, and Iggy Azalea sampled it for a song called "You" on her 2011 mixtape *Ignorant Art*.

This romantic ballad, which sometimes flirts with the explicitly carnal, has never been far from a Dave Matthews Band set list. A few years, it wasn't played much—across 2011 and 2012, it was played a total of nine times—but there's never been a year where it wasn't played, sometimes with Little Feat's "Dixie Chicken" added in the jam.

"Too Much"

A cynical ode to excess, "Too Much" was the first single pulled from *Crash*, which perhaps makes sense. It's a wild, rangy track—something that gives the impression of being a party, even though, at its heart, it indicts indulgence. It's essentially a funk jam—there's not much transition between the verse and chorus; they're all vamps around the same progression—so it's the kind of thing that could be extended onstage, which it often was. From the point of its debut late in 1996, "Too Much" was always in rotation, although there have been long stretches where the band has teased the song but never played it *in toto*; in 2009, DMB almost always indulged in it as a head fake.

"Too Much" received a heavy push from MTV upon its release but, as a single, it wound up playing only to an alternative and mainstream-rock audience: it peaked at #5 on *Billboard*'s Alternative chart and #9 on the Mainstream Rock chart. That makes sense: even if the song wound up as a staple within the DMB catalogue, it's something that plays to the band's strengths without roping in in new listeners.

"#41"

Allegedly written in the fallout of the falling out between Dave Matthews and his manager Ross Hoffman, "#41" is steeped in regret. At one point, Matthews sings, "Remember when I used to play for all of the loneliness that nobody notices now"—a fairly clear nod to the days he spent at the Warehouse, writing and singing with Hoffman—but what makes the song resonate is that it's not specific; Matthews could be singing about any kind of loss, not just his own personal experience.

The song was reportedly dubbed "#41 Police" in its original incarnation, a sign of how Dave Matthews Band—who spent most of its early years cataloging its songs by number—knew that there was a bit of a debt to the Police in this number. In reality, the connection is closer to solo Sting: this gently building, mid-tempo number never quite gets to the nervy new wave/reggae/pop of his trio. Instead, there's plenty of space for LeRoi Moore to play solos in the fashion of Branford Marsalis, and the open-endedness means that the group can bring in a bunch of other tunes when playing live—or can marry it with "Sojourn of Arjuna," a Béla Fleck and the Flecktones number, whenever DMB plays with Fleck.

This song has been in constant rotation since 1995, sometimes dipping to just eight performances a year—as it did in 2006 and 2011—but almost always in the set list at other times because it allows every member to flex their muscles.

"Say Goodbye"

First premiered in the autumn of 1993, "Say Goodbye" is a plea for one final night of passion in the face of a disintegrating relationship. Tomorrow, they'll "go back to being friends," but "tonight, let's be lovers"—and, fittingly, the music is urgent, building to a crescendo just the narrator ratchets up his desire.

At its core, it's a pretty adolescent song: it's how you'd separate in college, hoping for one more fling before calling it an end. Fittingly, the song was a staple in the '90s, played frequently all the way through 1999, and then back-benched in the 2000s. Since then, it has sometimes been taken out for an extended run—it was played almost daily in 2005, and unearthed six times in 2016—but usually surfaces just as a dose of nostalgia.

"Drive In, Drive Out"

"Drive In, Drive Out" is a song of escape—a message telegraphed in the chorus chant of "Drive in, drive out / I'm Leavin'"—but the distinctive element of the song is its churning, insistent sway, which feels like ocean waves crashing to the shore. Some of this urgency may derive from the fact that it was written when Dave Matthews was still young and hungry. It's a

Crash turned Dave Matthews Band into stars. *Author's collection*

very old song—one he brought to Dave Matthews Band as it was forming. The first time it was played onstage was in April 1992; the group touched upon it over the next two years. In 1995, it became a set list staple, and it remained in circulation for a decade. After 2005, "Drive In, Drive Out" was hauled out on occasion, resurfacing regularly during the 2014 tour.

"Let You Down"

A gentle breeze of a song informed by bossa nova, the Dave Matthews–Stefan Lessard co-write "Let You Down" never was part of the canon. This soft, slight number was played throughout early 1997 on tours by Matthews and Reynolds, but since then has been largely forgotten. It was not played at all between 1997 and 2015, when it was only aired twice as a solo Dave performance. The song may have been discarded, but it has its charms in its quiet, hushed vibe; where the rest of *Crash* feels forceful, this one lets you meet it on its own terms.

"Lie in Our Graves"

Dave Matthews Band first played "Lie in Our Graves" all the way back in March of 1992. From that point on, it became a regular part of the set, played continually in the '90s and often unearthed in the 2000s and the 2010s. "Lie in Our Graves" endures because it's one of the first songs to really capture Matthews's love of life and fear of death—there's a grim acknowledgment that this party of life will end at some point—and while the verses are pointed and melodic, it still offers plenty of space for the band to stretch, either to bring in themes from other songs or to just jam until the players run out of inspiration.

"Cry Freedom"

"Cry Freedom" dates from before Dave Matthews Band itself, first having been aired onstage in March of 1991. This moody, churning ballad cherishes its atmosphere, particularly in the incarnation Steve Lillywhite masterminded for *Crash*, which feels like it's swaying out at sea. For a while, this was a particularly popular song—during 1994, it was played almost nightly on the *Under the Table and Dreaming* tour, and it remained a staple throughout 1995, but after a spell in 2003 where it was played frequently, it was essentially shelved, only brought out for a dose of nostalgia a few times a year (or sometimes not at all).

"Tripping Billies"

One of the biggest songs in Dave Matthews Band repertoire, "Tripping Billies" first hit the stage in 1991, and it soon grew into an elastic, loose-limbed jam. Its name allegedly derives from one of the band's cohorts saying that it sounded like hillbillies on acid; "Tripping Billies" isn't quite so psychedelic as this description suggests, but it nevertheless contains the slightest hint of mind-bending, plus it pushes Matthews's "let's live for today" aesthetic. Musically and thematically, it exists at the foundation of Dave Matthews Band's legacy, which is why it was played constantly through the '90s and then regularly in the 2000s and 2010s. The fewest number of times it was heard was in 2011, when it was played a mere four times, but otherwise it has always been at the ready, because it is a rallying call for both the band and audience.

"Proudest Monkey"

First heard during the waning months of 1994, "Proudest Monkey" is a song that plays upon animal imagery—something that would become a staple for Dave Matthews Band—and it's a song of empowerment, with the narrator turning from a humble monkey into the proudest monkey you'll ever see. The song itself doesn't end on a note of triumph. Instead, it builds steadily, opening up to give LeRoi Moore plenty of space to take a saxophone solo. For a while, this was a regular part of Dave Matthews Band shows—particularly through the '90s, when it was often played in concert—but it was largely retired in the 2000s, before being moved into semi-rotation in the 2010s (2010 was the year it was heard most since 1999).

Recording

Crash was recorded quickly, between October 1995 and January 1996. The work was split between two different studios. Dave Matthews Band and Steve Lillywhite—along with auxiliary guitarist Tim Reynolds—returned to Bearsville, where they cut *Under the Table and Dreaming*, but also held sessions at New York City's Green Street Recording Studios. Lillywhite encouraged the band to stretch out and take risks and wound up recording most of the album live. Matthews recalled, "There was a lot more spontaneity on this album than on the one before. A lot of the solos were on the first take. It was created in a circle, everyone facing each other."

Even if this was made speedily, *Crash* feels considered in a way that *Under the Table and Dreaming* doesn't. It bursts with vivid color and is layered with details. It seems to split at the seams with ideas.

Release

RCA released *Crash* on April 30, 1996, on CD and cassette. There were no variations; in 1996, CD sales were robust, so there was no need for bonus tracks. *Crash* didn't receive a vinyl pressing until 2016, when the album reached its twentieth anniversary.

Reception

Fans flocked to *Crash*, sending it to #2 on *Billboard*'s Top 200. It went gold and platinum swiftly, earning both certifications on July 9, just two months after its release. By October of 1997, it had been certified platinum four times, before earning its seventh and final certification on March 16, 2000.

While fans were prepped to embrace *Crash*, the same can't quite be said for critics. This is a typical pattern for bands on their second album: on the debut, no conventional wisdom exists, but with the sophomore set, critics are dealing with a known quantity, so they're writing toward a narrative. This could be seen in the reviews for *Crash*, which usually placed it in the context of the success of *Under the Table and Dreaming*. Indeed, in his "Consumer Guide" in the *Village Voice*, Robert Christgau didn't bother with a full review, dismissing the album with a bomb—that is, an assessment that pivots off one of his other reviews; it'd be the last time he'd deign to entertain Dave Matthews—while Jim DeRogatis, reviewing *Crash* in *Rolling Stone*, claimed "eclecticism gives Matthews a slight edge over his peers, but that's sort of like saying you prefer vanilla ice cream to vanilla frozen yogurt." DeRogatis also drew a comparison between DMB and art-rock legends Roxy Music, and another art-rock group surfaced in Tom Sinclair's review for *Entertainment Weekly*, which cited cult act Mark-Almond as a DMB precursor. Sinclair wound up being the kindest to *Crash*, giving the album a B+ in a review that realized that "one of the nicest things about DMB's music is that its distinctive complexity serves as a virtual assurances against a flood of lame imitator bands." This has proven true over the years.

Legacy

With its seven platinum certifications, *Crash* is the most popular Dave Matthews Band album, and, for fans of different stripes, it's also considered one of the very best. Some of this may be due to timing—these were the boom years not only for alternative rock but also for CD sales, so *Crash* wound up in more households than any other DMB album, and became the kind of album that was often heard at parties and in record stores over the next few years, creating strong impressions among millions of listeners. Yet it's also the biggest, boldest album the band ever made—a record that captures its prowess in the studio and on the stage.

Much of this success lies in how *Crash* follows the same formula as *Under the Table and Dreaming* but is executed with slick precision. The reunion with Steve Lillywhite certainly helped, since the producer understood the band's strengths but also knew how to push it toward the future. Plus the album provided so many of the songs in the band's core catalogue. True, some of these songs were around long before the album itself—"Two Step," "Say Goodbye," "Cry Freedom," and "Drive In, Drive out" all existed prior to *Remember Two Things*—but that's part of the charm of the album. *Crash* feels like it ties a bow on the rise of the group, as the album that marks the culmination of the first act of DMB's career, and the place where the band finally aired out most of its early catalogue.

15

Before These Crowded Streets

The Masterpiece

The Album

A lengthy, seventy-minute album once again produced by Steve Lillywhite, *Before These Crowded Streets* was the first for which DMB didn't rely on previously written material, which may be the reason why it's also one where the group takes the most chances.

The lengthiest of all Dave Matthews Band studio albums, and packed with cameos, too, *Before These Crowded Streets* sprawls; it's a CD that feels like a double album. Such indulgences are a reflection of DMB's massive popularity—the band was at the point where it could do whatever it wanted—and while DMB would maintain its considerable popularity over the next two decades, this album effectively draws a close on its first act. This is the end of the band's ascendancy, the last record the band would complete with Steve Lillywhite, the last time the band would make something intimately connected with the jam-band scene. After this, DMB had transcended that designation.

It's possible to see the shift in the guests on *Before These Crowded Streets*. The group's old friend John D'Earth shows up twice, as does Béla Fleck, but so does the Kronos Quartet—an ambitious classical group too highbrow and refined for previous DMB excursions—as does Alanis Morissette, who in 1998 was perhaps the biggest star in rock, her presence signaling how Dave Matthews too was now a major star.

Certainly, when *Before These Crowded Streets* appeared in 1998, Dave Matthews Band was poised to become the biggest act in mainstream

American rock. By now, the shockwaves of the early '90s alternative-rock explosion were beginning to fade. Kurt Cobain was four years gone, and Green Day, the biggest punk band to cross over into the mainstream after Nirvana's success, wasn't necessarily old news—*Nimrod*, its 1997 record, produced a staple with the ballad "Good Riddance (Time of Your Life)"—but had been around long enough that the bloom was somewhat off the rose. Dave Matthews Band, on the other hand, was on the rise, its catalogue moving in increasing numbers, its concerts selling out, and, importantly, the band was embraced by the industry. It was time for superstardom.

Faced with this situation, it would've been understandable if DMB decided to go somewhat pop for *Before These Crowded Streets*, but that wasn't the path the band members chose. Instead, they decided to double down on their sense of adventure, something that's evident in the appearance of the Kronos Quartet and Béla Fleck but also apparent in the album's length and vague air of darkness. Although the band wasn't intent on alienating audiences, the album demands to be met upon its own terms—a sign of confidence, not cowardice.

The album is linked by a number of segues—ranging from interstitial music to audio clips—that only accentuate the record's atmosphere: such accouterments are not the province of a live show but exist solely within the studio, emphasizing how this record was designed to be a distinctly different beast than the rest of the catalogue. Nevertheless, there is a sonic continuity with previous Dave Matthews Band albums, including the prominent presence of Tim Reynolds, who plays guitar on every cut.

The Songs

By many measures, the compositions on *Before These Crowded Streets* are among the most ambitious Dave Matthews Band ever recorded. The band still flirts with good-time tunes on *Before These Crowded Streets* but also excels in moodier music, taking risks and threading in new influences, including jazz and world-beat.

"Panatela Naga Pampa"

A forty-one-second snippet, "Panatela Naga Pampa" effectively acts as a fanfare for *Before These Crowded Streets*, announcing the complex, world-beat overtones to come. It's also a sign of the band's impish humor. At one point, fans believed that the phrase was Gambian for "welcome to our home," but Gambian isn't a language, so the most likely explanation is that it means "I have a python in my pants" in Indian. If this song is ever played in concert, it's always played in conjunction with "Rapunzel," just like it is on record.

"Rapunzel"

Funky and deceptively complex, this retelling of the familiar fairytale finds Dave Matthews on the make. He's yearning for his Rapunzel, spitting out lyrics with intensity. What really distinguishes "Rapunzel" is the dense, jazzy interplay. The rhythms stop and start; the music swells to solos from LeRoi Moore. In that sense, it's one of the best full-band numbers: it shows how Matthews's vocals can be every bit as fluid, electric, and alive as Carter Beauford's rhythms or Roi's solos.

Played continually through the 1998 and 1999 tours supporting *Before These Crowded Streets*, "Rapunzel" has remained a reliable staple in DMB sets, popping up every year after its release. The fewest number of times it was played was in 2011, when it was aired just three times.

"The Last Stop"

Opening with an ominous swirl, "The Last Stop" is urgent and mysterious, a song that feels connected to the early classic "Minarets." The Middle-Eastern streak provides a great showcase for Stefan Lessard, who co-wrote the song with Matthews, but there is also plenty of space for Boyd Tinsley, whose violin is all over the song. On record, it also features Béla Fleck as a guest.

Played heavily in 1998, "The Last Stop" then essentially became a forgotten number. When DMB hauled it out—as they did in 2003, 2006, 2010 and 2016—they played it often, but it usually wasn't a song that remained in regular rotation.

"Don't Drink the Water"

The first single from *Before These Crowded Streets* didn't cross over into the Top 40—though it did peak at #4 on the Alternative charts—but it has become an enduring staple for Dave Matthews Band, played on every tour since 1998, and often showing up in every set.

At its core, "Don't Drink the Water" is a pro-environmentalism song, written from the perspective of natives who are pushed off their land by greedy forces. It's ominous and churning, sounding like a cross between Peter Gabriel and Daniel Lanois, and given a lift on record by banjo from Béla Fleck and vocals from Alanis Morissette. Fleck has often showed up onstage to play the song with Dave Matthews Band, and it has been performed regularly since its 1998 premier.

"Stay (Wasting Time)"

A lighthearted tune that skips along on a loose, cheerful acoustic guitar figure, this is a soulful party song, driven by jubilant vocal harmonies and burbling horns. It marks the studio debut of the Lovely Ladies, the backing singers who often supported Dave Matthews Band during this period, and they help goose this song into a party anthem. The song was performed often between 1998 and 2001 and also through the 2000s, especially during 2003 and 2007. It faded into the background in the 2010s, and was not played at all in 2013, but it showed up a lot in 2014 and 2015.

"Halloween"

Reportedly written about an early girlfriend of Matthews's called Julia, "Halloween" is a very early song. It was first played in 1992 and showed up often in 1993, before the band signed to a major label, before being revived in 1998 for *Before These Crowded Streets*. Here, DMB is augmented by the Kronos Quartet and John D'Earth, who together help to ratchet up the slashing, ominous tone of the song, which Matthews then undercuts with growls so guttural they verge on parody. This is something he'd often bring to concert performances, too, and it hurts what's otherwise a roiling piece of drama. "Halloween" may have enduring legs—it showed up regularly in sets from the 2010s, and was played often in 2012 and 2013—but there were times when the band barely played it—such as the 2000s, when it was only played a couple of times in 2000, 2002, 2005, and 2007.

"The Stone"

Fueled by staccato string stabs, "The Stone" is a better showcase for the Kronos Quartet than "Halloween." As on the song, John D'Earth arranged the strings, but here the Kronos Quartet creates a nicely tense atmosphere that suits a song about suspicions and worry.

"The Stone" was played often between 1998 and 2005 before slowly being put on the back burner. From that point on, it never left set lists entirely, but only in 2010 and 2015 was it aired often; it could be played as rarely as once (in 2011) or twice (in 2006).

"Crush"

The third single from *Beyond These Crowded Streets* only went to #75 on *Billboard*'s Hot 100—it did go to #11 on the Alternative chart and #20 on Adult Alternative—but it remains one of Dave Matthews Band's enduring songs. Like so many of the band's songs, it's a love song, but it's distinguished by an after-hours jazzy vibe, something that's evident in the supple rhythms, the single-note guitar lines by Tim Reynolds—who sounds like Wes Montgomery here—the textures from Boyd Tinsley, and the emphatic, nuanced singing from Matthews.

It's one of the most popular songs DMB has ever done—a staple onstage and on radio.

"The Dreaming Tree"

Clocking in at nearly nine minutes, "The Dreaming Tree" provides a journey—one that keeps developing and folding in on itself. It's fueled by memory and fantasies, with Matthews remembering an old man telling him about the dreaming tree. Quite quickly in the song, the dreaming tree winds up dying, and the whole song carries a sense of loss in its melancholy sway and percolating rhythms.

Given its majestic scale, "The Dreaming Tree" proved to be quite difficult to pull off on stage. The band played it with some regularity on the supporting tour for *Before These Crowded Streets*—it did, after all, give the album its title—and then attempted it often between 2006 and 2009, but there were years where the band never tried it, and several where it was attempted only once.

"Pig"

A low-key number that feels hushed and subdued yet has a cheerful undercurrent. It's another song wherein Matthews takes stock of the great human condition—sneering at the greedy little pig, encouraging everybody to open up and shake up their bones—and it's fittingly stuck between pop and arena rock, open-ended enough to invite jams but lacking a melodic through line.

"Pig" was played often during the *Before These Crowded Streets* tours, but 2002 was the year it was played the most, though it also showed up a lot in 2006. It regularly showed up in sets in other years, but was never played in 2001, 2001, 2008, and 2011.

"Spoon"

Tested out in 1997, "Spoon" provides a fitting closure to the album—reflective, without quite being sad. Béla Fleck once again shows up, as does Alanis Morissette, but their presence doesn't stop this from feeling stark and subdued. Played often in 1998 and 1999, "Spoon" would sometimes show up on Dave Matthews and Tim Reynolds's duo tours, but since 2003 has rarely been played by the band.

Recording

Sessions for *Before These Crowded Streets* started in October 1997, with Lillywhite and Dave Matthews Band heading to Sausalito's the Plant. Another round of sessions at New York's famed Electric Lady Studios followed in early 1998 before DMB wrapped up work.

Unlike the previous three albums, *Before These Crowded Streets* was written largely in the studio—a major shift for a band used to road-testing its material. There were only two exceptions to this rule: "Don't Drink the Water," which was aired early in a different version, and "Halloween," which was one of Matthews's first songs. Perhaps the fact that so many of its compositions were created in a concentrated burst is the reason why

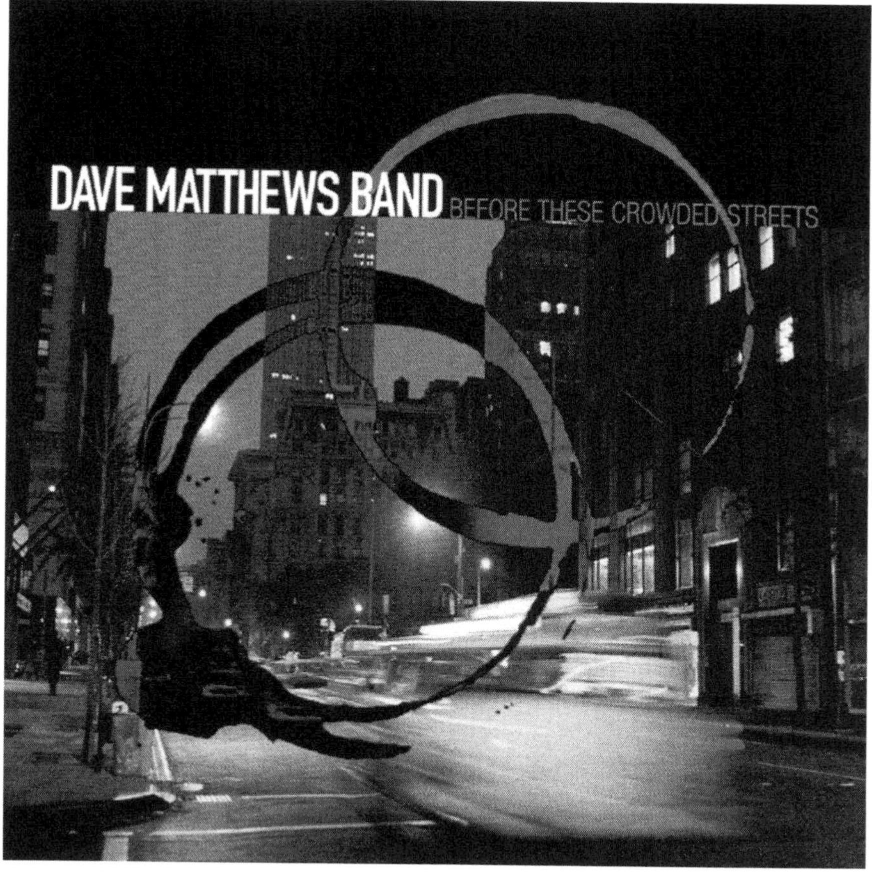

Dave Matthews Band stretched out on *Before These Crowded Streets*. *Author's collection*

the album feels unified in a way its predecessors don't. In Borzillo's 1998 book, Matthews says, "This album is less ambiguous, more connected. And there's a little more focused reflection on this album than there has been on others, whether that's good or bad. The lyrics and music seemed to happen much more together; it's more like a project from beginning to end rather than a collection of songs."

As lengthy as the album is, there were songs that were cut. "Help Myself" was turned over to the producers of *Scream 2*—initially, the band was planning to give the thematically appropriate "Halloween" to the filmmakers, before deciding to keep it for its own album—while other leftovers include "Get in Line," "#40 (Always)," and, most legendarily, "MacHead," an outtake so named because it apparently was a cross between Paul McCartney and Radiohead. Jake Vigliotti says he's heard six different demos of the song, some dating as early as 1997, but Boyd Tinsley said that the album was completed before the song, so it was left unfinished (although some fans speculate that it morphed into "Bartender.")

Release

RCA released *Before These Crowded Streets* on April 28, 1998—almost two years to the day after the release of *Crash*. Initially, the album was released on CD, cassette, and LP—the first time that a new Dave Matthews Band album saw a vinyl edition on the day of release. Indeed, when the group played "Don't Drink the Water" on *Late Night with David Letterman*, the host was seen fumbling with the vinyl, saying, "This is going to ruin your CD player."

Reception

Before These Crowded Streets debuted at #1 on the *Billboard* charts and swiftly earned gold and platinum certifications on June 2, 1998. A second platinum certification arrived in August, with a third and final one coming on September 15, 1999.

The album earned guarded but positive reviews that recognized the progress Dave Matthews Band had made since its previous records. Writing in *Entertainment Weekly*, David Browne zeroed in on the fact that "Dave Matthews is not a chugalug mirth-meister," noting the dark themes that flow throughout the album, along with the musical ambition. He praised the band for finding a "new style of unplugged prog-rock" but said it had "yet to learn the difference between virtuosity and bombast," claiming that at times Matthews "comes off as a post-alternative version of later-period Neil Diamond." In *Rolling Stone*, Anthony DeCurtis rightly asserted that "Dave Matthews Band has always been more about sound than songs" and praised the group's "extraordinary" rhythm section: "They anchor this unwieldy outfit without ever weighing it down. And when it's time to fly, they give the band wings."

Legacy

Despite these tentative reviews, *Before These Crowded Streets* is often considered one of the great Dave Matthews Band albums by fans and critics alike. It's earned that reputation partially due to its rich, layered atmosphere: it's an immersive record, one with a distinctly different feel than other DMB records. For that alone, *Before These Crowded Streets* would endure—it's an album designed for introspection—but the songs are equally compelling, showcasing both the adventurous and the romantic sides of Dave Matthews Band. Furthermore, the album functions like the close of its first act as a band. It is the culmination of all the labor and fun of the '90s. From this point on, the band's members would still work hard and have good times, but they were now older and were now stars, so things would be complicated. For as dark as *Before These Crowded Streets* sometimes gets, it never feels complicated: it's still the sound of the same band for which everything seemed to flow easily.

The Lillywhite Sessions

The Lost Album

The Album

Technically, *The Lillywhite Sessions* isn't a Dave Matthews Band album. The twelve songs on this "record" were abandoned, and while many of them were later revived for 2002's *Busted Stuff*, these recordings have never seen an official release. They were, however, bootlegged, first appearing on the internet in March 2001, roughly a year after the release of the Glen Ballard collaboration *Everyday*.

Fans flocked to *The Lillywhite Sessions*, finding it to be a tonic to the polished *Everyday* and turning it into one of the first heavily bootlegged albums of the internet age. Part of its appeal certainly derived from the fact that it was taboo: these were forbidden sessions, passed along as low-quality MP3s because that's all the technology could allow at the time. Another aspect of *The Lillywhite Sessions* that fans found appealing is that it was very much a continuation of *Before These Crowded Streets*, whereas the subsequent *Everyday* was as clear a departure as could be imagined.

Considering how fervently these abandoned sessions were embraced by fans, it's hard not to wonder why Dave Matthews Band didn't release the album. Why the sessions were scrapped remains something of an unanswered question, but there's no disputing that the group was having a difficult time finding its footing after a remarkable first act. Given all its success—the album sales escalated along with the tickets, the accolades began to pile up—it made perfect sense for the band to re-team with producer Steve Lillywhite, the man who helped translate its elastic fusion from stage to studio.

A crucial difference between *The Lillywhite Sessions* and *Under the Table and Dreaming*, *Crash*, and *Before These Crowded Streets* is that those three albums were all made in professional studios; it was Dave Matthews Band meeting Lillywhite on his home turf. These sessions were different: they were done near the home of Dave Matthews Band, in the Charlottesville house the group turned into a recording studio called Haunted Hallow.

Lillywhite and the group convened at Haunted Hallow in the winter of 1999, with the sessions spilling over into early the next year. During the sessions, Lillywhite posted an update on the DMB site, revealing that several songs had been tracked, including "Sweet Up and Down" and "JTR," a reworking of "John the Revelator" that Matthews wrote for Santana's star-studded 1999 comeback *Supernatural* but that wasn't included on the album. Everything appeared to be proceeding as normal, but there were warning signs, the loudest being Carter Beauford's confession to RCA A&R man Bruce Flohr that he "didn't feel" the recordings. Later, Matthews blamed the vibe on himself, specifically his heavy drinking—an indulgence that turned into a circular crutch. "I felt like I was in the process of failing, in the process of letting everyone down," he told David Fricke. "Inside that environment, I was continuing to do just that, come up with these sad bastard songs." Years later, Lillywhite expressed some bemusement about this narrative: "I've read a lot about how everyone [in the band] was very upset and sad but I didn't feel anything like that," he told *Rolling Stone*'s Greg Heller in 2001. "These sessions were nothing compared to a U2 album."

With the record label's deadline approaching, the band decided to shelve the recordings and go out on tour. "Grace Is Gone, "Grey Street," "Bartender," "Raven," "Sweet Up and Down," "JTR," and "Digging a Ditch" all showed up during the summer of 2000 tour, but while playing new tunes live usually helped DMB sharpen its songs, the record was no closer to release after the tour. During this stint on the road, *Rolling Stone* reported that the album was to be called *The Summer So Far*, but that was merely a title of a new song; the article extrapolated the title based on the scrawl engineer Stephen Harris put on eight CDs he made for himself, the band, Lillywhite, and Flohr. (Harris called it "The Story So Far," with "The Summer So Far" merely distinguishing the latest iteration of the sessions.) Matthews said he always intended to call the album *Busted Stuff* and, indeed, many of the songs would later surface under that title in 2002, albeit in new versions.

Before *Busted Stuff* came to fruition, there was *Everyday*, an album written quickly by Matthews and new producer Glen Ballard and recorded swiftly, too. *Everyday* not only contained none of the songs played on the 2000 tour, it back-benched the band and found Matthews

Dave Matthews Band on the March 15, 2001 cover of *Rolling Stone*. The accompanying story is the first time DMB went on record regarding the failure of *The Lillywhite Sessions*, all in the service of promoting *Everyday*. *Author's collection*

playing electric guitar—changes that irked hardcore fans and made them evermore eager to hear the music that was scrapped. All that needed to happen was for the music to make its way out of the studio.

Eventually, it did just that.

Release

Craig Knapp, the lead singer of a Dave Matthews Band cover band, was sent a CD in March 2001 containing the unreleased *Lillywhite Sessions*. Knapp was undoubtedly excited but unsure whether he should share the sessions with the world at large. He e-mailed Lillywhite directly and also posted his message on the Dave Matthews Band fan site DMBML.

He admitted in the e-mail that he had the bootleg—"I am blessed to receive this gift"—but rightly questioned the propriety of circulating the recordings. "I would really like to share these songs with the DMB trading community. However, I feel that if the Dave Matthews Band and Steve Lillywhite didn't release these songs, then what gives me that right? I don't want to disrespect the band, or yourself. I guess my question is simply this: Am I disrespecting the Dave Matthews Band and Steve Lillywhite by making these songs available."

Knapp then received an e-mail, purportedly from Lillywhite, claiming that it was kosher to circulate these tracks, so the singer posted them all to the net. This, of course, was no more than a ruse devised by another fan eager to hear the songs. Beholden to the speed of his modem, Knapp gave the tracks over to Drew Wiley, who then put the files online; initially, these were of poor quality, but as the tech improved, so did the bitrate. It wasn't long before *The Lillywhite Sessions* went from private trading among fans to the peer-to-peer trading of Napster, and the album became a public sensation.

An accompanying collection of demos also leaked to DMB fans sites. While some fans called this release "disc two," it wasn't a collection of polished recordings: these were rough demos, taped over the phone by Wiley. Such fly-by-night recording naturally resulted in exceedingly choppy audio, but the tape offered nascent versions of "Bartender" and portions of "Grace Is Gone," along with the unreleased "Build You a House," whose appearance is noteworthy for hardcore DMB collectors as the band never returned to the tune.

Reception

The bootlegging of *The Lillywhite Sessions* became a story outside of Dave Matthews Band circles because it was one of the first albums by a major act to be bootlegged on a peer-to-peer site (a few years earlier, Radiohead's *Kid A* spread like wildfire a few weeks prior to its release, but that album was slated for an official release; this was an outright bootleg). Not only did this bootleg earn articles in newspapers, but *Rolling Stone* and *Entertainment Weekly* reviewed it as a new album, giving it better reviews than *Everyday*.

Soon, fans were launching online petitions asking for RCA to "Release Lillywhite Recordings," a well-intentioned effort that was ultimately futile. Nevertheless, all this attention wasn't unnoticed by DMB or Lillywhite. The band began threading some of the songs into its 2001 set lists, and Lillywhite released a statement claiming, "I cannot condone the release of these unfinished recordings, although I feel these are some of the most moving pieces of music that I've ever recorded with Dave Matthews Band."

Dave Matthews Band then decided to combat the bootleg by revisiting the material with Stephen Harris, the engineer for *The Lillywhite Sessions* who now was hired as the group's producer. The band headed into the studio in 2002 to record *Busted Stuff*—the title the group had initially planned to give the scrapped album—and revived nine of the songs, leaving behind "JTR," "Sweet Up and Down," and "Monkey Man" (the latter having never found its way into the live set).

Legacy

Busted Stuff punctured the myth of *The Lillywhite Sessions* but didn't erase it, not by a long shot. Fans continued to trade the record, and one enterprising engineer even took the trouble to remaster the album in 2006, giving it its finest-sounding release to date. Even if it isn't an official DMB album, it's an important step in the group's career, the bridge between its first act and its second. Nevertheless, the reputation of the rejected recordings is somewhat inflated: since *The Lillywhite Sessions* was illicit, it carried a certain outlaw romanticism that's difficult to separate from the album itself. As a whole, *Busted Stuff* is a stronger and richer album, so *The Lillywhite Sessions* is best seen as a transitional work—an album that Dave Matthews needed to record but didn't need to release.

Everyday

The Crossover Album

The Album

Everyday may be the most divisive album within the Dave Matthews Band catalogue. Even if it hadn't arrived in the wake of the scrapped *Lillywhite Sessions*, *Everyday* would've been disarming, since it swaps out so many Dave Matthews Band sonic signatures for the markings of a modern-day pop album.

Chalk up the shift in direction to Matthews choosing to shake himself out of his creative doldrums by hiring producer Glen Ballard. At that moment in time, Ballard was best known for his work with Alanis Morissette, having produced her 1995 blockbuster *Jagged Little Pill*, a record that turned her into a superstar and made him a sought-after producer. Ballard's approach to recording was the opposite of Steve Lillywhite's. Whereas Lillywhite kept himself in the background, choosing to accentuate how the members of Dave Matthews Band interacted with each other, Ballard relied on his strengths and made an album where the studio was almost a sixth musician. Not for nothing is Ballard credited as a co-writer with Matthews throughout the album: he helped sculpt and shape the direction of the whole record.

Having Ballard work with drum loops and collaborate with Matthews on the songwriting was a huge shift for DMB. In the past, even if they didn't compose together, the band members at least wound up finding a song's heart through shared improvisation. None of that can be heard on *Everyday*. This may have revived a band that was going through a creative crisis in 2000, but the slickness of the album struck some fans as unwelcome—

a sentiment the musicians may share, since not a lot of the songs worked their way into lasting rotation on the road.

The Songs

The songs that comprise *Everyday* are different than those on any other Dave Matthews Band album. Unlike the records that came before or after, these songs were written without input from the members of the group who aren't Dave Matthews. He wrote these songs with Ballard, so they are unique in the DMB canon: tight, hooky, and succinct songs designed with a record in mind, not the stage.

"I Did It"

A bright, garish explosion of defiance and regret, "I Did It" feels designed to be a single. It has moments where Dave Matthews Band gets to flex its muscles, but it's a tight recording, flowing from verses to choruses, finding strength in its chorus. The chorus seems taunting—"Do you think I've gone too far?" carries an impish smirk, as if Dave knows that he's really pushed the limits.

As a radio single, it works quite well—and it did all right on the charts, peaking at #5 on *Billboard*'s Alternative chart and #20 on its Adult Alternative chart—but it's not the kind of song that withstands exploration. As such, it has had a very short shelf life with Dave Matthews Band. It was played regularly between 2001 and 2002, then its frequency fell precipitously in 2003 and 2004, before disappearing for years. After that, it was played four times in 2010, then twice in 2015.

"When the World Ends"

A light, tripping pop tune that cuts against the lyrics, "When the World Ends" was mooted as the third single from *Everyday*, and a video was even shot, but once terrorists struck the United States on September 11, 2001, it was pushed out of sight. It may never have received the commercial due it deserved, but "When the World Ends" is one of the best numbers from Dave Matthews Band's brief infatuation with mainstream pop. Here, Glen Ballard retains Matthews's winding narratives, polishing them and turning them into something gleaming, yet the song still has plenty of places of the band to roam. Perhaps that's the reason why it continued to be a popular item in the years after *Everyday*. Throughout 2001–2007, it was a regular, and though it wasn't heard much between 2008 and 2012, from 2013 on it has been a standard part of the band's repertoire.

"The Space Between"

By any measure, "The Space Between" belongs among Dave Matthews Band's biggest hits. It reached #22 on the *Billboard* Hot 100, #4 on the Adult chart, and #10 on the Alternative chart, then reached #35 on the UK chart—by any measure, that's one of the most popular songs in the band's catalogue. It was also heard in the ads to *Black Hawk Down*, and often in bumper music on television—in other words, it seems like one of the group's blockbusters. And yet . . . this is a song Dave Matthews Band has often avoided in concert. It was played a lot in 2001 and 2002, just after the release of *Everyday*, then essentially abandoned for a decade, played only five times in 2004 and twice in 2008, which is surprising, considering how big a hit it was. DMB did revive it in 2012, and it became a semi-regular inclusion during the 2010s, but that long stretch where it was absent might speak to how tightly composed the song is: it provides no avenues for the band to explore, and is a showcase only for the song itself.

"Dreams of Our Fathers"

A densely rhythmic work that feels tense in the verse and elastic in the chorus, "Dreams of Our Fathers" demonstrates a clear debt to Sting: Dave's voice is keening; the guitar echoes like Andy Summers. Curiously, this is the only song released on a studio album that Dave Matthews Band has never played live. The band attempted it during soundchecks in 2001 and 2003, but it never made it to the show. Maybe the song, which seems to be as dexterous and lively as any of the band's wildest moments, is too cloistered, too studio-bound; the rhythms are dense, and there are pliable moments on the bridge, but it's all tightly sealed.

"So Right"

"So Right" is loose-limbed, funky, and bright—a very rhythmic tune that's not especially melodic. At times, the song threatens to lift off—the chorus wants to soar—yet the whole production winds up feeling rather earthbound. One of the problems with the song, as far as DMB goes, is that it's too tight: the choruses float on punchy stabs of horns, but it's not especially hooky, nor does it give the band much place to explore. Consequently, it's a song that shows up sporadically in sets. The band is

Everyday was Dave Matthews Band's first album produced without Steve Lillywhite.
Author's collection

either completely committed—as it was in 2001 and 2002, or 2013 and 2014—or decides just to pepper it into the set.

"If I Had It All"

At its core, "If I Had It All" is searching and reflective, and, fittingly, it's the first song on *Everyday* that feels somewhat questioning in its intent, swaying between introspection and quiet urgency. There are also more studio effects here than on most Matthews tracks—there are moments where all the music seems swallowed up by a black hole—but this kind of meditation, which lyrically is typical to Dave Matthews, seems hermetically sealed, circling around the same kind figure without breaking free.

Dave Matthews Band played the song often between 2001 and 2003, then started to scale it back in 2004, when it was played seven times. After skipping it in 2005, the band played it nine times in 2006, but, after that, it was played once in 2007, once in 2010, and once in 2012—a sign that it was essentially abandoned.

"What You Are"

"What You Are" has a slightly Middle-Eastern flair to its rhythms and the melody—there's a drone to the verse that slowly surges into the chorus. In this sense, it's reminiscent of "Minarets" and feels very much designed for the stage, and it was often played there. It was a staple through 2001–2002, then it was played often in 2003, abandoned in 2004, and revived in 2005; it appeared a few times in 2006 and 2010—not to mention a handful of times over the rest of the 2010s—but has largely remained elusive in set lists.

"Angel"

A ballad that tilts toward the mainstream, "Angel" is an underrated song in the Dave Matthews Band catalogue. Somewhat grounded in a slow, soulful groove reminiscent of Jimi Hendrix's "Angel" and buttressed by a nice bit of Beatles-esque psychedelia on the chorus, it's a nice, polished pop song. Perhaps it wasn't an Adult Alternative hit but it feels like one. Nevertheless, it essentially wound up being discarded by Dave Matthews Band. The band played it a lot in 2001, on the tour supporting *Everyday*, then three times in 2003, but then it was abandoned from that point forward. It's not hard to see why: its charm is that it's concise, but there's no space for improvisation, so it's no wonder DMB doesn't play it much.

"Fool to Think"

"Fool to Think" is a slice of churning mid-tempo arena rock, sounding indebted to U2 and Sting. It's a heartbroken tune—the narrator thinks he's a fool to think that his lover looked at him with kindness—yet it's produced like an adult alternative love song, something where surface feel matters as much as the song. It feels designed to exist on record, so perhaps it's not a surprise that after the early 2000s, DMB put the song in mothballs. The band revived the song at the tail end of the 2010s, playing it often in 2017.

"Sleep to Dream Her"

"Sleep to Dream Her" glides along on light bossa-nova rhythms, accentuating the sweetness of the song with lots of washes of synths that help sell a melody that never quite sticks. It's a song that gains a lot of ground from its atmosphere: it feels warm and comforting, but there are no real hooks. "Sleep to Dream Her" was played often on the *Everyday* supporting tour in 2001, then a few times between 2002 and 2003, before being sent to the minor leagues; it was essentially forgotten after 2006.

"Mother Father"

Opening with a bit of single-string classical string guitar—a wash that recalls the world beat of Paul Simon—"Mother Father" gets complicated once it goes into half time for the breakdown. It's atmospheric, providing a natural space for the guitar of Carlos Santana, who swings by the studio to repay the debt he owed Matthews for the singer appearing on

Supernatural. It's an intriguing song but one that's very much a studio construction, so perhaps it's not a surprise that the band attempted it live a mere seven times in the summer of 2001 before abandoning it.

"Everyday"

One of the brighter songs on *Everyday*, the title track also seems like one that could fit on any other Dave Matthews Band album with ease. Much of this is due to how its roots lie in "#36," a song that was played frequently between 1993 and 1996 before eventually turning into this chipper paean to love and understanding. "Everyday" lies at the crossroads of the jam-happy Dave Matthews Band of old and the pop snap of Dave's collaboration with Ballard. Despite its polish, "Everyday" feels organic, and that may be why it remained a staple of DMB sets, played at least three times a year every year since its release.

Recording

Still nursing wounds from the unrealized *Lillywhite Sessions*, Dave Mathews Band attempted a different approach for what became *Everyday*. Matthews headed out to Conway Studios in Los Angeles to meet with Glen Ballard before the rest of the group, with the idea that they'd add a couple of new songs to the raw material Lillywhite had produced, but the singer and producer hit it off, creating nine songs within ten days. Once the rest of DMB arrived in Los Angeles, there was enough material for a brand-new album. By that point, it also had been decided that this album would be executed in a different fashion. All of the songs were in place, from the arrangement to the rhythm, and the others were not expected to flesh out the songs; they were simply to add to their parts.

To *Bass Player* magazine, Stefan Lessard recalled, "It was something I hadn't really been able to tackle before. It wasn't as organic as what I was used to. At the same time, I was psyched. Learning the lines was a lot of fun, and when I'd throw in my own ideas, Glen was open to them. The end of 'The Space Between' was something I came up with, and there are lots of other bits and pieces. It was great not being on my own—I had someone guiding me through the songs."

Carter Beauford seemed less positive in 2002. According to *Rolling Stone*'s David Fricke, "Beauford, a drummer of ferocious energy and forthright tongue, will tell you precisely what he doesn't like about *Everyday*: 'My creativity, my expertise, as well as that of the other guys in the band, was smothered. The record didn't need us.'" He underlined that this was not "the Dave Matthews Band. It is two people and they did an incredible job."

To that end, Ballard helped keep the circle closed. For the first time ever, Tim Reynolds was not invited to play guitar on a DMB album—instead, Matthews plays electric guitar—and the cameos are limited: Vusi Mahlasela sings backing vocals on "Everyday," but, more notably, Carlos Santana returned the favor Dave and Carter paid him on *Supernatural* by playing guitar on "Mother Father."

Release

Everyday saw an international release on CD and Cassette in February 2001, debuting at #1 on *Billboard*'s Top 200 and #1 in the Canadian charts. It was certified platinum three separate times by the RIAA: the first two certifications arrived April 2, two months after its release, with the third coming on January 8, 2002.

For the first time, there were variants in the CD release: in Australia and New Zealand, there were editions containing a *Live Bonus* CD featuring a Labor Day Broadcast of unspecified origin. To date, there has been no vinyl pressing of *Everyday*.

Reception

Upon its initial release, *Everyday* received positive reviews, with most critics praising the changes Ballard brought to Dave Matthews Band. *Time* claimed that his addition improved the band: "The change has been for the better. While the shelved songs had meandered, the new tracks are fierce and focused, powered by Matthews' electrified lead guitar lines." *PopMatters* went a bit over the top, exhorting, "Change is good, people! Keep in mind that Dave recently turned thirty-four and got married, so now he has more to do than stay on the road for five years straight. In short, he grew up, and slightly altered his style. Give him a break."

Writing in *Entertainment Weekly*, David Browne saw strengths and weaknesses in the album, claiming it was "a bumpy ride that finds Ballard attempting to rein in Matthews's self indulgent tendencies, while Matthews strives, with varying degrees of success, to ditch his jam band image for a sleeker sound. . . . What Matthews sacrifices in the process is distinctiveness; for much of the album, he might as well be backed by anonymous session men."

Legacy

In sheer sales terms, *Everyday* ranks right alongside *Before These Crowded Streets* as one of Dave Matthews Band's most popular albums. Still, sales can be deceiving. Despite this success—fueled in large part by the AAA hit "The Space Between"—the album is not well loved either by fans or the group.

Promoting *Busted Stuff* in 2002, Dave Matthews Band gave a lengthy interview to *Rolling Stone*'s David Fricke, who noted that there was once concert where a guy in the front row held up a sign reading "GLEN BALLARD IS THE DEVIL." Fans can occasionally be overheated, but the band itself quickly soured on *Everyday*, too. In that same article, Beauford told Fricke that the album "almost divided the five members. [*Everyday*], in a way, is Dave and Glen's record, really."

Ultimately, the root of all the problems with *Everyday*—in both conception and reception—was the collaboration between Ballard and Matthews. The producer's heavy hand is one of the reasons why *Everyday* feels more like a solo album than Dave's own 2003 solo album, *Some Devil*, which was a record that felt rooted in the exploratory folk of Dave Matthews Band; in that sense, it played like a continuation of the brooding *Lillywhite Sessions*. In contrast, the only true cousin to *Everyday* is its successor, the shiny, soulful *Stand Up*.

Despite its mainstream veneer, *Everyday* did generate a few DMB standards in "The Space Between" and "When the World Ends," but those were anomalies. Most of the songs from the record faded from view, and, as such, *Everyday* is the Dave Matthews Band album most fans choose to forget: it doesn't sound like Dave Matthews Band, nor does it feel like it, either.

18

Busted Stuff

Rescuing *The Lillywhite Sessions*

The Album

The simplest way to describe *Busted Stuff* is that it's Dave Matthews Band taking a second pass at the music of *The Lillywhite Sessions*. The title itself could be read as a passing allusion to that failed project—those sessions were broken or "busted," as it were—but in fact "Busted Stuff" is one of the songs that was first cut back in 2000, sitting here alongside nine other songs that were attempted back then. Two new tunes were added in the process—"Where Are You Going" and "You Never Know"—but those songs feel of a piece with the others, perhaps because they share a similar well-worn interplay.

That kind of weathered, knowing interaction is what was missing on 2001's *Everyday*, the album Dave Matthews Band cut in the wake of the failed Lillywhite record. Where *Everyday* seemed like a reaction to internal strife—the rough sessions pushed DMB toward working a heretofore alien method, with producer Glen Ballard directing the process—*Busted Stuff* feels like an answer to that album's gleaming AAA pop. Some of this about-face may be due to fans being unhappy with the Ballard production, but it also made sense for Dave Matthews Band to revisit its abandoned songs. Ever since its inception, this was not a group to leave tunes behind—songs would be tested for one album then polished on the next—so having a full album of material left to rot was not part of DMB's *modus operandi*. So, the band chose to revive the songs from *The Lillywhite Sessions* but not the existing recordings.

Busted Stuff stays true to the band's signatures and makes few concessions to a pop audience—"Where You're Going" is the closest, and it made sense that it was pulled as a single—and that's its strength: it feels like the true sequel to *Before These Crowded Streets*.

The Songs

Many of the compositions on *Busted Stuff* are derived from the abandoned *Lillywhite Sessions*, so it's perhaps not a surprise that they feel restless and searching. They were written at a time when the band wasn't sure where it was going, and, even if they were recorded at a time when they were assured, the songs retain a sense of unease that makes them compelling.

"Busted Stuff"

"Busted Stuff" takes stock of the destruction that happens when a relationship ends, or even when a "rolling stone" runs through the fields. It's a heavy subject, but the song shimmers on an elastic, mellow groove—one that gives Matthews plenty of space to indulge in his falsetto. The song was played often during the summer 2000 tour—the one that followed the aborted sessions—then seven times in 2002 and twice in 2003, before being shelved until 2010, when it was played six times.

"Grey Street"

Released as the third single from *Busted Stuff*, "Grey Street" didn't crack the *Billboard* Hot 100, but it peaked at #18 on the Adult Alternative chart. A tribute to the poet Anne Sexton, "Grey Street" went through many variations in lyrics over the years, before Matthews eventually settled on the version heard on *Busted Stuff*. This is one of his most ambitious lyrics, and it's also one of his tightest songs, inexorably building to a majestic conclusion. It's not divided into sections that would allow for intense jamming; instead, it's a fully formed piece that gains power in how it moves forward, and, in that sense, it hints at the music on *Some Devil*. Since its debut onstage in the summer of 2000, there's never been a year when Dave Matthews Band hasn't played this number, and it's often a staple of the band's set lists.

"Where Are You Going"

Unlike most of the songs on *Busted Stuff*, "Where Are You Going" wasn't a leftover from *The Lillywhite Sessions*. It first debuted in the autumn of 2001, and it's a song of questioning: "Are you looking for answers / Where do you go?" Matthews admits he has no answers—that he's no Superman—but the key to the song is how it keeps circling, meditating on the central point of directionless—a theme that seemed considerably poignant in the wake of the terrorist attacks of September 11, 2001.

"Where Are You Going" was also featured on the soundtrack for the Adam Sandler film *Mr. Deeds*, released in theaters just a month before *Busted Stuff* hit record stores. The single simultaneously promoted the movie and the new album, reaching #39 on *Billboard*'s Hot 100 and #3 on

Bassist Stefan Lessard dominates the cover to *Busted Stuff*. *Author's collection*

the Adult Alternative chart. It was frequently played in concert throughout the 2000s, but in the 2010s it was hauled out only a handful of times a year; nevertheless, it has never completely disappeared from set lists.

"You Never Know"

The other newly written song on *Busted Stuff*, "You Never Know" is distinguished by its evolving, shifting time signatures—a flourish that gives the song a sense of swaying on the sea. Like "Where Are You Going," the song is about pondering, but where "Where Are You Going" revolves upon the axis of its questions, there's a lift in "You Never Know"—a sense of accepting the uncertainty, of realizing that things can change at a moment's notice. After being played frequently following the release of *Busted Stuff*, "You Never Know" became a rarity, appearing infrequently apart from concentrated spells in 2005 and 2012.

"Captain"

One of the oldest songs on either *The Lillywhite Sessions* or *Busted Stuff*, "Captain" was first unveiled by a drunken Dave Matthews at an Agents of Good Roots show in 1996. He then played it with Tim Reynolds during a 1997 tour, but the song started to evolve and take shape during the 2001 recording sessions. By the time it got to *Busted Stuff*, the song had a jazzy, yacht-rock vibe—the kind of song that would be played in an after-hours lounge by a mustachioed DJ. DMB played "Captain" often in 2002, then left it behind for the better part of a decade, playing it only as a surprise before it was revived in 2013, followed by some appearances in 2015.

"Raven"

Dave Matthews started to test-drive the song that became "Raven" in 1995, but it really came into shape in 2000, when the group recorded it for *The Lillywhite Sessions* and played it on the summer tour. For *Busted Stuff*, the song received a free-flowing, appealing arrangement: it feels ever-expanding, which is a nifty trick.

Played often in 2002, then retired for three years, "Raven" returned to semi-regular rotation in the mid-2010s, yet it's essentially a cult song.

"Grace Is Gone"

One of the major songs on *Busted Stuff*, "Grace Is Gone" feels intimate and rootsy—an Americana song fused with the delicate sway of solo Sting. It's probably one of the most songwriterly songs Matthews has crafted: it feels like it wasn't made with the band's muscle in mind, which is appropriate, considering how it's written from the perspective of a dialogue between a drunk brokenhearted man and his bartender. "Grace Is Gone" was released as the second single from *Busted Stuff*, but it didn't show up on the charts. Nevertheless, it has been played often ever since its debut in the summer of 2000.

"Kit Kat Jam"

The very fact that "Kit Kat Jam" has the word "jam" in its title tells everything you need to know about this song. It is not a fully composed song but rather a vamp that came out of a jam. The band first tested it out for *The Lillywhite Sessions*, when Dave Matthews wrote some lyrics for the song, but by the time the group came to record it for *Busted Stuff*, the lyrics had been left behind. When it came to performing it onstage in the summer of 2002, Matthews once again sang lyrics—usually different variations, depending on the night. "Kit Kat Jam" remained in the repertoire through 2003, then it largely disappeared from view, surfacing four times in 2010 and twice in 2013.

"Digging a Ditch"

The somber "Digging a Ditch" first appeared in 1999, on a duo tour between Dave Matthews and Tim Reynolds, who performed it throughout the spring. During 2000, the band developed it onstage, getting it in shape for *The Lillywhite Sessions*. By the time it showed up on *Busted Stuff*, it was meditative and slick, easing from stark sections to reassuring swells from the band. Between 2001 and 2003, it showed up regularly in sets, but it wound up fading away in the back half of the 2000s, appearing only in the summer of 2006. During the 2010s, it became a semi-regular feature once again, played a fair amount in 2010 and picking up momentum toward the middle of the decade, always staying in rotation.

"Big Eyed Fish"

A moody, slightly unsettling, open-ended piece, "Big Eyed Fish" developed onstage and changed quite a bit, lyrically, between *The Lillywhite Sessions* and *Busted Stuff.* Matthews here uses nature as a metaphor, with fish, man, and monkey all finding themselves beset with problems when they decide to leave their homes. Unlike so many Matthews meditations on mortality, "Big Eyed Fish" doesn't end on a hopeful note, and its melancholy suits DMB's uneasy era of the early 2000s.

After playing the song often at the dawn of the 2000s, the band avoided it for the rest of the decade—the summer 2006 tour is the only time it was played regularly—but it showed up often in the 2010s, usually in conjunction with "Bartender," just like on the *Busted Stuff* album.

"Bartender"

The centerpiece of the material that comprises both *The Lillywhite Sessions* and *Busted Stuff*, "Bartender" began as a duet between Dave Matthews and Tim Reynolds, and was played often during their tours of 1999. During the 2000 tour, it started to expand, and it came to fruition during the *Busted Stuff* Sessions. "Bartender" is concerned with mortality and littered with religious imagery. Often, it seems as if the narrator is running away from pain, soothing himself in drink—a sentiment that underscores suspicions that *The Lillywhite Sessions* were a brooding, alcohol-soused time. "Bartender" may be a dark, roiling song that exists on the same plane with U2 and Peter Gabriel, yet Matthews's writing isn't imitative here: it achieves am ideal blend between introspective songwriting and expansive band arrangements. Maybe that's why "Bartender" proved so enduring.

Recording

Once Dave Matthews Band decided to revisit *The Lillywhite Sessions* material, the group hired Stephen Harris, a British producer who worked with the second wave of Britpop bands, earning his biggest hit with Kula Shaker's *K*. Harris and Matthews first crossed paths on Santana's *Supernatural*, where the former co-produced the track "Love of My Life," which featured contributions by both Dave and Carter Beauford.

Harris and the band headed to the Record Plant in Sausalito, California, in January 2002, and the sessions for *Busted Stuff* proceeded quickly. Unlike previous Dave Matthews Band albums, there were no guest musicians at these sessions: this was just the band, and nobody else—not even Tim Reynolds. Harris worked like his fellow Brit Lillywhite: he accentuated the interplay within Dave Matthews Band instead of bringing his own ideas to the table. In a sense, this was done on the fly, the band bashing out songs it had recorded once before and knew well through touring. The group did revive "JTR," "Sweet Up and Down," and "Monkey Man" from *The Lillywhite Sessions* but decided not to include these on the album. Similarly, DMB attempted "Save Me" and "Gravedigger," songs Matthews would take to his solo debut, *Some Devil*, the following year.

Once the sessions were complete, Matthews felt satisfied. "I feel like I've finished the picture," he told David Fricke in 2002. "I'd left those songs in an ugly little pile. Going back was like seeing old friends again."

Release

Busted Stuff was released on July 16, 2002. Initial US pressings included a bonus DVD called *Some Other Stuff*, which contained live performances of "When the World Ends" and "Bartender" shot at a concert in Boulder, Colorado, on July 11, 2001, along with the 5.1 mix of "Bartender." This was the only variation of the album, which did not see a release on cassette or vinyl.

Reception

Like its two predecessors, *Busted Stuff* debuted at #1 on the *Billboard* 200; it also reached #1 in Canada, the only other territory where it charted. On August 29, 2002, the RIAA certified the album gold, platinum, and double platinum, signaling that the record had shipped two million copies in a month and a half—a sign that Dave Matthews Band was at the peak of its popularity.

If the fans were enthusiastic about *Busted Stuff*, critics were too. Will Hermes rated the album 7/10 in the August 2002 issue of *Spin*, writing, "If serious art is the attempt of the artist to identify his depression, *Busted Stuff* is where Matthews finally gets serious—it's the sound of a man staring down his melancholy, albeit over a round of Jell-O shots." Hermes concluded, "The result is, as rumored, the best album of Dave Matthews' career—the most coherent and graceful, the least wanky and aw-shucks messianic." In *Entertainment Weekly*, Chris Willman gave the album a "B," admitting that he initially wished that the group hadn't re-recorded *The Lillywhite Sessions* but praising the new versions, which "feel altogether sweeter, cleanly separating the players an goosing the still-eclectic signature sound." Writing in *Rolling Stone*, Greg Kot made an argument for DMB's growth: "After years of trying to build memorable songs of an awkward mix of jazzy instrumentation and singer-songwriter introspection, *Busted Stuff* suggests a new lesson is starting to take hold: Sometimes simplicity is the best route to the heart of the song."

Legacy

Upon its release, several critics made a case similar to Will Hermes's, claiming *Busted Stuff* to be the best of the Dave Matthews Band albums. It didn't quite earn that reputation among Dave Matthews Band fans, who remain more fond of the career-making trilogy of *Under the Table and Dreaming*, *Crash*, and *Before These Crowded Streets*. Still, *Busted Stuff* belongs right up alongside those albums because it boasts one of the band's strongest collections of songs and was executed with precision that stays faithful to the group's inherent chemistry.

That said, the album is something of a detour in the Dave Matthews Band catalogue. Aesthetically and sonically, it feels like a continuation of *Before These Crowded Streets*, not *Everyday*, and its true sequel isn't 2005's *Stand Up*—technically, the next Dave Matthews Band album—but *Some Devil*, the Dave Matthews solo album that appeared the next year. This speaks more to growing pains within Dave Matthews Band; how its members tried to tackle its growth and status as one of the more popular bands in America in the early twenty-first century. They'd eventually settle, but during this time, they were still stretching and experimenting, and *Busted Stuff* is something of an oasis—a band momentarily reconnecting to its strengths.

19

Some Devil

Dave Matthews Goes Solo

The Album

Arriving in 2003, after *Everyday* and *Busted Stuff*—both aftershocks of the turbulent abandoned *Lillywhite Sessions*—it was hard not to see Dave Matthews's solo album, *Some Devil*, as the singer/songwriter establishing himself as a viable solo act in his own right. This, of course, is not a great leap. Casual observers may have assumed the "Band" in Dave Matthews Band to be mere supporting players, not a collaborative unit, and might have thought Dave could step away from the group and be no weaker. To an extent this was true, but only in the sense that he was indeed the band's main songwriter; *Some Devil*, like so many solo albums, not only puts his own talents in sharp relief but also reveals just how much Dave Matthews Band actually functions as a band.

The Songs

Some Devil may be the first solo album from Dave Matthews, but its contemplative nature makes it a cousin to the soul-searching compositions on *Busted Stuff*, a record comprised of songs written at the band's lowest point. The songs on *Some Devil* can be dark, but they aren't bleak: they're moody numbers where Matthews seems to reveal slightly more of his soul than he does on the songs he's written for DMB.

"Dodo"

Reportedly inspired by Matthews paging through a bunch of old *National Geographic* magazines, "Dodo" takes stock of how things can change over the years. Using the extinction of the dodo bird as a starting point, Matthews wonders, "This little game when nothing is sure / Why would you play by the rules?" It's one of Dave's "social conscious" songs, but the point is rather elliptical; and, fittingly, the music is rather subtle, distinguished on *Some Devil* by an appearance by the Dirty Dozen Brass Band, which gives a song that's essentially rooted in folk a bit of a soulful tilt. But as the sax solo concludes the coda, it's clear this song has a lyricism that is strikingly different than DMB: Matthews may be working from the same palette, but the concentration is on the song, not the performance.

Matthews would regularly return to "Dodo" on satellite tours—tours with his Friends, or duo performances with Tim Reynolds.

"So Damn Lucky"

A sweetly swaying folk-pop song, "So Damn Lucky"—as its title suggests—demonstrates a bunch of gratitude, but it was written at a time when Matthews often took scenic routes to his destination. This winds up giving the lyric a nice bit of tension—the details may be ambiguous, but the intent is clear—and, unlike music written for Dave Matthews Band, this is a powerfully melodic and tight song: it could've been a big Adult Alternative hit, if only the cards broke right. Alas, it was not released as a single, but it wound up becoming a staple—the rare *Some Devil* song to work its way into Dave Matthews Band set lists.

"So Damn Lucky" wound up becoming a regular song for Matthews, showing up not only at DMB shows but also in solo sets and duet concerts with Tim Reynolds. There wasn't a year since its 2003 debut when it wasn't played.

"Gravedigger"

"My father's been dead for more than twenty years. I still want him to be proud of me." These words are written in the liner notes to *Some Devil*, and while "Gravedigger" isn't precisely a tribute to Matthews's departed father, it is a meditation on mortality. Each verse finds the narrator pondering the fates of people buried within a cemetery. Matthews quotes the nursery rhyme "Ring Around the Rosie"—long rumored to be about the plague, although that theory has since been debunked—but its presence helps underscore the tug of death that runs through the song. Matthews asks to have the grave be shallow, because he's fighting death, and that's what gives the song tension: he's obsessed with death but doesn't want to succumb.

"Gravedigger" was pulled as a single from *Some Devil*, and it wound up peaking at #35 on *Billboard*'s Hot Adult Top 40 Tracks and Hot Alternative Songs charts. All this attention gave the song an extended life, with the tune becoming regular feature in Matthews concerts. Furthermore, Willie Nelson covered the song on 2008's *Moment of Forever*.

"Some Devil"

Stark and simple—in its studio incarnation, it features nothing more than a guitar and a voice, both heavily reverbed—the album's title track has a bit of a light melodic pull but a heavy heart. "Too drunk and still drinking / It's just the way I feel," opens the third verse, an acknowledgment that appears to conjure ghosts. If the narrator is trying to exorcise inner demons, the song actually doesn't feel haunting; there's something comforting in the melody, particularly when it's executed by Matthews himself.

"Some Devil" would show up regularly in concerts, occasionally attempted by Dave Matthews Band as a whole, and sometimes played in conjunction with Tim Reynolds, but usually performed by Dave solo, often as the first song in an encore at Dave Matthews Band shows.

"Trouble"

One of the distinguishing characteristics of *Some Devil* is that it's very much a songwriter's album, with few songs designed for a band to jam. "Trouble" falls into this category, and finds the narrator taking stock of his worries, wishing that all his troubles would leave. He's acknowledging that he wallows in these doubts, and that kind of self-questioning finds a nice fit with the slowly rolling clouds of echoing guitars: it sounds like Peter Gabriel fronting U2. "Trouble" was played a few times in the 2003–2004 tour supporting *Some Devil*, then once each in 2005 and 2006, then retired.

"Grey Blue Eyes"

A circular number in which the narrator obsesses over his departed lover's grey-blue eyes, this song is distinguished by the ringing chords by Trey Anastasio. His guitar gives "Grey Blue Eyes" a bit of a hypnotic feel, but the song also feels slight, like something that can slide away in the slipstream. Played a few times on the *Some Devil* tours of 2003 and 2004, it faded from view after 2006.

"Save Me"

The funkiest number on *Some Devil*, blessed by backing vocals from a gospel choir, "Save Me" is also the number that feels closest to a traditional Dave Matthews Band song—a composition that mashes up folk, rock, gospel, soul, and a hint of jazz. It is a cry for redemption, and that salvation seems to come from the music, which is big, bold, and openhearted: it's a rallying cry in the midst of navel gazing. Its similarities to DMB tunes may be the reason why it wound up being a regular in Dave Matthews Band sets in the 2010s.

"Stay or Leave"

Another relationship song, and one existing at the fulcrum of where a romance could either grow stronger or splinter. The narrator is asking his lover whether to stay or leave; "I want you not to go / But you should" is an acknowledgment that things may not be going as well as they could be. A lot of the song is tied up in reflection and the realization that the decision is ultimately outside of the singer's reach, but what makes it work is the wonderful sway of the melody, a melodic line that acknowledges the

Dave Matthews appears contemplative and skeptical on the cover to his solo album, *Some Devil.* *Author's collection*

heartbreak of the situation; the idea that this relationship is essentially over even as the narrator asks his sweetheart to stay.

"Stay or Leave" proved to have long legs in the Dave Matthews universe, showing up at solo shows, duet performances with Tim Reynolds, and Dave Matthews Band concerts proper.

"An' Another Thing"

"An' Another Thing" is the title given on *Some Devil* to a song that otherwise has been known as "Little Thing," a number first debuted in 1995 and played frequently between 1996 and 1997, then revived a few times a decade later. In all these cases, it was known as "Little Thing"—this includes a *Live Trax* volume that digs out a concert from April 30,

1996—but on *Some Devil*, it's heard as "An' Another Thing," a title that makes as much sense as "Little Thing," since neither phrase appears in the lyrics. On *Some Devil*, it's another moody place—one filled with images of broken hearts and rain—and delivered in a keening falsetto by Matthews. On record, the SeattleMusic string ensemble helps give this a lush, spooky feel, and that's actually what elevates it above "Little Thing." Here, it feels not designed for the stage, just a little bit of a dreamscape that's come to life.

"Oh"

"Oh" is a place where Dave Matthews's two main obsessions intersect: it's a love song couched in the idea that the world is falling apart. The opening lines admit as much—"The world is blowing up / The world is caving in"—but the narrator finds solace in the fact that his lover is still there with him. Appropriately, this song gains strength from its lightness: it's slight, but that's its charm.

"Oh" wound up being one of the enduring numbers from *Some Devil*, often showing up in Dave's solo shows and his collaborative concerts with Tim Reynolds.

"Baby"

Another song accentuated by a prominent string section—on *Some Devil*, it features nothing more than Matthews's acoustic guitar and a string quartet—this is a number that offers consolation to the narrator's girlfriend. That's the crux of the chorus—"Baby it's all right / Stop your crying now"—and the rest of the song offers similar reassurance. It's a nice sentiment, but "Baby" is a slight song—an opinion supported by how it essentially disappeared after no more than five performances in 2003 and 2004.

"Up and Away"

A mellow, soulful number where the narrator pledges allegiance to the love of his partner, "Up and Away" kind of departs from the mournful character of *Some Devil*, but, placed near the end of the album, its lightness comes as a reprieve. Despite the washes of jazz organ, it's essentially a tight pop song, and one that's slightly disposable, as evidenced by how the song disappeared from view after 2006; it was played only fifteen times total.

"Too High"

The concluding number on *Some Devil* is as hushed as so much of the rest of the album, but it feels lighter, even if the lyrics are rather ambiguous. It's a dramatic number—one where it feels like the power is consciously restrained, but the entire thing feels amorphous. The words are a mishmash, pledging allegiance and absence, and the music churns without a crescendo. Not surprisingly, the song faded from view after the accompanying *Some Devil* tour, airing just once in 2006 before disappearing.

Recording

"I hadn't really been thinking about doing a solo album until I had a handful of songs that didn't really fit with the band, so I started with those and it just grew into a full record," Dave Matthews told MTV during the promo junket promoting *Some Devil*, and these words, alongside others, helped soothe fans who were afraid that the appearance of this record and Boyd Tinsley's *True Reflections*, released in the summer of 2003, signified to permanent fractures in the Dave Matthews Band foundation.

Once he decided to cut a solo album, Dave Matthews chose to reunite with Stephen Harris, the producer who helped bring the remnants of *The Lillywhite Sessions* to life on *Busted Stuff*. Choosing to work near Matthews's new home in Seattle, the pair set up shop in Studio Litho and brought along Tim Reynolds, Phish guitarist Trey Anastasio, bassist Tony Hall, and drummer Brady Blade, with Harris playing keyboards. Sessions ran between October 2002 and June 2003, and the recording was methodical—Matthews told *Rolling Stone* he and Harris wound up "playing a click track and getting ideas down, building songs piece by piece, taking things apart and rearranging things on the computer"—but the end result feels full and robust.

Release

Some Devil saw release on September 23, 2003, and was made available in two separate physical formats—a standard CD, then a deluxe version featuring a five-track bonus CD from the 2003 tour by Dave Matthews and Tim Reynolds—and as a digital download. This was the first time a Matthews-related studio album was released digitally.

Reception

Some Devil debuted at #2 on the *Billboard* 200, and within a month it would be certified both gold and platinum by the RIAA; these would be the last certifications it would receive. Early in 2004, "Gravedigger" took home the Grammy for "Best Male Rock Vocal Performance," an award that suggested the song was popular, but it wasn't a major hit: it peaked at #35 on both the Adult Top 40 and Modern Rock Tracks charts.

Most of the reviews of *Some Devil* were kind, noting its similarities with and differences from the rest of the Dave Matthews Band catalogue. *Slant*'s Sal Cinquemani claimed, "*Some Devil* might just be the jam-band front man's best work since *Before These Crowded Streets*." Writing in *Entertainment Weekly*, Greg Kot noted that it "falls in line with the last couple Dave Matthews Band studio albums, which de-emphasized open-ended jams in favor of a more sculpted, song-oriented approach," but concluded, "Matthews better rejoin his band and get back to the arenas, where he belongs."

Legacy

As it turns out, the solo projects by Matthews and Boyd Tinsley were a passing phase—a way for the group to grow, a way to get out of a fairly rough spot. Naturally, Matthews's album was a bigger deal than Tinsley's: it was treated not as a solo album but like another Dave Matthews Band album, and pushed toward radio. "Gravedigger" worked its way into Dave Matthews Band's setlists, often appearing as a solo showcase for the songwriter, and it wasn't the only *Some Devil* number to be revisited by the DMB at large. "So Damn Lucky" appeared in set lists in 2008, and "Stay Or Leave" showed up in 2009, but the rest of the tunes were comfortably ensconced on this record, and feel at home in this moody, melancholy affair. This supple sullenness separates *Some Devil* from the rest of Matthews's work; while there might be moments of sadness on the group's studio albums, this feels like a "dark night of the soul" record, the occasional levity functioning as a counterpoint to the album's essential darkness.

Stand Up

The Modern R&B Album

The Album

Dave Matthews Band took its time following up *Busted Stuff*, which itself felt something like a quick corrective action from the band—a neo-apology for the crossover of 2001's Glen Ballard–produced *Everyday*. When *Stand Up* finally emerged in 2005, it seemed like the time was ripe for DMB to return to its '90s form with a record that accentuated its long-limbed rhythms and freeform jams.

Despite the appearance of the group's long-standing Fire Dancer logo on the album cover—a graphic Dave Matthews designed years earlier, inspired by the revelry he witnessed in the audience—*Stand Up* isn't a throwback to old-school DMB, nor is it much of a continuation of *Busted Stuff*. Instead, it bears the heavy influence of modern R&B producer Mark Batson—who had previously worked on Seal's fourth album, and would go on to collaborate with Eminem, Jay Z, and Alicia Keys, as well as James Blunt—and wound up doubling down on the group's slick crossover aspirations, delivering a record that felt like a sequel to *Everyday*.

The Songs

Like those on *Everyday*, the songs on *Stand Up* are unlike most of the rest of the Dave Matthews Band catalogue. Usually, DMB writes together, or interprets the songs Matthews writes on his own, but here the producer Mark Batson wields a heavy hand, steering the group toward a lithe, modern

R&B sound that bears traces of the band's DNA but is slicker, smoother, and hookier than most of its other work.

"Dreamgirl"

Fittingly, given its title, "Dreamgirl" shimmers. This love song is subdued, an ode to a lover who remains just out of reach, and that melancholy undercurrent is what gives the song—it's what lends the song an air of poignant mystery. Perhaps that elusiveness is why the song didn't wind up charting, despite a heavy push via a video starring Julia Roberts. "Dreamgirl" saw regular play on the tours surrounding *Stand Up*, but since then has been revisited rarely.

"Old Dirt Hill (Bring That Beat Back)"

Quite clearly built around a sample in the studio, this is the closest Dave Matthews Band ever got to straight-ahead contemporary R&B. With its looped rhythm and mellow vibe, it's not a far cry from something that Babyface might attempt, and that smooth surface helps soft-peddle a nostalgic song about childhood. Dave Matthews Band played "Old Dirt Hill (Bring That Beat Back)" often during the tours for *Stand Up*, and it has remained in relatively regular rotation, picking up spins during the mid-2010s.

"Stand Up (For It)"

Functioning as the album's title track, "Stand Up (For It)" could be heard as a nod to Sly and the Family Stone's classic "Stand," and it's certainly one of the funkier numbers Dave Matthews Band has ever done. It's essentially a vamp that seems designed for the stage, but it wasn't played there much: it was a staple in 2005, revisited in 2007, and then revived in 2018.

"American Baby (Intro)"

A bridge to "American Baby," this also stands as something distinct in itself, offering Dave Matthews Band ways to explore themes of patriotism and sacrifice by contrasting sounds of war with a jazzy, atmospheric swirl. It seemed designed to be played onstage, too, and it was often played in the mid-2000s, when the band was joined for it by such guests as Rashawn Ross and Rage Against the Machine guitarist Tom Morello. Following those three years in the spotlight, it was quietly dropped from set lists.

"American Baby"

The hit single from *Stand Up*, "American Baby" is a vague protest song—one more concerned with playing to America's better nature than throwing firebombs in the middle of George W. Bush's second term. Here, Matthews is hoping that America stays beautiful through all of its turmoil—a patriotic message that could play to listeners of either political persuasion—and the song has a similar gloss, which turned this slow groove into a pop hit. It wound up climbing to #16 on *Billboard*'s Hot 100—the Dave Matthews Band's highest ever chart placement—yet the song didn't have legs. DMB played often it in 2005 and 2006, but after that it was largely abandoned.

"Smooth Rider"

Highlighted by Mark Batson's organ, which feels channeled from soul-jazz of the '60s, this song has a nice, deep groove, a vamp that digs deep. For a while, the group figured out how to ride this onstage. It was played throughout 2005 and 2006 and well into 2007 before starting to peter out in 2008. After that, it was played only twice in 2009 and 2015—perhaps a sign that this kind of vamp is too funky for Dave Matthews Band onstage, but on record it's one of the band's better deep cuts.

"Everybody Wake Up (Our Finest Hour Arrives)"

One of the few songs on *Stand Up* that seems designed to fill a stadium, "Everybody Wake Up (Our Finest Hour Arrives)" speaks to our finest impulses—an anthem in the vein of Bob Marley's "Get Up, Stand Up." Despite this rallying cry, Dave Matthews Band doesn't follow a straight line. Although the chorus is insistent, the verse is winding, both melodically and lyrically, so it's not as rousing as intended. Maybe DMB realized this: it was not played often on the *Stand Up* tour, appearing just eight times in 2005, which is the same number of times the band played it in 2012. After that, it faded away.

"Out of My Hands"

A moody ballad that almost seems to exist at a standstill, "Out of My Hands" feels a little out of step with the rest of *Stand Up*. Generally, it's a buoyant record, but this is insular and meditative—the sound of somebody giving up control—and some of that churning gloom recalls the darker moments of Dave Matthews Band, particularly portions of *Before*

Dave Matthews Band's trademark "Fire Dancer" logo finally makes an appearance on an album cover on *Stand Up*. *Author's collection*

These Crowded Streets. Maybe that's why the song found legs onstage. Played often during 2005, right after the album's release, it then was heard in 2008, but its real revival came in 2012, since when it has popped up on occasion.

"Hello Again"

"Hello Again" stands out on *Stand Up* but also among Dave Matthews Band songs in general. It is one of the rare times Matthews tells a story. He fashioned "Hello Again" as his version of a murder tale, which may explain the country-and-western lilt in its rhythms—another rarity for a band that usually avoids country. DMB played "Hello Again" often in 2004, just before the recording of *Stand Up*, then played it throughout the summer of 2005, then revived for six shows in the summer of 2010 before benching it for several years. It was hauled back out in 2018.

"Louisiana Bayou"

A funky workout that naturally carries a hint of New Orleans in its rhythms, "Louisiana Bayou" offers plenty of opportunities for Dave Matthews to indulge in a bit of Cajun patois—something that Mark Batson buries in his soft, amorphous production, which does give the recording warmth but also diminishes its earthiness. In the studio, Batson's clavinet gives the recording a hint of classic '70s funk, but the fact that at its core "Louisiana Bayou" is a loose, rhythmic workout its why it was a *Stand Up* song that endured in the back half of the 2000s, often featuring in DMB concerts between 2005 and 2009.

"Stolen Away on 55th and 3rd"

One of the better fusions of Mark Batson's R&B sensibility and Dave Matthews's balladry, "Stolen Away on 55th and 3rd" breezes along, the gentle acoustic strums intertwining with a drum loop to create a mood that is undeniably romantic. It's the loveliest moment on *Stand Up*, and feels like something of a reprieve amid all the funkier workouts. It was played often in 2005—Matthews usually sang it while perched on a chair—and then sporadically over the next three years before once again becoming a staple in the 2014 set.

"You Might Die Trying"

Mark Batson gave this funky bit of *carpe diem* a somewhat hushed production, but the inspirational message shines through nearly as expertly as the polyrhythms, breakdowns, and vamps. "You Might Die Trying" is one of the few songs on *Stand Up* that really showcases LeRoi Moore and Boyd Tinsley, and that might be why the song wound up being the one tune from the album that was played constantly over the next decade. Every year from that point on saw a performance of the song.

"Steady as We Go"

A reassuring piano ballad—one that preaches togetherness and solidarity in a long-term relationship—"Steady as We Go" bears some similarities to previous introspective Dave Matthews numbers, but the difference is that piano: played by Mark Batson, the piano lends the impression of a Paul McCartney tune, with the melody building in a manner not dissimilar to "The Long and Winding Road." Played all the way through 2005, it was aired five times in 2006 and then essentially forgotten until a 2018 revival.

"Steady as We Go" has an interesting side history. The song played a pivotal role on the John Edwards presidential campaign of 2008—a campaign that ultimately was doomed. It was later revealed that "Steady as We Go" was a shared favorite song of Edwards and his mistress, Rielle Hunter. Furthermore, Edwards often reassured Hunter that once his terminally ill wife died, he'd marry her in New York on a rooftop wedding featuring Dave Matthews Band. It seems highly unlikely that DMB knew any of this at the time.

"Hunger for the Great Light"

A stirring album closer, "Hunger for the Great Light" expresses the need for something bigger than oneself, and while there's a weird disdain in the opening verse ("Here you go, you dirty girl"), such reservations are undercut by the thick, funky verses, spiked by an organ from Butch Taylor. Once the songs moves into the bridge section, it expands into Beatles-esque psychedelic harmonies—a nifty bit of conscious expanding. It's the kind of song that could be opened up onstage, and it was throughout 2005–2007.

Recording

Ironically, this commercially minded record was largely recorded on Dave Matthews Band's home turf. The band hunkered down in its own Charlottesville studio, and, determined to get funkier this time around, was open to the suggestion of A&R man Bruce Flohr to work with Mark Batson. Some of the recording sessions were filmed and put together in a loose documentary aired on the band's website prior to the album's release. Apart from Batson himself, who played a number of keys, and DMB touring keyboardist Boyd Tinsley, there are no auxiliary players.

For his part, Stefan Lessard was excited about his experience on *Stand Up*. Talking to *Bass Player*, he said, "Mark Batson taught me a lot about bass in hip-hop—he'd show me by playing keyboard with the kind of feel he wanted. I listened to hip-hop when I was growing up, but now I have a better understanding of what the bass is doing, and how it's not just haphazard."

Release

Stand Up saw release on May 10, 2005. Early promotional copies from Australia suggest that a song called "Trouble with You" once existed in the position where "Hello Again" wound up. This was the first Dave Matthews Band album to see many physical variations. All preordered CDs of *Stand Up* came with a five-track companion bonus disc that contained the unreleased songs "Joyride" and "Trouble with You," plus three live performances from 2004. If the album was preordered through the Warehouse online store, there was a second bonus disc with further live cuts. Furthermore, the album appeared as a DualDisc—a short-lived format featuring a disc that was simultaneously a CD and a DVD—but it never was pressed on vinyl.

Reception

Stand Up debuted at #1 on the *Billboard* 200 and was quickly certified gold and platinum by the RIAA on June 23, 2005, just over a month after its release, but would gain no further RIAA certifications.

Fans embraced the record, and critics also were positive about it. Reviewing the album in *Entertainment Weekly*, Tom Sinclair praised Batson, claiming he'd done "what the wisest producers have always done—that is, stir a band's creative juices, inspire great songwriting, singing, and playing, then get the results down while everything's fresh." In *Rolling Stone*, Christian Hoard called *Stand Up* "a quintessential summer record, a collection of tight, group-composed grooves and breezy tunes that sometimes float by too easily. . . . Batson met with each band member individually, taping instrumental ideas from which *Stand Up*'s fourteen tracks were later constructed. The result is a disc whose unfussy demeanor conceals a mountain o overdubs and deftly edited jam," he added, before concluding, "If the thoroughly good-natured *Stand Up* proves anything, it's that Dave Matthews Band has learned to temper its considerable chops with enough restraint and pop smarts that it no longer seems possible for even the most ardent punks to hate the group."

Legacy

Like *Everyday* before it, *Stand Up* isn't especially beloved by hardcore fans of the group. Once again, it's easy for the devoted to place blame on the producer. Marc Batson may have consulted closely with each member of Dave Matthews Band, but he's a modern pop producer whose method was to digitally cut and paste instead of relying on the grooves of this archetypal jam band. As such, *Stand Up* gleams and shines in a manner that fit Adult Alternative radio but not necessarily the band itself: there are glimmers of the group's personality, but it doesn't have the exuberant, boundless energy of Dave Matthews Band's best recordings.

Stand Up wound up being the last full album recorded with saxophonist LeRoi Moore. It was never intended as a farewell—nobody could've foreseen the accident that took Roi's life—but it's nevertheless his last testament. It's an odd sendoff for somebody so important to the band—one where his presence isn't heard so much as suggested. It's not a stretch to think that so much of the back-to-basics approach of *Big Whiskey and the GrooGrux King* stems from the fact that *Stand Up* didn't feel much like a Dave Matthews Band album, particularly in how it fails to showcase Moore.

Big Whiskey and the GrooGrux King

Requiem for LeRoi Moore

The Album

When Dave Matthews Band headed into the studio with producer Rob Cavallo—a mainstream alternative-rock producer best known for his million-selling productions for Green Day—the intent was to strip away the gloss that covered the band during the early days of the twenty-first century. Ever since the failed *Lillywhite Sessions*, the group had pushed itself toward the mainstream, first through the slick pop of the Glen Ballard–produced *Everyday* and then through the R&B undercurrents of *Stand Up*, but this album was intended to be different: it was supposed to get back to the band's funky, multicultural, polyrhythmic roots.

Big Whiskey and the GrooGrux King did indeed do that, but it turned into something unintended: a requiem for founding member LeRoi Moore. During the recording of the album in 2008, Moore suffered an accident while driving an ATV on his Virginia property, and he subsequently died from the injuries he sustained in the crash. Understandably, this loss shook the remaining members of the band, but they continued to work—they played a concert the day of Moore's death—and the album in progress turned into a tribute to their departed brother, its title a tip of the hat to the larger-than-life saxophonist. "GrooGrux" was a nickname for Moore but also for drummer Carter Beauford, Tim Reynolds, and Tim Wicks, a Charlottesville saxophonist who occasionally sat in with DMB. The musicians believed their invented word captured the spirit of their "wild-sounding rhythms." ("Big Whiskey" derived from a local street musician who asked the band for money so he could buy a "big whiskey.") This helped turn the 2008 album into a reset for Dave Matthews Band as it discarded the pop and got down to what really matters.

The Songs

Dave Matthews Band began writing the songs for *Big Whiskey and the GrooGrux King* while LeRoi Moore was still alive, and wrapped the album after his death. This means the album isn't strictly a tribute to the departed saxophonist. Instead, the record bears his imprint and then reckons with his ghost, which means the songs on *Big Whiskey* are rich and resonant, celebrating both life and its absence.

"Grux"

A minute-long montage of LeRoi Moore playing, "Grux" kicks off *Big Whiskey and the GrooGrux King* with a tribute to the departed saxophonist. It's bittersweet, not haunting—a fitting tip of the hat to a fallen partner—and opens the album on a fittingly elegiac note.

"Shake Me Like a Monkey"

Big, brash, and rhythmic, "Shake Me Like a Monkey" makes it clear that Dave Matthews Band has left muted modern R&B behind and returned to an organic, rhythmic kick. This song separates itself from the past through the presence of a full, complete horn section, making it plain what Rashawn Ross adds to the mix. "Shake Me Like a Monkey" entered regular rotation in 2009 and hasn't left set lists since.

"Funny the Way It Is"

Maybe the best example of how Dave Matthews can spin sad, bemused tales of humanity into something comforting—"Somebody is going hungry, somebody is eating out . . . Somebody's broken heart becomes your favorite song"—"Funny the Way It Is" sounds a bit like a fusion of

Paul Simon and Sting. The song boasts a soothing, expansive verse, but it lurches forward once it hits a bridge that emphasizes the rediscovered rhythmic attack of DMB. One of the more accessible songs on *Big Whiskey*, it was released as the album's first single and peaked at #37 on the Hot 100 and #21 on Adult Alternative. "Funny the Way It Is" became a regular part of DMB sets after its debut.

"Lying in the Hands of God"

Moving at a faster clip than its relaxed feel suggests, "Lying in the Hands of God" has its roots in folk, but it also recalls early Sting in the way Matthews's pretty melody gets answered by the clarion call of LeRoi Moore. This gentle song was played often on the tours supporting *Big Whiskey*, then played on occasion over the next few years.

The cover of *Big Whiskey and the GrooGrux King* was designed as a tribute to the late LeRoi Moore. *Author's collection*

"Why I Am"

A bright, buoyant tribute to LeRoi Moore, "Why I Am" is the closest Dave Matthews Band gets to straightforward pop on *Big Whiskey*. Perhaps the big hooks wouldn't have given Moore room to roam, but when Matthews sings, "And when my story ends it's gonna end with him / Heaven or hell I'm going there with the GrooGrux King," it's hard not to sense Roi's spirit. "Why I Am" was released as a single, but it didn't chart. Nevertheless, it turned into a DMB standard, played regularly ever since.

"Dive In"

One of the gentler moments on *Big Whiskey*, "Dive In" sways with a hint of romanticizing and climaxes with a lyrical guitar solo from Tim Reynolds. The lyrics find Matthews coming to terms with all the pain in the world, and the struggle has a counterpoint in the soft sweep of the song. "Dive In" faded out of set lists a few years after its debut, but was then revived in 2016.

"Spaceman"

Not quite as spacey as the title suggests, "Spaceman" has traces of fatalism—"Doesn't everybody deserve to have the good life / But it don't always work out," is its refrain—but Matthews winds up drawing sustenance from his lover. "Spaceman" does drift: the song moves from folky verse underpinned by hyperactive rhythms from Carter Beauford, then opens up on the bridges. It's the kind of song that feels designed for the stage, where it was played often in the years after its introduction.

"Squirm"

Allegedly inspired by the serious, unsettling films that Dave Matthews Band were watching while recording *Big Whiskey*, "Squirm" is melodramatic, creating anxiety in the verse and then exploding on the chorus, assisted by a horn section and surging strings. This tension makes it an ideal vehicle for the stage, where the band can create drama, so it's not a surprise that the group regularly included it in set lists over the next five years.

"Alligator Pie (Cockadile)"

A rangy, multipart piece that gains speed in the choruses and slows down in the verses, "Alligator Pie"—which carries the subtitle "Cockadile" in the liner notes—bears a distinctive New Orleans flavor. However, the way that the song ping-pongs from tempo to tempo, it feels like it was designed to showcase the dexterity of the rhythm section of Carter Beauford and Stefan Lessard. They move fluidly from polyrhythmic clusters to elastic breakdowns—transitions that often overshadow whatever lyrics Matthews sings. Given that it's such a showcase for the band, it's not a surprise that it was a staple throughout 2009, but from there it dropped precipitously out of the spotlight.

"Seven"

A surprisingly soulful entry for Dave Matthews Band, "Seven" opens up with a careening falsetto from Matthews, who moves into a lower register for the chorus. It's a love-and-devotional song with a carnal edge—"I can still taste you and I won't wash my hands" and "Wanna drink it wanna drink it" suggest sex—but the track works because it is a neo-soul song in the vein of Peter Gabriel's "Sledgehammer," which DMB started covering in 2009. Perhaps it's not a direct Stax homage, but it's fueled by gritty guitars and stabs of horns that are hard to resist. "Seven" was one of the songs from *Big Whiskey and the GrooGrux King* to stay in rotation throughout the years following its release.

"Time Bomb"

A deceptively subdued song, "Time Bomb" is effectively a song about the quiet neighbor next door—the one that nobody would expect to go mad, "A ticking time bomb / Waiting to blow my top." Appropriately, the hushed arrangement gives the song a bit of intensity, which sets up the band's full-blooded explosion at the end. This is the most effective part of the song: the band's building of tension pays off through a volcanic conclusion. DMB played "Time Bomb" quite often in the years surrounding Big Whiskey, then abandoned it after 2013.

"Baby Blue"

A delicate love song in which the narrator is pledging eternal love in the wake of a broken heart—a sentiment that certainly brings to mind the recently departed Moore—"Baby Blue" is graced by subtle strings on its studio arrangement, but its small scale made it ideal for palette-cleansing moments in a concert. "Baby Blue" showed up often in the years after *Big Whiskey*, then it faded away.

"You and Me"

The second single from *Big Whiskey and the GrooGrux King*, "You and Me" is another devotional love song, and it's one that stresses the long-term over immediate gratification: "We can always look back / At what we did." It's anchored on acoustic strumming—indeed, the iTunes deluxe version of the album features an acoustic take on the song—but at its heart it's a pop song, given a nicely baroque treatment by Rob Cavallo. Nevertheless, the tightness of the song is why it works well in concert, where it has showed up often every year since its release.

Recording

The sessions for *Big Whiskey and the GrooGrux King* began in November 2007 in Charlottesville, at DMB's Haunted Hollow studio. After two sessions in Seattle—Studio Litho in February 2008, Studio X in December 2008—the album was finished in January 2009 at Piety Street in New Orleans. Although the album wound up as something of a tribute to LeRoi Moore, the group already was making strides to turn *Big Whiskey* into something of a return to roots. Compatriot Tim Reynolds, a staple of the group's '90s LPs, was brought back to play in the studio for the first time since 1998's *Before These Crowded Streets*, while members of the touring band found their way into the studio as well, including Rashawn Ross, a trumpeter who at this point was a *de facto* member of the group. Apart from these two, the cameos were few—only banjoist Danny Barnes, along with Jeff Coffin, who filled Moore's shoes after his death—which was another way of underscoring how this record focused on the inherent idiosyncrasies and signatures of the band.

Release

Big Whiskey and the GrooGrux King saw release on June 2, 2009, and—typically for albums of its time—was released in a number of different variations. In addition to the standard thirteen-track album, there was an iTunes edition that included live versions and behind-the-scenes videos. The bigger deal was the deluxe box of *Big Whiskey and the GrooGrux King*, which contained an EP called *Little Red Bird* featuring four exclusive songs: the group composition "Write a Song," and three by Matthews, "Little Red Bird," "#27," and "Beach Ball," with the latter two working their way into regular rotation in concerts. In Europe, the album was expanded to fifteen tracks with the inclusion of "Write a Song" and "Corn Bread," which was another song that became a regular at DMB shows. It was also the first Dave Matthews Band album to be released on vinyl on the day of its release since *Before These Crowded Streets* in 1998.

Reception

Like its four predecessors, *Big Whiskey and the GrooGrux King* debuted at #1 on the *Billboard* 200, shifting 424,000 units in its first week of release. In August 2009, it was certified both gold and platinum; it never received another certification.

Big Whiskey and the GrooGrux King earned Dave Matthews Band its best critical reviews. In *Spin*, Mikael Wood called *Big Whiskey* "harder edged and more bottom heavy than DMB's usual fare," concluding that it's "a fond, funky farewell" to Moore. At *Rolling Stone*, David Fricke carried through on this theme, saying the album "is a lot like a New

Orleans funeral parade—mourning and zest balled into big, brawny music." Danny Clinch in *Entertainment Weekly* echoed this sentiment: "Throughout, the specter of death rarely recess, but life—embodied by the proto-DMB revelry of 'Why I Am'—still prevails."

At the Grammys, *Big Whiskey and the GrooGrux King* garnered nominations for "Album of the Year" and "Best Rock Album," and although it didn't win in either category, these honors suggest how warmly this album was received.

Legacy

In the grand scheme of things, *Big Whiskey and the GrooGrux King* marks the start of DMB's third act—the place where the band starts to settle into its own skin and ease into veteran status. The group was still aiming for hits—the presence of Rob Cavallo behind the boards suggests a band looking for a fresher, dynamic sound—but the approach is a continuation of what began nearly a decade earlier, when DMB entered the studio with Steve Lillywhite to record its fourth album. The musicians were now older, wiser, and ready to abandon their awkward adolescence, so they returned to what used to work. The sound may be familiar, but the execution is different—streamlined and tighter, something that suggests the adventure of jazz but keeps the focus on the songs. This intense concentration on vivid, lively tunes points toward the direction Dave Matthews Band would follow.

22

Away from the World

Back to Basics

The Album

Big *Whiskey and the GrooGrux King* may have been an expansive return to roots for Dave Matthews Band, but it was haunted by the death of LeRoi Moore. Despite this tragedy, the album found DMB discovering a way to connect to its past while moving forward into the future, and 2012's *Away from the World* is a continuation of that sensibility, sounding rich, mature, and settled while also being proudly tied to the band's roots.

Part of that line is a reunion with Steve Lillywhite, the producer of the band's first three albums. The last time Dave Matthews Band worked with Lillywhite, the group was in the process of change, figuring out how to deal with superstardom while also navigating a brand-new home studio. It was such a rough process that the band decided to abandon the sessions—infamously, they'd later be bootlegged—and work with star producer Glen Ballard, heading down a road that took DMB far away from Lillywhite's textured renditions of the band's live sound.

That sensitive sensibility returns to the forefront on *Away from the World*, but this is the work of a different band. DMB had lost a brother and gained some new permanent members—Tim Reynolds, a compatriot from the start, is now part of the band, as is longtime touring trumpeter Rashawn Ross and newer recruit Jeff Coffin—but the fundamental difference stems from all the years the band has accumulated. It had been two decades since the band started its professional career and twelve years since it worked with Lillywhite, and that time is not dismissed—it's felt. The group bears the bruises and scars of experience, and since this is a group that always favored complex fusions and is fronted by a singer obsessed by the passage of time, it wears its age well.

The Songs

It's easy to see the songs on *Away from the World* as the most mature tunes Dave Matthews Band has recorded. None of the songs seem like they were written with the charts in mind; they play upon themes and styles the group has essayed on previous albums. As such, the songs are a little subtler than what came before, but they can also be a bit richer, suggesting that DMB had figured out a way to ease into middle age.

"Broken Things"

Co-written with John Alagía, an old friend of the band, "Broken Things" is pinned by a romantic chorus, but this provides a tonic for images of disarray and questioning. War surfaces, as does the acknowledgment that you "can't always know what's coming / You can't always trust a twist of fate," suggesting that the narrator finds some measure of solace in the quiet harbor of peace. It's a rather meditative opener—it's not a rallying call, it's searching—and it doesn't quite feel urgent, which may be one reason that it wasn't played often, appearing in set lists a grand total of nineteen times in the year surrounding the release of *Away from the World.*

"Belly Belly Nice"

Co-written by Rashawn Ross, "Belly Belly Nice" is a funky, soulful workout that showcases the new Dave Matthews Band horn section. It is also another one of Matthews's carnal songs: "When the juice is dripping' off your chin / One peach is not enough," he sings, not disguising his entendre at all. It's essentially a party song, so it works well in concert, where it was played often in the years following the release of *Away from the World.*

"Mercy"

Unfolding slowly, "Mercy" is hushed but urgent—a plea for understanding, empathy, and forgiveness in a cruel work. "Stand up for what we need to be / 'cause crying won't save or feed a hungry child," Matthews sings on the second verse, making it a rallying call in the face of hopelessness. It's a strong message, but the setting is soft—it feels warm and cozy, a message of reassurance, not defiance.

"Mercy" was the first single from *Away from the World*, debuting on April 24, 2012, on *Late Night with Jimmy Fallon*, where Matthews performed it with "Captain" Kirk Douglas of the Roots. The single didn't go any further than #95 on the charts, but it was played continually through 2012 and 2013 tours supporting *Away from the World*, and featured regularly from that point forward.

"Gaucho"

One of the more complex songs on *Away from the World*, "Gaucho" is structured as a time-shifting suite, all building up tension and urgency, underpinning the geopolitical protest of the lyric. It's a protest song, but one whose message is almost overshadowed by the complexity of the arrangement—one that's so overstuffed that the children's chorus that floats into the coda almost avoids being floral, although it does slide into the cliché of kids singing protests about war. After receiving a lot of play in 2012, it was phased out of rotation the following year.

"Sweet"

A simple—and, yes, sweet—song, "Sweet" is built on a Dave Matthews strumming a ukulele and singing about his son learning how to swim. It's a little song, but its specificity makes it work: he's cheering his son on, waiting for him to emerge from the deep; when he does, he'll discover it's so sweet. "Sweet" debuted in 2011, prior to the release of *Away from the World*, and it has stayed in rotation from that point forward.

"The Riff"

"The Riff" isn't driven by a strong, powerful riff—instead, it's a play on "The Rift," the drama and tensions that come from a couple cleaving in two. The song is peppered with imagery of regret and the past, ending with the narrator saying, "You stay with me baby / You and me we'll change the game," but the music suggests that the relationship has already come to an end. It's starts ruminative, then builds three times to intense crescendos, the last highlighted by a Tim Reynolds guitar solo. It's a good showcase for the muscle of a band, and it was played often in 2012 before slowly fading away.

"Belly Full"

A quiet song of love, "Belly Full" is a sweet little folk song, one with a nicely contoured melody and delivered with understated passion. It's designed to be played by no more than one person, and it infrequently served as a solo showcase for Dave between 2012 and 2015.

"If Only"

One of the highlights on *Away from the World*, "If Only" simmers to a mellow soul groove, turning into one of the tightest and slickest songs on the album. Matthews is pleading for his love to take him back—or at least to return things to the way they used to be—and he undersells his vocals, crooning and seducing in a manner that fits the song. There are some excellent Steve Cropper–inspired leads from Tim Reynolds, and, on the whole, it feels like a great adult-alternative hit that never was. "If Only" wound up staying in rotation in the years following its 2012 debut.

"Rooftop"

A throwback to the earliest Dave Matthews Band songs—its very title feels like a nod to "Warehouse"—"Rooftop" is built on a winding acoustic-guitar figure that builds to a big band explosion on the chorus, where the tempo slows, the harmonies build, and the horns come out. The narrator gets Dutch courage in a drink, so he can scream out his devotion from the rooftop—and, when we arrive at the bridge, it feels as if the narrator has achieved the moment of transcendence he desires. The song is open-ended, allowing plenty of opportunity for jams and solos, which is certainly why it became a regular part of DMB sets over the next few years.

"Snow Outside"

A nicely arranged love song, "Snow Outside" is built on a skipping acoustic-guitar figure, but as the song unfolds, there are harmonic washes, soulful horns, slide guitars—lots of inventive flourishes that help turn the tale of love into something warm, even if the narrator is promising

Dave Matthews drew the album art for *Away from the World.* *Author's collection*

something chilly outside. Such understated arrangements are a testament to both the band and producer Steve Lillywhite, who always knew how to maximize the band's range. It's one of the rare Dave Matthews Band songs that sounds best on record, although it works well onstage, too, as evidenced by its regular appearances in sets between 2012 and 2015.

"Drunken Soldier"

At nearly ten minutes, "Drunken Soldier" is an epic, which is fitting, because it's a song that Dave Matthews Band had in the works for a long time. The band first attempted it for *Stand Up* and tried it again for *Big Whiskey and the GrooGrux King*, but re-teaming with Steve Lillywhite allowed the musicians to dig into the inherent drama of the piece. He allows them to build tension, giving them plenty of space to play with mood and solos, to let the newfound horn section punch up the crescendos while also allowing the starker sections to sparkle. The lyrics appear to be a protest of sorts, but it's a bit ambiguous: it's one of the songs where Matthews opts for imagery over clarity. Given that it's such an ambitious piece, it's not surprising that the band hauled it out with regularity over the years following *Away from the World*. It wasn't played all the time, but its subdued melodrama did provide a showcase for every member of the group.

Recording

Dave Matthews Band and Lillywhite began work on *Away from the World* in January of 2012, holing up in a Seattle studio. By May, the record was finished. The group worked quickly—Boyd Tinsley told www.dmbnews.net, "Some of the songs that you hear on this album, the basic tracks came out, like, the first or second time we played them"—and the album does feel fresh. DMB and Lillywhite kept their circle this time—Tower of Power's Roger Smith is the only cameo on the album, lending organ on a few tracks—and that helps accentuate the impression that this is Dave Matthews Band returning to the basics.

Release

Like so many other albums of the 2010s, *Away from the World* arrived in a variety of incarnations, both in the US and elsewhere. There was a Deluxe Edition, containing three live tracks recorded in May and June of 2012; two different Super Deluxe Editions, one containing five live tracks on a second disc, the other available through Warehouse and featuring three additional live cuts, all recorded in the summer of 2012; and for those who preordered the album through Warehouse, there was also a DVD of live performances from the same timeframe. Finally, there was a separate European bonus edition containing live selections recorded between 2007 and 2010.

Reception

Released on September 11, 2012, *Away from the World* sold 266,000 copies in its first week, debuting at #1 on the *Billboard* 200—the band's sixth straight #1 studio album. By the end of October, it was certified as gold by the RIAA, but it is the first Dave Matthews Band studio album to not go platinum.

Away from the World was greeted to generally positive reviews from critics. Jon Dolan in *Rolling Stone* claimed, "This is no nostalgia trip back to the quad. . . . He wears his grown-'n-grumpy honesty like a champ," a review that accentuated DMB's maturation. Megan Ritt followed a similar line in *Consequence of Sound*, noting that "by pulling away all the layers of guitar and production, Dave Matthews Band has unearthed a simple truth: these are genuine craftsmen." Notably, the album placed at #29 on *Rolling Stone*'s list of the Top 40 albums of 2012—the band's highest placement in the magazine's year-end lists to date.

Legacy

Upon its release, *Away from the World* appeared to be a consolidation of strengths: a return to the band's roots that took into account the musicians' increasing maturity. Chalk this up to a successful reunion with Steve Lillywhite, who helped the group tap into its classic '90s sound while navigating its expanded lineup. In retrospect, *Away from the World* carries a bittersweet twinge, given Boyd Tinsley's departure from the band during the making of 2018's *Come Tomorrow*. This is the last time this founding member played with DMB in the studio and, as such, *Away from the World* winds up feeling like the closing of an era as much as it is the start of a new one.

Come Tomorrow

Easing into Middle Age

The Album

Come Tomorrow, the ninth studio album from Dave Matthews Band, appeared in the summer of 2018, a few months after Dave Matthews turned fifty-one years old. The milestone was on the mind of the singer/songwriter. Speaking to *New York Magazine* journalist David Marchese while promoting the album's release, Matthews admitted, "After I turned fifty, something happened." While Matthews couldn't articulate the details of this change, it was spurred in part by his belief that he had allowed *Away from the World* to be scrubbed clean in the final stages of completion. Matthews was determined not to make that mistake with *Come Tomorrow*.

This change in philosophy may initially seem to be slightly ironic, as *Come Tomorrow* arrived six year after *Away from the World*, shattering the record for the longest gap between Dave Matthews Band albums (it was previously held by the four years separating *Away* and *Big Whiskey and the GrooGrux King*). Such a lengthy span usually suggests a band was fussing with a record—a suspicion strengthened by how the album contains songs DMB have had lying around for years. As an album, *Come Tomorrow* quickly dispels such notions. Unlike nearly every Dave Matthews Band album that precedes it, it is filled with loose ends and rough edges, benefitting from its varied sources.

Compared to *Away from the World*, *Come Tomorrow* also sounds like a new beginning. Some of that is due to unfortunate circumstances. During the final stages of recording, Dave Matthews Band parted ways with Boyd Tinsley. At first, the violinist's absence was depicted as a matter of health, a situation requiring nothing more than a hiatus, but after that initial statement in February 2018, a story surfaced where James Frost-Winn—a former trumpeter for Crystal Garden, a band produced by Boyd—claimed he was sexually harassed by Tinsley. Tinsley denied these allegations, but Dave Matthews Band fired its founding member on May 18, 2018.

The Songs

Tinsley is credited with one song on *Come Tomorrow*, but even there he's not heard on the record; only his ghost is present. With the violinist absent, Dave Matthews Band sounds burlier yet retains its inherent eccentricity, the players leaning into dense polyrhythms with the same fervor as they embrace quieter moments. This leaner sound helps emphasize how *Come Tomorrow* is a collection of songs connected by empathy. Matthews emphasized this point in an interview with NPR's Talia Schlanger upon its release, tying it into the wave of nationalism sweeping the globe in 2018: "That is bizarre and terrifying to me that someone might think of a person that's looking for a better life as a parasite simply because they're looking for a better life." This compassion isn't a new development for Dave Matthews, but given the politics of 2018, this sentimentality felt timely, just like how the stripped-down sound gives Dave Matthews Band a newfound vitality.

"Samurai Cop (Oh Joy Begin)"

Taking its title from a 1991 exploitation flick starring nobody you've ever heard of, despite its snarky title, "Samurai Cop" is an earnest paean to birth and all the firsts that follows: first steps, first broken bones, first kiss. As the band climbs to skyscraping peaks on the back of an echoing guitar riff reminiscent of U2, Matthews implores listeners to not "lose our way in fear and hate," to keep focused on the joy that begins life. Such sentimentality seems like an awkward fit for the song's campy name, and there was a brief spell where Matthews toyed with another name. In July 2016, he introduced it as two concerts as "Joy Begin," a title that became a parenthetical when it was released as "Samurai (Oh Joy Begin)" on *Come Tomorrow*.

"Can't Stop"

An old song written with producer Mark Batson during the *Stand Up* sessions in 2005, "Can't Stop" is one of Dave Matthews's ribald sex songs. Driven by a dexterous rhythm and fueled by a ravenous carnality—one that equates physical longing with a junkie getting a fix—"Can't Stop" seems designed for the stage: it's a party song, one that will get the crowd moving, but also functions as a showcase for the group's skills. Appropriately, the group played it often from its 2006 stage debut to its 2018 unveiling on *Come Tomorrow*.

"Here On Out"

Simple as a sketch yet graced with an orchestra, "Here On Out" sounds particularly diminutive when heard after the cheerful cacophony of "Can't Stop." Debuted onstage by Dave in 2016, who played it with Joshua Bell and the Chamber Orchestra of Havana in a concert called Seasons Of Cuba—a performance that aired on PBC in December of that year—"Here On Out" is a devotional to a girl who has him under her spell. It's a delicate number—so delicate it would seem that the orchestra would drown out the intent—but the arrangement is so subtle that the focus remains on Matthews's sweet, satisfied croon.

"That Girl Is You"

Opening with a dark, textured groove—too simple to be called jazz and too straightforward to be called African, although it contains elements of both—"That Girl Is You" is a master class in sustained mood. Dave Matthews Band keeps building upon that vamp, slowly escalating in attack and volume. This tense melodrama counters the simple lyrics, which find Matthews's narrator entranced by the way a girl dances. The singer is so bewitched by the moves that she "changed the way I see the world," and appropriately the song climaxes with a cascade of yelps, claps, and stomps, a cathartic coda that crests and recedes back to the groove that started the whole affair.

"She"

Opening with a riff so heavy it recalls nothing so much as Pearl Jam during its prime, "She" is a rocker that showcases the six-string pyrotechnics and provides plenty of space for Dave Matthews to stretch out his voice. Alternating between a guttural growl and smooth high notes, he navigates chord changes that recall the post-grunge glory days of the 1990s. Dave Matthews Band never attempted this sound when surrounded by bands wearing flannel, but better late than never.

"Idea of You"

Debuted in 2006, "Idea of You" was a staple in live sets for over a decade before Dave Matthews Band recorded it for *Come Tomorrow*. When the song was still fresh in 2007, Matthews introduced it onstage by claiming it was inspired by a babysitter he had as a child, which could explain some of the juvenile imagery that floats through the song. The narrator flirts by saying he won't pull her hair—an idea that still places him somewhere within the vicinity of childhood. As a piece of music, "Idea of You" is more complex than its inspiration, reaching an apex on its jazz-spiked chorus: the confluence of horns and elongated melody suggests the salad days of yacht rock. Here, it's possible to hear echoes of the old Dave Matthews Band, and that's not just imaginary: on *Come Tomorrow*, the recording of "Idea of You" opens with saxophone from the long departed LeRoi Moore, and this is also the only track to feature Boyd Tinsley. Their presence almost makes "Idea of You" feel elegiac within the context of *Come Tomorrow*.

"Virginia in the Rain"

The Virginia in the title of "Virginia in the Rain" doesn't necessarily refer to a woman. Instead, it appears to be a valentine to the state of Virginia, the place Dave Matthews Band called home in its earliest days. Appropriately, the song has a hazy, nostalgic quality: with its soft, shimmering keyboards and Matthews's understated falsetto, the track creates a specific vibe more than place, conjuring a feeling that a summer can last forever. Dave Matthews Band debuted the song in the summer of 2015, played it regularly through that summer, then revived it in 2017, just prior to beginning serious work on *Come Tomorrow*. Oddly, the song was played only twice during the album's supporting tour.

"Again and Again"

First unveiled as "Bob Law" in 2016—a title that appears to be an allusion to Bob Loblaw, Scott Baio's memorable character from the cult sitcom *Arrested Development*—"Again and Again" is another love song on *Come Tomorrow*. This time, the subject is a long-time lover, one who remains the subject of desire time and time again. Matthews paints vivid, sensual portraits during the verses, but the song takes off on its soaring chorus—a transition that seems designed for the stage, which is where "Again and Again" resided in 2016. The group played it often that year, always calling it "Bob Law," then changed its name to "Again and Again"—a title that reflects its intentions—for the 2018 release of *Come Tomorrow*.

"bkdkdkdd"

"bkdkdkdd" is merely a clip of a composition called "Be Yourself," which was played on tour during 2015. It doesn't last even thirty seconds, just offers a funky palette cleanser between the love songs and introspection.

"Black and Blue Bird"

Perhaps the weightiest song on *Come Tomorrow*, "Black and Blue Bird" is a love song whose romantic notions are undercut by the narrator's obsession with mortality and the state of the world. Matthews sings so sweetly, it's possible to miss that he's crooning, "God is troubling when you consider / Believers that would welcome the end of the world," but he's not being intentionally subversive here. Instead, "Black and Blue Bird" is delicately balanced between the knowledge that death comes to us all yet love provides us with all with reasons to keep living.

Dave Matthews Band first played "Black and Blue Bird" in 2015, and it was a staple of sets that summer. It returned to regular rotation yet was rarely heard on the supporting tour for *Come Tomorrow.*

"Come On Come On"

"Come On Come On" swells with strings as it reaches its climatic chorus, where Dave Matthews implores a "beautiful, beautiful girl" to take it easy and "come on." In other words, this is another one of the songs where Matthews intertwines love and sexuality, camouflaging carnal inclinations with sweetness. Thanks to Mark Batson, who co-wrote the song with Matthews, "Come On Come On" feels like it could fill up an arena, but its intent is decidedly more intimate.

"Do You Remember"

Dave Matthews gives away the game with the title of "Do You Remember." The title makes it clear that this is a dose of nostalgia, a trip through the past inspired by the loss of a dear friend many years ago. Fittingly, "Do You Remember" is a song spiked with melancholy memories of childhood, filled with fantasies but grounded by nature. Despite its sad undercurrent, it's a joyful tune with percolating rhythms—one that focuses on the good times that were had, not the loss that came later.

"Come Tomorrow"

Appropriately for the title song of an album, "Come Tomorrow" sums up the themes that run through the album. Melodically, it plays like a melancholy inverse of "You and Me," yet where that 2009 song was a testament to the power of a couple, "Come Tomorrow" is an ode to the promise of the future. Supported by the harmonies of Brandi Carlile, Matthews pleas to "let the children run the show"—a sentiment that places itself as an opposition to the xenophobia of the Trump years. Matthews doesn't offer this song as a protest, though: it's an understated anthem that appeals to the heart as much as it does the head.

"When I'm Weary"

Sweet and slow, "When I'm Weary" is a song that encourages the listener to endure in the wake of "dark, dark days." At times, it's not clear whether Matthews is speaking to the audience or himself, and that's why it works in the context of *Come Tomorrow*: in troubled times, this is an oasis of empathy.

Recording

Dave Matthews told David Marchese "the newest music on the record is only a few months old and the oldest is from twelve years ago," and given the long gestation of the album's songs, it makes sense that Dave Matthews Band chipped away at *Come Tomorrow* for a while. During the course of the sessions, DMB worked with several different producers, including many from the group's past, spending time at studios in Los Angeles, Charlottesville, and Seattle. Initially, the group revived some shelved tunes recorded with Mark Batson, then began working with Rob Cavallo, who produced *Big Whiskey*. Once those sessions faded away, they looked toward John Alagía, who previously produced many of the group's live albums. Alagía helped DMB corral the old songs while also working on new material.

Release

Sporting a cover by Béatrice Coron, an artist known for her cut designs, *Come Tomorrow* was released globally on June 8, 2018. In addition to its digital incarnations, RCA/Bama Rags released the album on CD, cassette, and vinyl, with a limited-edition white vinyl set available through DMB's official store.

Reception

Come Tomorrow debuted at #1 on the *Billboard* 200. This was notable in a number of ways. First, this debut represented the biggest chart week for a rock album since *Billboard* revamped its charts to reflect plays on streaming services like Spotify and Apple Music. With album-equivalent plays from these services factored in, *Come Tomorrow* racked up a total of 292,000 units moved in the first week—285,000 coming from traditional album sales, a number that constitutes the best number of 2018. More importantly, *Come Tomorrow* was DMB's seventh album to enter the charts at #1—a record no other band could match.

24

So Much to Say

The Videos

Videos always were a tricky area for Dave Matthews Band. There's no denying that they provided a pivotal avenue for the group to expand its audience—in fact, if MTV hadn't picked "What Would You Say" as a *Buzz Bin* clip in 1994, it's conceivable that the group never would've become much more than a regional sensation, like so many bands of its ilk. But, MTV *did* pick "What Would You Say" as a *Buzz Bin* clip, the first sign that the network had embraced the band wholeheartedly. From that point through 2005, when the group started to lose its cultural currency and was phased out by the music-video network, Dave Matthews Band was something of a staple on MTV, and the band often spent resources to develop striking clips to accompany its singles—a smart move, considering how powerful MTV was in peddling music during the '90s and 2000s.

Matthews himself was somewhat ambivalent about the idea of a hit single. Talking to *Billboard* in 2007, he couldn't help but convey his distaste for singles: "Very often singles are songs that I'm not crazy about, for whatever reason and I don't feel indebted to that part of the culture of music. That really hasn't been our strength. Our strength has been more compilation, more our live shows and the body of work, rather than individual songs being particularly catchy."

Once videos started to decline in the early 2010s, Dave Matthews Band chose to opt out of them, not making a single video for its 2012 album, *Away from the World*. Despite this disdain, Dave Matthews Band did have hit singles, and they were crucial in shaping the arc of the group's career, especially in terms of the public consciousness. Perhaps these songs weren't always embraced by Dave Matthews Band diehards—although they often were, particularly in the case of the videos that showed up a little bit further down the line in a promotional cycle—but they were the songs that the average observer would know, often because they *saw* the songs as much as they heard them. And the videos were an essential part of the narrative, helping construct the picture of Dave Matthews Band for the general public, which is why it's important to look at them as a body of work: they're how the world at large saw Dave Matthews Band.

"What Would You Say"

The first video Dave Matthews Band ever filmed is also one in which the band takes something of a backseat to the video itself, which is a bit of an eye-popping colorful salute to the glory days of the '60s. In his DVD commentary for *The Videos 1994–2001*, director David Hogan claims that the clip is "an homage to 60s pop," and it is indeed possible to see echoes of Peter Blake and *Sgt. Pepper* throughout his work.

Hogan didn't pick these images out of thin air. He admits he "took the images (that) kind of fit the lyric," so there's a bit of a carnival-esque quality to the film, with lots of sly, colorful clowns vying for space with the band onstage. It was shot quickly, a two-and-a-half-day experience that the director admits was a "tough shoot."

It's a vibrant video, partially because Hogan didn't use any special effects, and that's why it crackles: this was not big budget; it was pulled together on a shoestring, which may be why the director calls it "kind of [an] anti-music video." Among the surprising things tucked away in the video is the "flaming lady" animation—Hogan stole this dancing figure from an early T-shirt, but it became a signature symbol for the band, later figuring prominently on the album cover for 2005's *Stand Up*.

"Ants Marching"

David Hogan returned to direct "Ants Marching," which wasn't the second single pulled from *Under the Table and Dreaming*—"Jimi Thing" and "Typical Situation" were both worked to radio, without much results—but it was the one that RCA decided to emphasize. In his commentary for *The*

Videos 1994–2001, Hogan says the group wasn't available for close consultation. He maintains that there was "no talk about what it was gonna be," so he wrote a treatment inspired by the lyric and his interactions with Matthews.

In the commentary, Hogan says the song is about Dave's childhood, how you're "always slapped upside the head by somebody." The director adds that he's "not afraid of a literal interpretation of a song," and that "Dave Matthews is the kind of artist to stick with the literal," so he wound up with a video that follows a couple skittering around New York City, sometimes hitting major life events but always interrupted by the *Sturm und Drang* of the metropolis. As the director puts it, "New York is the best place to see what an anthill might look like if it was inhabited by humans," and so the video mirrors the song: it is metropolis madness, something that emphasizes how we're all just dust in the wind.

Hogan decided to set up Dave Matthews Band to play live on a wharf, and then cut the performances into his narrative. "I don't think MTV knew quite what to think," the director adds. "I know VH1 embraced them right away." This strikes to the core of the Dave Matthews Band conundrum: musically, the band could play to the softer side that could be heard on VH1, but aesthetically this was a group that belonged to MTV, particularly in those early years when it was catapulting from the college circuit into the mainstream.

"Satellite"

The last single pulled from *Under the Table and Dreaming* is also the sweetest song on the record—a song that could certainly have crossed over into the adult-alternative mainstream. "Satellite" did manage to get to #18 on the *Billboard* Alternative chart, but based on its video, it seems like RCA had faith that the song would go further.

Wayne Isham, who directed his first big video back in 1984, when he helmed Mötley Crüe's "Smokin' in the Boys Room" (quickly followed by "Home Sweet Home"), wound up directing the clip. In his commentary for *The Videos 1994–2001*, Isham notes how he was inspired by the song to accentuate the disconnection people feel between themselves and a media-saturated world—a concept that has only gained strength over the years.

Isham came up with the concept of a guy holed up in his trailer, watching videos piped in from throughout the world. He secured the rights for a number of old cartoons, B-movies, and horror flicks, all of which are seen on screens in the trailer, along with footage of Dave Matthews Band playing live. (In an interesting footnote, MusicSpace shows up on one of the screens, an early attempt at branding by Coran Capshaw.) He hired Johnny Galecki—then known for his co-starring role on *Rosanne*, later to be seen on the *Big Bang Theory*, and an actor who was a fan of the band—to be the guy in the trailer. Galecki had the comedic chops to pull off the punch line of stepping outside of the trailer and finding the world to be so beautiful. "It really doesn't pertain to the lyrics of the song," Isham says in the commentary, yet it feels like it does: the images match the openhearted sentiment of the song.

"Satellite" was the last thing released from *Under the Table and Dreaming*, and the band was in the midst of recording its second album when the video was shot. In the commentary, Isham remembers, "The guys were finishing up the album, so we went up to Woodstock and shot up there." All the live footage was cut in a rehearsal studio, sometimes seen on screens in the trailer, often in bubbles that float outside the trailer. "In 1995 when we shot this, it was hard to shoot bubbles like this on computer," Isham says on the commentary, yet it still feels rather effortless—a sweet film to accompany a sweet song.

"Too Much"

"Too Much" is an ode to excess, so perhaps it's no surprise that its video is a cornucopia of indulgence. Dave Matthews Band gave director Ken Fox a break here, allowing him to helm this first single from *Crash*. In his commentary track for the video, Fox describes "Too Much" as "kind of subversive, in a way," in how Matthews battles with his own predilections for gluttony. "I thought it would be good to subversive with the images, too," Fox admits, so he constructed a video filled with faceless men stuffing themselves at orgies of food and wine. Every person onscreen wears cartoonish glasses, which are equipped with magnifying lenses, so the actors were effectively blind during the filming. "Most of the time I'm yelling at, them because they couldn't see anything," says Fox, who helped direct them through a concluding sequence where they're all feasting on raw meat—whole, uncooked fish and pink, bloody ribs. "That end scene with the feast is disgusting," Fox admits. "It's kind of sick, but it looks great." He's right, but only to an extent: though exceptionally well shot, this is an amazingly gross video—the kind of thing that churns the stomach and leaves a mark, which makes it a strange choice for the first video from a record. It may underscore the song's themes, but at the expense of alienating a potential audience.

"So Much to Say"

"We're inside Dave's mind right now." So says Ken Fox, who returned to direct "So Much to Say," the second single pulled from *Crash*. In his DVD commentary track, Fox claims, "This video is all about the band," which is true, even if much of the video is focused on Dave, who is depicted bouncing around in a rubber room, sometimes duetting with himself on a microphone—a visual that suggests he's on the precipice of madness. Despite this, Fox may only be following through on his presupposition, "What's better than one Dave Matthews? Two Dave Matthews."

Fox came to this conclusion through hanging with the band, realizing that Matthews is "a goofy guy," and that's a big part of the fun of the video: he's hamming it up, enjoying the camera—an act that might be at odds with the feel of the song but still reflects part of Dave's personality. To Fox, "I think that's what intrigues people about videos. They really want to get to know the artist," and that's what he attempted to do with "So Much to Say." He emphasizes Carter Beauford because Dave told him, "He's the glue that holds it together. [Matthews] also told me that Carter is the one running the show. Carter kind of dictates what kind of show they're going to have." If Beauford anchors the group, "Stefan is probably the coolest hepcat in the music business . . . the great thing is that he doesn't try to be cool." Of Moore, he says, "LeRoi never smiles," so he's proud he captured a smile from Roi.

At the conclusion of his commentary, Fox claims, "I'm actually going to go on record and say that Dave Matthews will be a gigantic actor if he ever decides to do it." This didn't really pan out. Matthews would show up onscreen in comfortable surroundings, but he never pushed the limits of his skills, so he never became a star, although his performances—whether in film, television, or video—highlight his inherent charisma.

"Crash into Me"

"Crash into Me" is a sultry ballad that provided Dave Matthews Band with its biggest hit to date. What role did the video play in this success? It's impossible to gauge, but the video is evocative and seductive, suiting the song's hazy romanticism. Dean Carr, the director, claims in the commentary heard on *The Videos 1994–2001* that "this was the only video I've ever done that didn't really have a video treatment," so he wound up following his instinct, instead of storyboard. He had certain images that he wanted as anchors, so he picked the actors and created prompts for the band members—he also had fun by dressing Tinsley Boyd in an outfit made of violins—then "made up 80 percent of the video on the fly."

Much of the video benefits from its connection to its northern New York setting. Carr drafted a modern dance group outside of Woodstock, and he hired "two Chinese girls [who] were working at a Chinese restaurant and wound up being in the video as geisha twins." Such choices as adding texture to every frame of the print lends the entire clip a feeling that is both dreamlike and grounded; there are fanciful images, but it's all derived from people and images that are earthbound, not celestial.

"Tripping Billies"

"Tripping Billies" was the first live performance video Dave Matthews Band ever released, and it arrived by pure circumstance. Director Ken Fox says in his commentary that he was told at the last minute that the band needed a video but didn't have much time to shoot a clip, so they had to shoot something live. This sounds simple, but the band members weren't in the mood to shoot a video, plus they were concerned that the filming would distract from the concert. They asked him to "shoot a live video," but on the proviso that "[we] don't want to see that you are there."

This is a trickier proposition than it might initially seem. As Fox says, "There is really nowhere to hide in that big stadium," so his challenge was to be transparent—to not draw attention to his cameras as he documented the band in its natural element. Fox devised a number of clever methods to disguise his crew. He put unobtrusive lipstick cameras on Dave's mic and Stefan's bass, and he let the audience know about the taping, encouraging them to go nuts when DMB finally played the song. This doesn't mean that everything went off without a hitch. The guy

Dave Matthews Band: The Videos 1994–2001 DVD cover.

Author's collection

operating the Steadicam got nervous and screwed up the footage, but "Tripping Billies" still feels alive, probably because it was shot not at the soundcheck—which is where so many live videos are shot—but during the actual concert, so it has an electric energy.

"Don't Drink the Water"

The most ambitious video Dave Matthews Band ever made, "Don't Drink the Water" wears its politics on its sleeve. Dean Carr batted ideas around with Dave Matthews, realizing that the song was about "a person or a people who had lost their land." Originally, Carr was thinking along the lines of Native Americans, but the concept "then got translated to the destruction of the rainforest"—a dramatization of the ecological issues that are near and dear to the heart of Matthews and the rest of DMB.

Dave Matthews Band didn't fly down to the Amazon, instead shooting the clip in Pasadena, because there was a dedicated rainforest area in the Los Angeles Arboretum. Carr managed to convey the thick, steamy atmosphere of the rainforest, and he populated the shoot with different tribes, several of whom didn't necessarily talk easily.

To this, he added a prosthetic head of Dave Matthews. Carr did this in part because Dave Matthews Band was stuck on a tight touring schedule, so he needed to find a way to put Dave in the clip when he wasn't physically present. He developed the conceit of Dave's head being passed from tribe to tribe—an unsettling choice that pulls "Don't Drink the Water" in line with other DMB's other album-opening videos. Like "What Would You Say" and "Too Much," "Don't Drink the Water" is garish—purposefully so—but it's something that targets the initially converted, and it's not something that would hook in crossover audiences.

"Stay (Wasting Time)"

"A big part of the creative of this is was, we were really trying to find something to complemented the song—sort of like a feel-good piece for summer," Dean Carr says in his commentary for "Stay (Wasting Time)" on

The Videos 1994–2001, and that's a good starting point for this cheerful video. He sets Dave Matthews in a barbershop to sing the song, intercutting that with frivolity on the streets. The two intercut well, creating a vibrant portrait of a neighborhood ready to party; there's an unmistakable *Mardi Gras* feel here. It feels unified, which makes it interesting to learn that the clip was shot in both Virginia and Jamaica—a move that adds a nice directorial flair but also suggests how we're all the same in different cities in different countries. This may be colorful, but Carr put in some interesting quirks. While he was scouting for locations, he found a guy called Joe Louis at a barbershop. "He had the largest goiter that I've ever seen on a living person," Carr recalls, and casting like this added a bit of Federico Fellini flair to this funky celebration.

"Crush"

"Crush" may be the most romantic song Dave Matthews Band ever released, so it's only fitting that it received a sultry video treatment in the form of a lustrous black-and-white film. This look didn't come out of left field. Director Dean Carr says the approach is rooted in how the group approached him, telling him "they wanted to portray their roots in the jazz background of their musicianship." This immediately made the director think of black-and-white photography—the kind of images that Francis Wolff shot for Blue Note album covers. He contacted William Claxton, a renowned photographer who captured Duke Ellington, Frank Sinatra, and Thelonious Monk on film, but is perhaps best known for his portraits of the doomed trumpeter Chet Baker. Those pictures are the direct antecedent for "Crush," which is set in a moody nightclub, where Dave Matthews Band—complete with Tim Reynolds—is playing onstage while Dave sits at the bar. He sings the lyrics to himself, then winds up rushing to the stage in the midsection, joining with the group for the last minute.

What's appealing about the "Crush" video is its lushness. Carr admits that it was a departure for him to go in and not hire the hottest director of photography of the time; instead, he decided to follow his instinct to not only use Claxton's work as a foundation, but to have the photographer on set to take snapshots of everything that was happening on the set. It's easy to see why "Crush" would be ripe for black-and-white portraits: it's gorgeous and self-consciously retro yet lacking any kind of winking smirk. "Crush" is also cinematic, and that makes it the best video Dave Matthews Band ever released.

"I Did It"

Dave Matthews Band shook up its sound for 2001's *Everyday*, hiring Glen Ballard to produce the record. Similarly, the band decided to shake up the visuals for the album's videos, hiring Dave Meyers—a film director who previously made *Foolish* with comedian Eddie Griffin—for the first single, "I Did It."

In the commentary for *The Videos 1994–2001*, Meyers revealed the video's origins. "I got to go meet Dave and have a vibe session with him," he says. "A month later I got these pictures from Dave in an e-mail that were so hard to understand that I had to call the label and ask for their interpretation of them and no one at the label understood exactly what he was trying to do." With nobody except Matthews able to explain the illustrations, Meyers had to eventually reconnect with the singer/songwriter, who explained that he wanted each band member to be represented by a larger-than-life avatar.

In other words, Matthews wanted to create a kind of live-action cartoon, turning everybody into an exaggerated caricature. To that end, "I Did It" is perfectly in line with how the first video from a Dave Matthews Band album leans toward the garish—and that's certainly true with "I Did It," which opens with Dave Matthews marinating in a dumpster. From there, Meyers indulges in a bunch of visual trickery: Matthews flies out of the dumpster; Boyd Tinsley is a giant; LeRoi Moore kicks the leg out of Matthews. Things get progressively weirder and sillier, before the clip culminates with the group being snapped back to earth: we enter a reality where the members are garbage men, working a regular gig, not the cartoon characters they've been until this point. The "rubbish" conclusion is clever—it shows why the singer was in the dumpster to begin with—and helps emphasize that this isn't really a flashy band but a group of musicians who treat their job seriously.

"The Space Between"

Continuing its collaboration with Dave Meyers, Dave Matthews Band brought in the director for "The Space Between," the ballad that turned out to be the group's biggest crossover hit. "This time Dave was interested in doing 180 degree turn from what we did last time—doing something 'bleak,'" Meyers relates in his DVD commentary. But with the single planned for the summer, he adds, "they were worried that doing something monochromatic would turn off MTV," so Meyers came up with the idea of painting the clouds in the sky different colors, thanks to the magic of postproduction.

Clouds loom throughout "The Space Between," which is set in a bay—a couple is fighting on the shore, the band is playing on the dock, and somehow, somewhere actress Jaime Presley plays a mother clutching a baby. She's somewhat out of the narrative of the video—the emotional thrust is with the couple orbiting the dock where Dave Matthews Band is—but everything adds up to convey a sense of emotional disconnect, which culminates with the storms passing and the clouds lifting. We end with a beautiful night, complete with Matthews smiling at the camera. The jumbled narrative helps accentuate the ambiguousness of the song—its swirling angst and emotions—which Meyers captures very well.

"Everyday"

A replacement for "When the World Ends," which was going to be the third single from *Everyday* until the 9/11 terrorist attacks made its title somewhat problematic, "Everyday" is a jubilant song with an appropriately life-affirming video directed by Chuck McBride that emphasizes connections between standards. Comedian Judah Friedlander stars, essentially playing a variation of his Frank Rossitano character from the sitcom *30 Rock*—he's decked out in the same jeans, T-shirt, and ball cap—as he wanders through the streets of Charlottesville and New York, trying to coax strangers into giving him a hug. This proposition doesn't get too many takers at first—he's shunned and scorned—but soon he wanders onto a news broadcast and becomes a viral sensation, and that's when "Everyday" starts featuring tons of cameos. Friedlander wanders into a DMB rehearsal, dances at Coyote Ugly, hugs Sheryl Crow and *The Sopranos*' Big Pussy, and winds up with Conan O'Brian and the Blue Man Group. It's a virtual cavalcade of new-millennium celebrities, and that's the charm of the piece: it's a time capsule for a specific moment, when the country was rallying to get back to good times.

"Where Are You Going"

The first single from 2002's *Busted Stuff* doubled as a song from the Adam Sandler film *Mr. Deeds*, so it's not surprising that the video itself functions as a twofer: a showcase for the song itself, and a showcase for the film. As directed by Digital Kitchen, the ever-present camera wanders over landscapes—many computer-generated—which serve as a backdrop for Dave Matthews Band, but also for televisions and drive-in screens showing clips from *Mr. Deeds*. It's a fairly standard way to promote a film, but the clips provide an odd contrast with the performance, which taps into the moodiness of the song. Also, the visuals seem chipper in a way the music doesn't.

"Gravedigger"

Dave Matthews headed up to Montana to shoot "Gravedigger," the first single from his first solo album, *Some Devil*. He was accompanied by a heavy-hitter: director Mark Pellington, who made his bones with a version of U2's "One" (there were multiple versions of the video; his is the one with running buffalos) and Pearl Jam's "Jeremy." He had recently started directing feature films, too—he did the nifty thriller *Arlington Road*—but he went back to music videos for Matthews.

Appropriately, "Gravedigger" feels something like a mini-movie. It's a gorgeous-looking video with oversaturated colors, and Matthews gives a moody performance that's eventually intercut with evocative visuals—images of loss and despair from the past to the present. Matthews reportedly lost his wedding band while filming in the grave that he inevitably enters—it was later found—but even if the video builds to that somewhat predictable conclusion, there's a real grace and power to this clip that sets it apart from most Dave Matthews videos.

"Save Me"

The second single from *Some Devil*, "Save Me" is a laid-back, funky affair, one that benefits from the presence of Phish guitarist Trey Anastastio, who, not coincidentally, is seen in close-up in the first seconds of the video—the second face we see after Dave Matthews himself. This is a strong tip of the hat from Matthews, and an acknowledgment that Anastasio provided a big assist on *Some Devil*, even though he didn't actually *play* on "Save Me," so it should be seen as a roundabout way of trying to push the album: perhaps diehard Phish fans will realize their guitar hero can be heard here. Compared to "Gravedigger," "Save Me" is quite intimate: it's essentially a performance video, albeit one set at a rehearsal studio. The band members are shown joshing around with each other, which suits the levity of the tune—it's the only unabashedly fun song on *Some Devil*.

"American Baby"

As directed by David Meyers, the video for "American Baby," the first single pulled from *Stand Up*, finds Dave Matthews Band playing outside a rusty old warehouse—not the pink Warehouse of lore, but certainly there to evoke memories of that storied structure for hardcore DMB fans—but the band's performance is almost beside the point. What matters in "American Baby" is a series of vignettes from across the United States that spends as much time on the landscape as it does in urban territory. It's a celebration of the diversity of America—the diversity of its people, culture and landscape—which carried an understated political undercurrent in the turmoil of George W. Bush's presidency; it's not a protest, but rather a celebration of everything that matters in America. It's also firmly in the vein of "The Space Between" and "Gravedigger": even if it has no narrative, it's polished, and plays like a mini-movie. It's one of the slickest videos in the DMB canon.

"Dreamgirl"

Several notable actors and actresses have appeared in Dave Matthews Band videos over the years, but there never was a bigger star in the DMB universe than Julia Roberts, who is the leading light in "Dreamgirl." In 2005, when the *Stand Up* album was released, she was about five years removed from her Academy Award for "Best Actress" for *Erin Brockovich*, so she had the luxury of doing only projects she wanted to do. Roberts, as it turns out, was a fan of the band; Matthews joshed to MTV in 2005 that "she's been struggling as of late. Things haven't been unfolding exactly the way Julia wants them, so we thought we'd politely give her a hand up."

Appropriately enough for a video featuring a movie star, director David Meyers frames "Dreamgirl" as if the action with Roberts is from a film—one that Matthews is watching in an empty movie theater. In the film, Roberts is on the run from a faceless figure, eventually encountering every member of Dave Matthews Band in one fashion or another. It belongs to the series of DMB videos that play like mini-movies; it's elaborate, and ends on a joke as Roberts winds up not with our lead singer but Stefan Lessard—a nice kicker to an imaginative video.

"Funny the Way It Is"

For the first video from *Big Whiskey and the GrooGrux King*, Dave Matthews Band elevated longtime lighting director Fenton Williams into the director's chair. He shared duties with Jeff Crane, the pair creating a clever stop-motion video, pieced together to suggest that it was all directed in one take. It has a clear antecedent in "Eh Hee," Dave Matthews's digital solo single from 2007, which was accompanied by a video co-directed by Williams that also uses stop-motion.

Matthews is at the center of "Funny the Way It Is," donning different outfits and mugging up a storm for the camera, the frivolity cutting against the somewhat sorrowful song. As Matthews takes stock of how there's both pleasure and pain, loss and love, within the world, he gets his faced smashed by tape and covered with chocolate syrup, and eventually winds up hooded in an orange jumpsuit—an image that is designed to touch a nerve. These visuals aren't exactly pretty, but they're certainly not as lurid as those in "I Did It," and the video winds up digging a bit deeper than "Don't Drink the Water." All the humor and pathos in the images captures all the mixed emotions of the song.

"Why I Am"

Directed by Sam Erickson, "Why I Am" is the second live performance video from Dave Matthews Band, but like "Tripping Billies," there's a trick here: this was filmed in London, England, not necessarily one of DMB's strongholds. It's easy to see this as a way to break the group into the United Kingdom—or at least show that the band does have a considerable number of fans there, as suggested by the long lines outside the Brixton Academy—and much of the video emphasizes that crowd, spending as much time with fans waiting to get into the venue as it does onstage. It's a nice video for a good song, but ultimately rather forgettable.

"You and Me"

The last single pulled from *Big Whiskey and the GrooGrux King*, "You and Me" was designed as a sweet epilogue to a sometimes-heavy album, so it also happens to work as a nice conclusion to Dave Matthews Band's career in music videos. Director Michael Baldwin staged the video in a big, open performance space filled with empty chairs. At first, Dave is there alone, strumming an acoustic guitar, but soon the rest of the band—including Rashawn Ross, Tim Reynolds, and Jeff Coffin, who all appeared onstage in "Why I Am," but this marks the first time they're all in a production—join him, followed by a number of amateur musicians. It's a sweet, communal gesture that fits how openhearted the song is—and its warmth makes for a good final video from Dave Matthews Band.

Too Much

Stray Songs and Detours

Most of the major Dave Matthews Band songs appear on the official studio albums, but there are also a host of stray songs. Some of these popped up on B-sides or as bonus tracks; some cuts showed up on movie soundtracks or various artist collections. Usually, these orphans were aired onstage, occasionally making their way onto official live albums.

This is the kind of miscellany a band builds up over the course of its career, but with Dave Matthews Band, these odds and ends say a lot about that career and the times. Certainly, DMB built up a lot of this backlog through the practice of testing songs onstage prior to recording them—some songs were attempted, then abandoned—but being a major band in the 1990s and 2000s meant that you maintained your profile by donating songs to charity albums or filling out different music formats with rarities.

By their very nature, some of these songs aren't especially memorable, but the surprise is that several of these tunes are indelible, and an important part of DMB's legacy. When they're all seen together, these stray songs form an alternate history of the band—one told through the margins of pop culture and the deep recesses of Dave Matthews Band live shows.

Stray Songs

These are the songs that Dave Matthews Band never put on their albums. Instead, they showed up on B-sides, were played in concert or released as one-off singles, or otherwise showed up in places that only hardcore fans would ever know about. Some of these are clear throwaways, while others are as good as anything the band put on its official studio albums.

"#27"

Dave Matthews Band started playing the song called "#27" in 2007, roughly a year before heading into the studio to record the album that became *Big Whiskey and the GrooGrux King.* The fact that this numerically named song appeared after such DMB staples as "#40" signals how, sometime in the 2000s, Dave Matthews Band reset its numbering system; now, the numbers apply to the songs generated at a specific session.

This song showed show up on the bonus EP for *Big Whiskey*, sounding lean, bluesy and muscular—a sound that suits its bitter sentiments, where the narrator is sick of everything this world throw his way. Some protest surfaces at the conclusion, but the ennui feels internal. It's tougher than much of the music on *Big Whiskey*, so that may be why "#27" didn't make the cut, but it wasn't forgotten: it surfaced on the EP and was played often in the summer of 2014.

A postcard promoting the July 16, 2002 release of *Busted Stuff*. *Author's collection*

"#40"

A delicate acoustic love song, "#40" wound up being played often in the spring of 1995 and surfaced in a brief version on the 1999 live album *Listener Supported*, but otherwise it was abandoned—probably because it was never finished. In a documentary made around the time of *Big Whiskey and the GrooGrux King*, Matthews notes how fans always ask for the song and insist there was a version with complete lyrics, because there was one performance were it was played until the end. He, however, doesn't remember that performance, and claims all of the words came off the top of his head. This didn't stop him from teasing the song throughout the years, though, before finally playing a full version on July 4, 2015.

"Beach Ball"

A piece of elongated folk-rock—the melody is winding, not hooky, the lyrics elliptical in how they take stock of the world—"Beach Ball" saw its stage debut in April of 2009, suggesting that it was a song written during the sessions for *Big Whiskey* but never test-driven onstage. For a long time, the song wasn't played much, but fan demand for this nifty miniature escalated, and it was played somewhat often during 2015.

"Blackjack"

A moody song written with producer Mark Batson during the *Stand Up* sessions, "Blackjack" didn't make its live debut until half a decade later, when it started showing up in set lists throughout the last half of 2010. The band played it often that year, then wound up working it into its Gorge set list in 2011—a performance in which DMB hit the funky back half really hard—but then let it loose the next year.

"Blue Water"

A moody, still number that gives a lot of space to Boyd Tinsley's violin, "Blue Water" was played frequently during 1992 and 1993—the early years when the band was still figuring out what worked. Often, it was paired with "Minarets," which had a similar roiling undercurrent, but the group wound up abandoning the song. Dave played it with Tim Reynolds in 1996, but apart from that, the band has been reluctant to complete it, despite the pleas of fans. It did, however, show up on the twentieth volume of *Live Trax*.

"Break Free"

A churning mid-tempo vamp that slowly gains strength through its understated groove and sometimes sounds like a funkier "The Space Between," "Break Free" is a leftover from *Stand Up*. After playing it often in 2006, the group left it unplayed for years, then tested it out in 2011 before returning it to rotation during the summer of 2016.

"Can't Stop"

A song that grew out of jamming on the solo Dave Matthews song "Save Me," "Can't Stop" is another leftover from *Stand Up*. Like so many songs on that album, it's a bit of a groove song, but this is a low-key funky affair that opens itself nicely to extended solos. DMB played the song a lot in 2006, and kept returning it, playing it frequently in 2010 and having Gary Clark Jr. sit in for a version in 2012.

"Corn Bread"

Another leftover from the *Stand Up* sessions, co-written with producer Mark Batson, "Corn Bread" appeared on the bonus CD included with the European edition of *Big Whiskey and the GrooGrux King*. It's one of Matthews's most ribald songs—one of the main refrains is about how he wants to "go down on you"—but the lyrics take a backseat to the dense, cloistered rhythms, which are accentuated by a nimble banjo on the studio version. Even though the verses are heavy and funky, it's not a tight song: the focus drifts on the bridge and breakdown, neither having a strong hook, yet things are salvaged by the horn section. Perhaps the rhythms suggest what this would've been, had it showed up on *Stand Up*, an album whose beats were largely pieced together on the computer, but the band manages to cook up a real head of steam here, and that's why the song stayed in sets between 2007 and 2016: it's a song that invites long, open-ended jams.

"Crazy Easy"

A lively, sunny little number debuted during 2004—the dead zone between *Everyday* and *Stand Up*—"Crazy Easy" was played often in 2004, then abandoned until 2013, when the band tested it out for five shows in the summer and then left it behind.

"Deed Is Done"

A percolating song whose ominousness is undercut somewhat by its intimate arrangement, "Deed Is Done" essentially existed for about a year, played often by Dave Matthews and Tim Reynolds during the winter 1996 tour, then on Dave and Tim shows in 1997 and 1999 before being abandoned. Even if it was forgotten, hints of the riff can be heard on *Before These Crowded Streets*, in a jam following "Pig."

"Dream So Real"

The rare Dave Matthews Band song that features Matthews on a keyboard, "Dream So Real" plays a bit like his variation on a Sinatra saloon song: the verses are certainly that kind of tears-in-beer mournful, but the song lightens on the chorus. The group tested it out often during 2007, tried it again in 2008, then left it behind.

"Dreamed I Killed God"

An intense, minor-key number played by Dave Matthews and Tim Reynolds during their winter tour of 1997, "Dreamed I Killed God" was often paired with "Typical Situation," but the union didn't last long. It existed only that February, but its haunting murmurs linger, suggesting that it could've developed into something larger and lasting.

"Eh Hee"

Initially released as a solo song before Matthews brought it to Dave Matthews Band at large, "Eh Hee" made its debut during a cruise by Dave Matthews and Friends in February of 2006. At that point, it was called "Ayhee." It then drifted into the background, popping up for a solo performance in Manchester, then was hauled out for a duet concert with Tim Reynolds at the Radio City Music Hall in 2007. This performance showed up on the *Live at Radio City* live album, where Dave introduces the song with a tale of how he heard Khoisan music in South Africa and wanted to know more about it, so wrote this as an "homage to meeting . . . the most advanced people on the planet."

A magazine ad promoting the release of *Before These Crowded Streets*. *Author's collection*

To most ears, "Eh Hee" will sound like a Peter Gabriel song: it relies heavily on rhythms and harmony, all existing in a primordial soup. The murkiness is an attribute, giving the track a darkly pulsating undercurrent. "Eh Hee" was released as a solo Dave Matthews song—the first since *Some Devil*—and he not only played every instrument and sang every note here but also co-directed the video with DMB lighting director Fenton Williams. The pair developed a distinctive stuttering stop-motion effect for Matthews, who spends the clip sitting in a chair while the Seattle-based dance troupe Zoe Juniper cavorts around him. It was a lot of effort for a song that's not quite a throwaway but not really canon, either. ATO/RCA pushed it out as a free download in September 2007—something that didn't please *Riverfront Time* music critic Annie Zaleski very much. "Dave, placate your white guilt some other way and stop doing this stuff," she wrote. "Please. Just take your Fratboy Idol franchise on the road and stop trying to be a diversity-obsessed cultural spokesperson." The song remained a familiar figure in set lists between 2008 and 2012.

"Good Good Time"

Considerably mellower than its party-hearty title might suggest, "Good Good Time" nevertheless does feel warm and friendly: it's a song for evenings around a campfire, not a beer bash in a rental house. Dave Matthews Band tested it out often in 2004 but then let it linger for a decade, bringing it back for a series of shows in the summer of 2014.

"Granny"

Not actually released on *Under the Table and Dreaming*, "Granny" was an important part of the Dave Matthews Band's early repertoire, showing up in concerts in late 1992 and throughout 1993. "Granny" may not have made the cut for *Under the Table and Dreaming*, but it's remained one of the most popular DMB songs, showing up in concert through the '90s and never entirely benched from that point on. There were a few years when it wasn't played very much—just twice in 2007, five times in 2011, and six in 2012—but it's a flexible song that allows for call and response. Even if it's grounded in a folky guitar figure, it gives plenty of opportunity for the band to stretch out and play, which is why it's so often part of the group's set list.

"Idea of You"

"Idea of You" is another outtake from the *Stand Up* sessions, and another song written with Mark Batson. Unlike a lot of the chipper songs on that album, this tune has a melancholy undercurrent, despite its skipping tempo and bold melody. It didn't fit into the feel of *Stand Up*, but it plays to all of the strengths of Dave Matthews Band, which may be why the group played it often between 2006 and 2008. After a few years in mothballs, it showed up again in 2013, and it would continue to be brought out on occasion from that point on.

"Joy Ride"

A bright, cheerful tune propelled by a stop-start rhythm that encourages crowd participation, "Joy Ride" didn't make the cut for *Stand Up*. It showed up as a bonus track on the supplemental EP and was played often in 2004 before being retired, then revived for a few shows in the summers of 2006 and 2013.

"JTR"

One of the songs from *The Lillywhite Sessions* that wasn't revived on *Busted Stuff*, "JTR" is an acronym for "John the Revelator"—which is itself a title of a classic prewar blues song popularized by Blind Willie Johnson. The Dave Matthews song has nothing to do with that tune, but it's a dense, exciting number with a stronger jazz undercurrent than most DMB songs. Ultimately, that jazziness winds up carrying more power than Matthews's vague words of devotion. Dave Matthews Band played it throughout 2000 and 2001, then added it to sets in 2006, 2010, and 2013.

"Kill the King"

This was a song that got a test run in 2006, when it was played throughout the summer, then abandoned, only to return in the summer of 2011, during the Dave Matthews Band Caravan tour. It's unclear why this song was left to rot: it's funky and forceful, and has a stronger sense of momentum than most songs from 2001–2006. It did wind up getting showcased on the 2011 release *Live in Atlantic City*, which is regarded as one of the great Dave Mathews Band live albums.

"Little Red Bird"

A gentle little folk tune with a strong Beatles-esque bent—this is the closest Dave Matthews came to sounding like Paul McCartney—"Little Red Bird" lent its name to the bonus EP included with deluxe editions of *Big Whiskey and the GrooGrux King*. It doesn't fit the tone of the rest of the sessions, and its delicate melodicism is unique within Matthews's catalogue: this is as intimate and mellifluous. After a tentative start, the song started to be played more often during the course of the 2010s, and it was played often in 2015.

"Loving Wings"

First debuted in the summer of 2002, "Loving Wings" has showed up on six live albums, which makes it the song that shows up most frequently on Dave Matthews Band records without appearing in a studio version. It's a delicate little love song that benefits from its hushed atmosphere. The group played it often in 2002 and 2003, then pushed it again in 2006 and 2007, but after that it would only return to set lists as an occasional surprise.

"Shotgun"

Not a cover of Junior Walker's Motown classic, "Shotgun" isn't a manic rocker: it's a moody, textured number where the narrator bears some grievances against a lover. The song carries a sense of drama that means it sounds good onstage. The band played it often in 2006 and 2007, then revived a few times in 2009, 2011, and 2012.

"Sister"

Dave Matthews first wrote a song called "Sister" in 1994, but that was abandoned and swapped out for an earnest acoustic ballad in 2006. A sweet, quiet song whose familial bent certainly suits *Every Mother Counts*, a benefit album for Christy Turlington's childbirth foundation of the same name—it's another song that's dedicated to Dave's sister Jane—it has a lovely lilting lyrical melody whose lightness distinguishes it from other Matthews ballads, which can occasionally be heavy-handed. Dave Matthews Band started playing the song in 2006, and it was in regular rotation over the next three years, before slowly fading into the background. By the time of 2012, it was down to being played only four times a year, but it never completely left set lists after the point it was debuted in 2009.

"Spotlight"

Debuted as early as 1991, "Spotlight" stayed in circulation until the fall of 1993, when it was dropped and never heard again. Matthews is reportedly not a fan of the song, but it has an insistent pulse and a winding melody that are of a piece with other early numbers; it's not a great song, but one that has a period charm.

"Sugar Will"

A churning ballad where the narrator is yearning for escape—the sugar in the title isn't a term of endearment but an acknowledgment that too much of a sweet thing can kill you—"Sugar Will" is a song Dave Matthews Band tested out throughout 2004 but didn't bring to the *Stand Up* sessions. The band attempted it in 2008 but really attempted to bring it into its own in 2016, when it was played throughout the summer.

"Sweet Up and Down"

The second song from *The Lillywhite Sessions* that was not carried over to *Busted Stuff*, "Sweet Up and Down" is a funky and filthy number that hints at oral sex throughout its lyrics. It's lighter in tone than the other *Lillywhite Sessions* songs, but also slighter, as if designed for stage. It has been put onstage several times since—in 2007 and 2010 it seemed like a regular number—but it essentially feels like a throwaway.

"Trouble with You"

Included on the bonus CD *A Limited Edition Companion to Stand Up*, "Trouble with You" is a smoldering groove that pledges devotion to a wild lover. Initial promo pressings of *Stand Up* in Australia had "Trouble with You" in place of "Hello Again," but it feels like a B-side: an extension of the mood of the record that lacks distinguishing factors. The band never played the song live.

"Water into Wine"

First played in 1994, "Water into Wine" is a slight song in the best possible sense: it's delicate and fleeting, built upon a plucked acoustic figure and Matthews's murmuring melody. It showed up in sets throughout 1995, then was faded away until 2008, when it not only showed up onstage but also appeared on *Live Trax 13* and *Live Trax 15*. Since then, it's been played infrequently.

"Write a Song"

Appearing alongside "Cornbread" as a bonus track on the European CD edition of *Big Whiskey and the GrooGrux King*, "Write a Song" isn't literally about composing a song. Instead, it's a love song disguised as a mid-tempo arena-rock groover: our narrator is writing a song to make his queen high; to make her dance, sing, and swing. It's a tightly written pop tune that the band decorates with flourishes, but it doesn't allow the group much place to play, which may be why it has only been in limited rotation since 2010.

Compilations

Like many groups of its stature, Dave Matthews Band has been invited to contribute songs to albums consisting of multitude of stars. Usually, DMB has participated in compilations intended for charity, but the band has also taken the time to salute an idol, as when appearing on a star-laden salute to Bob Dylan. What follows are highlights from these records.

A Very Special Christmas, Vol. 3

On the 1997 release *A Very Special Christmas, Vol. 3*—the third in a series of albums designed to benefit the Special Olympics—Dave Matthews and Tim Reynolds team up to deliver a live version of the Matthews original "Christmas Song." This was first heard in a studio version on *Remember Two Things*, so it had been kicking around for a little while, but the hushed rendition by Dave and Tim showcased on this compilation is relaxed and reflective, suiting both the spirit of the season and the earnestness of the project.

Every Mother Counts 2012

This 2012 compilation was the second volume assembled to benefit the Every Mother Counts charity, an organization designed to assist in maternal health. Dave Matthews Band contributed a live version of "Sister," a song that was often performed live by Matthews and Tim Reynolds.

The Bridge School Concerts: 25th Anniversary Edition

In 1986, Neil and Pegi Young held a benefit concert for the Bridge School—a nonprofit based in Hillsborough, California, designed to assist children with serious physical and speech impediments. Pegi Young was one of the founders of the school, joining with Dr. Marily Buzolich and Jim Forderer to establish the institution. It was personal for the Youngs: their son Ben has cerebral palsy. The 1986 concert helped open the institution; starting in 1988, they held a concert every fall. Dave Matthews—either with Dave Matthews Band, with Tim Reynolds, or on his own—appeared no less than seven times. DMB made its first appearance in 1997, playing again in 2000; Dave played alone in 2001, showed up with Reynolds in 2005, brought the band in 2006, then returned with Reynolds in 2011, before reappearing as a solo act in 2016.

Sometimes, accompanying charity albums were released—there was a digital release in 2006 that contained three selections from Matthews, including a duet between DMB and Neil Young on "Cortez the Killer"—but Reprise's 2011 set is the big kahuna of these, a lavish anniversary edition celebrating twenty-five years of the Bridge School Concerts. Dave Matthews Band has just one song, a perfectly fine and not terribly surprising version of "Too Much," but its presence is enough to illustrate the band's deep connection with the organization.

Chimes of Freedom: The Songs of Bob Dylan

A massive, triple-disc tribute to the Bard that also functions as a benefit album for Amnesty International, *Chimes of Freedom: The Songs of Bob Dylan* contains a live version by Dave Matthews Band of "All Along the Watchtower," the song that is a standard in its concerts. This particular one is an early version, given at Philadelphia's Mann Music Center in 1995, when the band was still in the first throes of success, feeling rangy, wild, and open. Matthews leans a little too hard into his phrasing, but LeRoi Moore provides an elegant counterpart in his solo, so the entire thing winds up as a nice, brief snapshot of a band on the rise.

Soundtracks

During the 1990s and 2000s, movie soundtracks were big-budget affairs, filled with splashy new recordings from the biggest stars, all designed to push the soundtracks up the charts. Dave Matthews Band never wound up on a soundtrack that turned into a blockbuster as big as *Singles* or *Titanic*, yet the band played a key part on several soundtracks, which are chronicled here.

Black Hawk Down

Black Hawk Down, Ridley Scott's dramatization of a failed mission in Mogadishu, Somalia, in 1993, was the first war film to be released in the wake of the 9/11 terrorist attacks, so marketing the film proved to be something of a tricky proposition. To that end, Columbia—the studio releasing the film—decided to place "The Space Between" in the trailers and commercials. Its slow, spacey sadness struck a melancholy chord suited for the doomed military mission, but the song also has a certain sense of sweetness that helped sell the film to a perhaps skeptical audience.

Scream 2

"Help Myself" is an early song, one that first was debuted in 1992 and stayed in the set throughout 1994. Afterward, the group tried it out in the studio, initially recording it during the sessions for *Crash* but then putting it on the back burner. When DMB was approached to contribute a song to *Scream 2*, the sequel to Wes Craven's 1996 blockbuster, the group initially considered handing over the horror-appropriate "Halloween" but decided the version with the Kronos Quartet was too good to give away, so instead contributed "Help Myself," a skittish and fun number that isn't necessarily spooky but suits the billing of a throwaway: the vibe is good, the melody hooky, and it wouldn't fit on a Dave Matthews Band record.

We Were Soldiers

The soundtrack to Mel Gibson's 2002 film *We Were Soldiers* included an unexpected collaboration—a song performed by Dave Matthews and country legend Johnny Cash. The pair met in 1999 at a Cash tribute concert and wound up staying in touch, eventually recording the Paul Brandt/Steve Rosen composition "For You" together in 2002. It opens the soundtrack to *We Were Soldiers*, and it somehow manages to exist on a plane where the moodier moments of Dave Matthews Band and Johnny Cash's Rick Rubin–produced later recordings intersect. Sonically, it's meditative and slowly churning, but the song itself feels a bit elusive: there aren't hooks so much as burbling murmurs. Still, "For You" is a fascinating document—a collaboration that proves that Dave Matthews's star was burning brightly at the dawn of the 2000s, and suggests just how firmly Johnny Cash was in the mainstream after his *American Recordings* revival of the '90s.

26

Pay for What You Get

Tape Trading

What Is Tape Trading?

Tape trading is a self-explanatory name for a complex phenomenon—namely, the process of recording live rock concerts, and then, once those homemade cassettes were in hand, of fans trading the recordings between themselves. At first, it was friend to friend—people who helped spread the word—but as the group's profile started to rise, a whole system of trading music between strangers was established.

Tape trading began with the Grateful Dead, who decided to combat the onslaught of pirated unofficial live shows by embracing the tapers. The bigger concern for the Dead was pirated albums—when the band launched its own record company, it saw a deluge of shoddy bootlegs, all cutting into its bottom line—and viewed the live tapes as something akin to fan currency: something the hardcore could trade, using the tapes as something like advertising. The Dead had its own taping system, at first fronted by Owsley Stanley, who was also well known as a manufacturer of LSD.

Given this beginning, it's not surprising that the concept of taping seems slightly antiquated. Certainly, taping concerts is easier to do than ever, given the quality and ease of digital recording. Any fan can make a respectable recording with their own phone, and there are plenty of live performances posted onto YouTube—so there is a flood of performances that can be heard easily.

It's also hard not to discount the impact of the proliferation of official live albums from Dave Matthews Band. If digital technology helped improve the quality of amateur taping, it also allowed the DMB organization to quickly release official versions of these shows, in effect cutting into the audience for unofficial live tapes.

How Were Tapes Made?

Fans brought their own cassette decks to a concert, some taping through open-air microphones but most plugging into the soundboard through a system provided by DMB soundman Jeff "Bagby" Thomas. Hooking up a deck to the soundboard—initially with analog cassettes, but Digital Audio Tape would yield a better result—always sounded better than the recordings that were made from microphones set up in the audience. In the early days, audience recordings were the most common kind of tape, but as Dave Matthews Band instituted a pro-taper policy, hooking up to the soundboard was encouraged, albeit at a price: the designated taping section by the soundboard required a special ticket.

These audience tapes became the source recordings that were dubbed and traded among fans. Some recorders earned reputations for high-quality tapes, but the most familiar designation among traders was when a tape was labeled a "Bagby"—meaning that it was a recording made by plugging directly into Thomas's soundboard.

Did Dave Matthews Band Embrace Tape Trading?

Deadhead that he was, Dave Matthews Band manager Coran Capshaw embraced this patchwork solution to an existing problem as a practical business plan. From the outset of DMB's career, he decided this was the road to follow, so he baked tape trading into the promotional plan, encouraging hardcore fans to trade recordings because that was the best way for the word of mouth to leap from campus to campus across America. Matthews himself told MTV Online that trading "was the best free promotion we've come across," so it's not a surprise that it didn't take long for Dave Matthews Band to develop an official policy for taping, designating a certain portion of the audience for tapers, while insisting that these recording were for personal, not commercial, use. Most fans obeyed this rule.

How Were Tapes Traded?

Once the tapes were made, the next step was to trade cassettes of live performances with other fans. Initially, these fans connected either through word of mouth, snail mail, or listservs, but once the internet began to mature—simultaneously with Dave Matthews Band beginning to climb the charts—fans developed systems to trade cassettes among each other.

Usually, newbies—fans looking to dip their toes into trading—would post to a listserv and ask for help getting started. Some good-hearted souls would often help out these fledgling traders, provided that they were sent blank tapes and postage. Once those tapes were in hand, fans could start trading the tapes, usually through a system called a tape tree. In a tape tree, a fan would announce that they had a particular show and solicit requests for a tape. Once those were received, the labor of copying the tapes was divided into groups, with one person making dubs for a

A live shot of Dave Matthews Band from 2004 that was distributed exclusively to members of DMB's Warehouse fan club. *Author's collection*

group of people, and those people dubbing for another group, so the tapes could be disseminated quicker.

All serious tapers would keep track of the performances they owned by maintaining a tape list, detailing the date, venue, source, and quality of the recording. This not only helped fans maintain their own collections but also encouraged taping, because fans could compare and contrast tape lists whenever they were in search of rare concerts.

How Did Bootleg CDs and the Internet Change Taping?

The harmony of the tape-trading community began to curdle around 1996, during the rise of bootleg live CDs. Unlike the bootleg vinyl of the '70s and '80s, bootleg CDs were cheap to manufacture and easy to distribute, so they started to flood the US marketplace during the mid-to-late '90s under the guise of "import CDs." This is how these illegal recordings were labeled in independent record stores, which was just enough of a ruse to keep them in the bins and available to fans.

Hardcore tapers saw this as an affront, for a couple of reasons. First, tape trading was a communal activity that reinforced ties among the fans; these bootleggers were interlopers, looking to profit off of their community. To combat this scourge, traders distributed "Bagbies," repurposing an old tape-trading term for nicely recorded live concerts and handing them out at concerts, illustrating to unenlightened fans that quality live performance could be heard at low cost—not for the twenty five or thirty dollars the bootlegs commanded in stores for a single disc.

If the fans were fighting back, so was DMB's management. In November 1996, the band hired a New Jersey lawyer called Jules Zalon to investigate the sale of unofficial Dave Matthews Band CDs in independent record stores. That month, Zalon launched a lawsuit against four New Jersey record stores, which led him to the source of a bootlegger called Gnarly Music in New York. Zalon quickly expanded his investigation to other states in the Northeast, confiscating numerous bootlegs and launching hefty lawsuits against the indie stores, claiming that DMB was owed $100,000 for each bootleg live album.

Such strong tactics engendered a backlash from numerous stores, some of whom launched boycotts of Dave Matthews Band albums. Coran Capshaw dialed this activity back by a notch, claiming that Zalon may have overstepped his boundaries and accentuating that the concern was stopping the bootlegs. Ultimately, this tactic was successful, not just for Dave Matthews Band but for the rest of the record industry. In the summer of 2007, the Recording Industry Association of American picked up where DMB left off, cracking down on a New York–based bootlegger with 425,000 illicit albums. From that point on, CD bootlegs were on the wane.

The other way that the Dave Matthews Band organization decided to combat the bootleggers is by launching its own official live releases. The first of these, *Live at Red Rocks 8.15.95*, arrived in October 1997, less than a year after the band started its crackdown on illegal CDs. From that point on, DMB released its own official live albums on a regular basis, only gaining momentum during the course of the 2000s. By the dawn of the 2010s, these were no longer reaching the Top 10, the way the first official Dave Matthews Band live albums did, and they were no longer hitting the stores but were released on the internet on a steady basis, offering a combination of recent shows and archival releases.

An unexpected side effect of these live albums is that they wound up undercutting the culture of tape trading. It still existed, to be sure, but most of the active online trading websites that flourished at the dawn of the twenty-first century started to wither away. Tape trading was no longer at the core of the Dave Matthews Band fan community, but was merely one part of the tapestry, and all the curious newbies who wanted to hear a great live performance from Dave Matthews Band had plenty of official live performances to choose from . . . although there's still something to be said by being taken under the wing of an experienced fan who only wanted to spread the word.

Two Step

Official Live Albums

From the beginning, Dave Matthews Band allowed its concerts to be recorded. This altruism started to turn against the band in the mid-'90s, when unofficial CDs started flooding record stores. Dave Matthews Band fought back in part by releasing its own live albums. Manager Coran Capshaw made it plain that bootlegs were the reason the group started its official live series in 1997. "A lot of this resulted out of interaction with stores that were selling bootleg CDs of the band for an average of $30 for a single disc or between $50 and $60 for a two-disc set," he told *Billboard*. "There will always be people who want bootlegs, but we can start doing these records out at a more reasonable price."

What started as a defensive move for DMB turned into a tradition. Between 1997 and 2011, Dave Matthews Band released thirteen official live albums, each of them designed to be sold for the mass market. The first of six of these were such huge hits that they'd wind up spawning a separate series called *Live Trax*, which was sold exclusively online. While that series is quite interesting, the live albums released between 1997 and 2011 are the official canon: the albums that helped build DMB's audience by establishing the band's live prowess.

The Hit Live Albums

The first seven live albums released by Dave Matthews Band were strategically planned to appear between studio albums. In other words, they were released to a market hungry for new DMB material and, as such, they wound up being huge hits, charting in the *Billboard* Top 10 and sometimes becoming platinum hits.

Live at Red Rocks 8.1.95 (1997)

Released on October 28, 1997, *Live at Red Rocks 8.15.95* is noteworthy as the first official DMB album, but the show itself was something of a pivotal moment, too, marking the third occasion the band had played the celebrated venue and the second as headliner. DMB first showed up there in 1993, supporting the Tragically Hip and the Samples, and came there next in support of 1994's *Under the Table and Dreaming*, but this August '95 show occurred as the band was marshaling strength between its major-label debut and its 1996 sequel, *Crash*. "Drive in, Drive Out," "Two Step,"

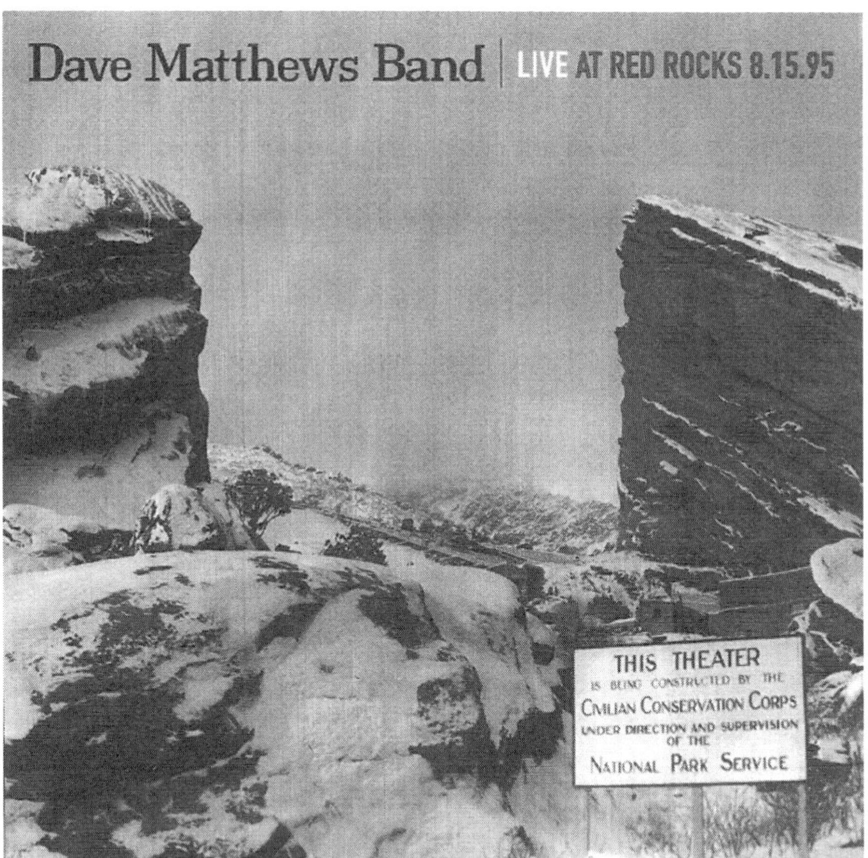

Album art for *Live at Red Rocks 8.15.95*. *Author's collection*

"Proudest Monkey," and "Lie in Our Graves" were all teased from the new album, as was "#36," a song that would become "Everyday" in 2001.

As good as the performance is—and it is, the band playing at a peak in an ideal location, supported by auxiliary guitarist Tim Reynolds—the really noteworthy aspect of *Live at Red Rocks 8.15.95* is how it transferred the notion of releasing old live tapes to the mass audience. The Grateful Dead tentatively made this move in 1993 with its *Dick's Picks* series, but that was an archival series designed for a limited audience; its inaugural release unearthed a celebrated show from twenty years prior. Dave Matthews Band pulled a full show from the recent past, spruced it up, and marketed it as somewhere between a new album and something for the hardcore.

Prior to this, live rock-and-roll albums were usually composites: for instance, Cheap Trick's celebrated *At Budokan* was taken from several dates. *Live at Red Rocks 8.15.95* boasted its date in its title, so there was no mistaking that this, like so many audience tapes and grey-market bootlegs, came from a specific show. RCA put some marketing muscle behind the album, because it arrived during the period between 1996's *Crash* and 1997's *Before These Crowded Streets*. In other words, it was thrown into a market hungry for new Dave Matthews Band product, so the lengthy double-album was snatched up, reaching #3 on *Billboard*'s Top 200 on its way to double-platinum certification. This smash success—aided, no doubt, by perfect timing—established that there was a considerable market for official live releases from DMB, and, from this point out, there would be absolutely no shortage of those to offer.

Live at Luther College (1999)

Appearing on January 19, 1999, *Live at Luther College* was the second Dave Matthews Band–related live album to see release, and it was different from both its immediate predecessor and its successor by showcasing something that was yet to be heard on a DMB album: Dave solo, supported only by his old friend Tim Reynolds. These gigs had been happening for a while—they date back to the group's earliest days, when the two guitarists would jam—and this particular release showcases an older show, given at Iowa's Luther College on February 6, 1996. The intimate acoustic nature made it appealing to hardcore fans, but there were additional enticements here, too: the first unveiling of some songs that would show up on *Crash*, plus "What Will Become of Me?," a song that didn't show up on other albums. The intimacy is the appeal here: Matthews isn't as florid as he sometimes is when he's playing with the full band, and there's a nice, warm interplay between the two old friends. Upon its release, *Live at Luther College* debuted at #2 on the *Billboard* 200, and by 2001 it had been certified platinum three times.

Listener Supported (1999)

The second major live album from Dave Matthews Band, *Listener Supported* is a double-disc set capturing a concert given at the Continental Airlines Arena in East Rutherford, New Jersey, on September 11, 1999. It was released just two months later—a remarkably quick turnaround that emphasizes how this official live series was designed to cut the legs out from underneath the bootleggers. Dave Matthews may be in the center of the album art, but he's obscured on the cover, blurred by a spotlight and smaller than the rest of the band. LeRoi Moore is the most prominent figure, occupying half the cover, then the rhythm section: Boyd Tinsley is in the background with Dave. This live album was the first to showcase supporting keyboardist Butch Taylor—additionally, the band's supporting backing singers, the Lovely Ladies, are in full view—and it also unveiled the previously unreleased songs "#40" and "True Reflections," the latter sung by Boyd Tinsley. *Listener Supported* peaked at #15 and was certified double platinum.

Live in Chicago 12.19.98 at the United Center (2001)

Released on October 23, 2001, *Live in Chicago 12.19.98 at the United Center* was the fourth official live Dave Matthews Band release. The group's December '98 show in Chicago was first broadcast as a webcast, which made it a natural candidate for an official release. Here, Victor Wooten sits in on "#41," while Maceo Parker—best known as the saxophonist for James Brown's J.B.'s—plays on "What Would You Say." Wooten comes back for a cover of Daniel Lanois's "The Maker" (which Mitch Rutman plays on, too), and there are plenty of showcases for Tim Reynolds. *Live in Chicago 12.19.98* entered the charts at #6 and was certified platinum.

Live at Folsom Field, Boulder, Colorado (2002)

As the fifth official live Dave Matthews–related album, *Live at Folsom Field, Boulder Colorado* captures a show given at the University of Colorado on July 11, 2001. In addition to the CD component, the show was released as a live video on both VHS and DVD. Once again, the Lovely Ladies appear as vocal support throughout the record, while the other cameo is Butch Taylor, who sits in on "All Along the Watchtower." A lot of *Lillywhite Sessions* material appears here, too, including "JTR," which hadn't made it to *Busted Stuff* earlier in 2002. *Live at Folsom Field* debuted at #9 upon its release on November 5, 2002, and was certified platinum.

The Central Park Concert (2003)

The Central Park Concert followed the previous live Dave Matthews Band album by a year—a sign of a bit of a product slowdown as the group took its time to follow up *Everyday*. Dave spent time on his own, recording and releasing the solo album *Some Devil*, which saw release on September 23, 2003—the day before the DMB gave this concert in Central Park. By November 18, the show had appeared as a triple-disc set accompanied by a DVD, and it's something of an extravaganza. Warren Haynes sits in for a cover of Neil Young's "Cortez the Killer," along with a sixteen-minute workout of "Jimi Thing," and such long-running times are not atypical here; "Two Step" almost makes it to the twenty-minute mark. It's a heavy dose, as Thom Jurek put it in his *Allmusic* review, but there's a sense of celebration here. Debuting at #14 upon its release on November 18, 2003, the album would be the last Dave Matthews Band live album to be certified platinum.

The Gorge (2004)

Following rather quickly on the heels of *The Central Park Concert*—it appeared on June 29, 2004, just over half a year after that 2003 release—

Album art for Dave Matthews and Tim Reynolds's *Live at Luther College*. *Author's collection*

The Gorge captures highlights from Dave Matthews Band's three-night stint at the Gorge Amphitheater in George, Washington, in September of 2002. This makes it somewhat different than the previous Dave Matthews Band live albums: those captured a single show, but this a selection of culled highlights, designed to showcase the band at their best.

Like its immediate predecessors, *The Gorge* arrived as a joint package containing two CDs and one DVD. This mirrored a trend in the early days of the twenty-first century, when all live albums became a two-part experience, containing audio and video—the better to be ripped for MP3 audio players and then shown off on home surround systems. A wrench was thrown into the works by a companion limited-edition release, which contained the entirety of the three shows performed between September

6 and 8; this was available either as a six-disc boxed set or as a digital download in MP3 or FLAC format.

As a double-disc consolidation, *The Gorge* plays almost like a live greatest hits, touching upon most of the familiar set items—"The Song That Jane Likes," "Granny," "Gravedigger," "Two Step," "Warehouse"—but thankfully sidestepping "All Along the Watchtower." Apart from touring keyboardist Butch Taylor, there are no additional musicians—not even the backing vocals of the Lovely Ladies—and that makes this something of a back-to-basics set for the group: it's just the band, playing standards and playing them well at a venue that is beloved by DMB and its fans. *The Gorge* peaked at #10 and was certified gold.

The Rest

With the exception of *Live on Lakeside*, these live albums, all released between 2005 and 2011, appeared as traditional releases marketed to the mass audience. The difference is, unlike their predecessors, they were not platinum-selling hits. This is a reflection of the band's maturation, as well as the shift from a CD-driven music marketplace to digital consumption. After 2011, Dave Matthews Band would only release live albums through its online store.

Weekend on the Rocks (2005)

Released on November 29, 2005, just three months after Dave Matthews Band held a four-day stint at the Red Rocks Amphitheatre, *Weekend on the Rocks* represents a notable shift in the design and fortunes of official DMB live releases. Although it charted well—it entered the *Billboard* 200 at #37, a very nice showing for a band that had been around for a decade and had a surplus of live albums to its credit—it was never certified platinum, which signals how the bloom on the rose was starting to fade: Dave Matthews Band no longer shifted millions of units of its live albums, which instead appealed only to the hardcore.

Fittingly, *Weekend on the Rocks* feels a bit transitional in how it was released as two separate sets, one being a basic two-CD/one-DVD package designed with a wide audience in mind, and then a mammoth eight-CD box containing the entirety of all four shows—a box that was made for the hardcore. Such hoopla might be fitting for Dave Matthews Band's return to Red Rocks, such a regular haunt for the group that the band inaugurated its series of live albums with the 1997 release of a 1995 show. In a sense, this recording bookends that show; where that presented a band fired by hunger, this is a group settling into a comfortable superstardom, able to shake off the relatively underwhelming *Stand Up*—a record that performed nicely on the charts but is not greatly loved among fans—by delivering the goods in concert.

Here, DMB is joined again by Butch Taylor and trumpeter Rashawn Ross, with Robert Randolph making a guest appearance on pedal steel. The condensed version highlights new songs and tunes that don't often make it into the rotation of either radio or live sets, while the DVD doesn't mirror the CD—the video contains such staples as "Crash into Me," "So Much to Say," "Too Much," "Recently," and "Jimi Thing"—but all the old favorites are somewhere to be found on the big box, all performed with grace, if not necessarily gusto.

Live at Radio City (2007)

Live at Radio City is the first on-record document of a Dave Matthews and Tim Reynolds concert since *Live at Luther College*, a 1999 release of a 1996 concert. That means nearly ten years separates the actual performances captured on the two records, but the essential vibe is the same: a warm, intimate performance between two friends. Unlike *Live at Luther College*, which was at heart an archival release, this one was a quick turnaround: the concert was on April 22, 2007, and the CD/DVD set showed up in stores on September 4.

There are some unusual elements to *Live at Radio City*. Matthews relies rather heavily on *Some Devil*, digging up six songs from that solo set, plus he plays piano for the first time on a live record. *Live at Radio City* also showcases the previously unreleased "Sister," and there are a couple of new songs making their debuts, along with covers of two songs by Daniel Lanois—"The Maker" and "Still Water"—plus Woody Guthrie's "This Land Is Your Land" and Neil Young's "Down by the River."

Matthews cedes the spotlight to Reynolds for "Betrayal" and "You Are My Sanity," underscoring how this is a collaborative affair. *Allmusic*'s Thom Jurek cited Reynolds as a highlight, saying that the album "demonstrate[s] what a wonder Reynolds is. . . . Somebody should sign this guy up, and quick."

Live at Piedmont Park (2007)

Recorded at a gig in Atlanta, Georgia, on September 8, 2007, and released not long afterward—the double-album hit the stores on December 11, 2007, just three months later, just in time for the holiday season—*Live at Piedmont Park* differs from several of its immediate predecessors by virtue of the fact that Dave Matthews Band created space for some of Georgia's favorite sons. Gregg Allman and Warren Haynes of the Allman Brothers Band sit in for two songs, playing their own "Melissa" and also DMB's "What Would You Say." The two musicians also played elsewhere on the Piedmont Park bill, the concert being a benefit for the park itself, hoping to raise a million dollars for a project to expand its parameters. Butch Taylor and Rashawn Ross—auxiliary players who at this point were nearly full-time members of the band—also appear. Although it's a solid set, Kevin O'Donnell in *Rolling Stone* claimed, "If you've got one of the previous six [official live releases], you've heard it all before," and while DMB diehards would certainly dispute this fact, it does signal how the big-budget physical releases from the band were starting to saturate the market a bit. *Live at Piedmont Park* debuted at #68 on *Billboard*'s Top 200.

Live at Mile High Music Festival (2008)

Dave Matthews Band selected its performance at the Mile High Music Festival, in Denver, Colorado, on July 20, 2008, to be its annual live album for 2008, releasing the double album on December 16 of that year. Notably, this was the first live album by DMB to not feature LeRoi Moore. The saxophonist suffered an ATV accident a few weeks earlier—at the

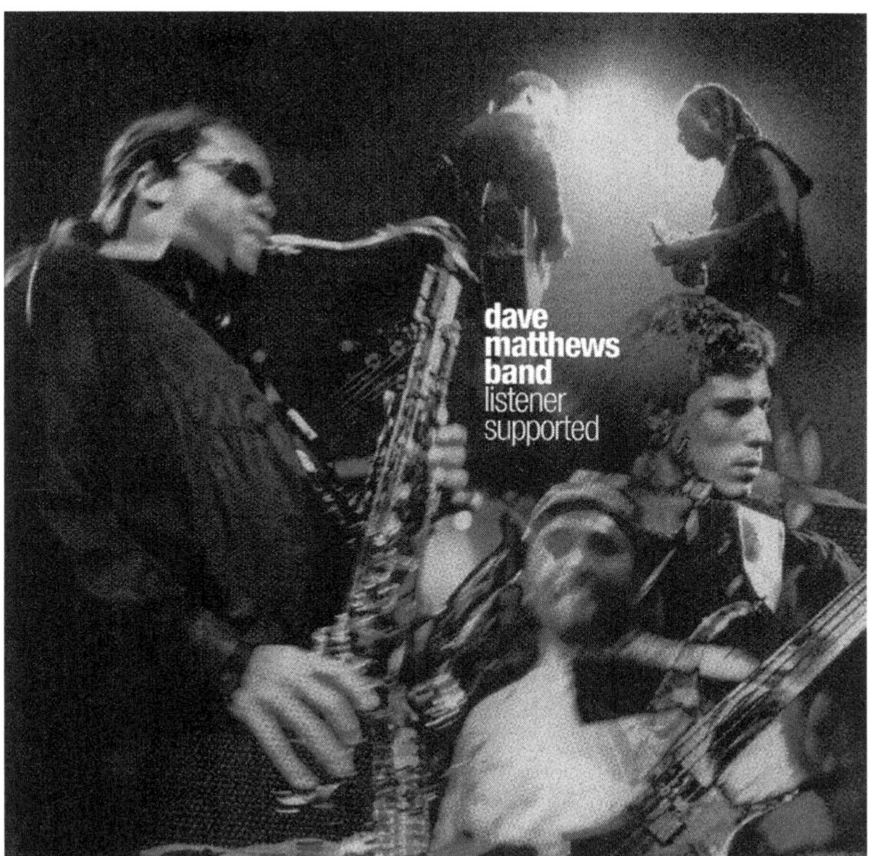

Cover art for *Dave Matthews Band: Listener Supported.* *Author's collection*

time of this concert he was still alive, but he would die from his injuries almost exactly a month later—and his spot here is filled by Jeff Coffin of Béla Fleck and the Flecktones. Coffin would later become a permanent member of Dave Matthews Band, but here he was a friend in need, sitting in alongside Tim Reynolds and Rashawn Ross. Maybe all this turmoil is the reason why DMB decided to stick close to the favorites on this twenty-one-track set, finding space for covers of Peter Gabriel's "Sledgehammer" and Sly and the Family Stone's "Thank You (Falettinme Be Mice Elf Agin)," but generally marching out a lot of favorites, plus a few works in progress that'd show up on *Big Whiskey and the GrooGrux King*. The album debuted at #97 on the *Billboard* 200.

Europe 2009 (2009)

The packaging looks quick and cheap—a stamp on a cardboard sleeve, a careless efficiency bringing to mind old artless bootlegs of the '70s, or perhaps the endless series of Pearl Jam live releases from earlier in the twenty-first century. Either way, the cover art suggests that *Europe 2009* marks a considerable downshift in the amount of money being poured into Dave Matthews Band live albums, or perhaps a dawning realization that these recordings are for the diehards alone: there is no longer any chance that these could be turned into a crossover hit.

The artwork isn't the only notable thing about *Europe 2009*. This was the first live album to feature Tim Reynolds, Jeff Coffin, and Rashawn Ross as official members. Furthermore, the very location of its recording was noteworthy, for DMB have long been an American phenomenon, never making great strides on the continent. The group started to target Europe in the back half of the 2000s, and this set contains selections from two different locations: the audio is taken from a concert given at the Piazza Napoleone in Lucca, Italy, on July 5, 2009, while the DVD is from a gig at London's Brixton Academy on June 26, 2009. The set lists do not precisely mirror each other, but there is considerable overlap in song selection, with the band general avoiding early singles and major hits—the exceptions being "Crash into Me" and "Ants Marching"—to emphasize newer material, or at least compositions that allow the band to stretch out. The album debuted—and peaked—at #120 on the *Billboard* 200.

Live in Las Vegas (2010)

The final big-budget, mass-market live duet album from Dave Matthews and Tim Reynolds, *Live in Las Vegas* was a quick turnaround. The pair performed at the Planet Hollywood Resort and Casino on December 12, 2009—something of a holiday gift for all their fans—and the CD/DVD set showed up in stores on February 9, 2010, a swift production by any measure. What is noteworthy about *Live in Las Vegas* is that it features some of the first recorded acoustic renditions of songs from the acclaimed 2009 album *Big Whiskey and the GrooGrux King*, but apart from that, this is a fairly expected turn of affairs. The two old friends wander through their back pages, pulling rather heavily from Matthews's *Some Devil*—five tracks from the record appear here; three years earlier, it had provided six cuts on *Live at Radio City*—and there's a solo showcase for Matthews along with two for Reynolds, which finds the guitarist playing Led Zeppelin's "Kashmir." Initial pressings of the album available through the DMB Warehouse site included a "Double Down" bonus disc with selections from two previous shows at Planet Hollywood. "Kundalini Bonfire," the second of Reynolds's solo numbers, earned a nomination for "Best Rock Instrumental Performance" at the Grammys.

Live in New York City (2010)

Following its standard practice, Dave Matthews Band rounded out 2010 by delivering a live album from a splashy gig earlier in the year. This time, it was a show at Citi Field in Queens, New York, on July 17, 2010—the second night the band headlined the venue that summer. There were no special guests—at this point, Tim Reynolds, Rashawn Ross, and Jeff Coffin were not officially members of DMB, but everybody acted as if they were—and the group also wasn't pushing a new record, so hauled out a few deep cuts to balance the standards, with "Warehouse," "Crash into Me," "Proudest Monkey," "Dancing Nancies," "Gravedigger," "Two Step," and "All Along the Watchtower" once again making appearances in a live set. Ultimately, the show feels a little meditative and moody—not necessarily avoiding a party, but not pushing one, either. A third CD—dubbed *Big Apple Bonus Disc*—digs further into the first date for songs not played on the 17th, offering up "Why I Am," "#41," "Little Red Bird," "Rapunzel," and "So Damn Lucky," among its eight cuts. The record debuted well, hitting #36 on the *Billboard* 200.

Live at Wrigley Field (2011)

Released not at Christmas, as had become standard for Dave Matthews Band, but at the start of the summer of 2011—just when the band should've been heading out on tour, but was not due to a planned year-long hiatus—*Live at Wrigley Field* captures a concert at the famed ballpark on September 18, 2010, the second of two shows the band played at the venue. This is the standard edition; there's also a *Live at Wrigley Field Double Play* boxed set containing the entirety of the two shows.

There isn't much in the way of surprises in either version. The lineup is the standard post-Moore Dave Matthews Band lineup—the core four, augmented by Tim Reynolds, Rashawn Ross, and Jeff Coffin—and the band plays a set heavy on crowd pleasers, tipping the scales toward hits not played on the *Live in New York City* set of a few months prior. It's a good show, but it's more remarkable for being the end of an era. This was the last Dave Matthews Band live album to debut on the *Billboard* charts—it went in at #49—and from this point on, the group pushed its live albums toward the hardcore.

Live in Atlantic City (2011)

The big Dave Matthews Band project for 2011 was the Caravan package tour—a traveling festival that hit four American cities, beginning with a showcase in Atlantic City, where the group set up shop at Bader Field. *Live in Atlantic City* captures the concert given on June 26, 2011—the final date in a three-night Caravan stand. The group mixes up its set list, relying on old staples—"Warehouse" is one of the first songs played, along with yet another version of "All Along the Watchtower"—but also threading in some deep cuts and newer material along the way, closing the set with the now familiar Sly Stone cover "Thank You (Falettinme Be Mice Elf Agin)."

Crucially, the difference between *Live in Atlantic City* and its predecessors is that this set was not marketed as a major release by RCA. It was something the band put out on its own website in conjunction with the label—a practice that would become standard from this point forward.

Live on Lakeside (2011)

Live on Lakeside was the first DMB live album to not be released on CD, thereby bringing this era to an end. It showed up on Google Play in November 2011, but it's since disappeared, and is difficult to find online.

28

The Riff

Live Trax and *DMBLive*

From the very beginning, Dave Matthews Band fans demonstrated an unquenchable thirst for live performances. Traded tapes became currency during the earliest years, and the band's organization capitalized on this market through its official mass-market live albums, but that wound up opening the door for another kind of release: archival concert releases targeted at the most dedicated fans.

Ultimately, there would be two different series: *Live Trax*, which debuted in 2004, and *DMBLive*, which arrived four years later. The best way to understand the difference between *Live Trax* and *DMBLive* is to think of the two online-only live series like this: *Live Trax* is the Rolls-Royce, the gold standard of live albums; *DMBLive* is a funky second-hand vintage car. *Live Trax* releases sound spiffy and elegant thanks to how they're largely sourced from soundboard recordings; with *DMBLive*, the quirks are its charm. As the cassette-worshipping cover art suggests, *DMBLive* albums rely on recordings that are a bit rougher.

Both series have their charms and their values—and both feature performances from Dave Matthews and Tim Reynolds, plus Dave on his own—but each has a distinct audience: *Live Trax* plays to a wider audience, with *DMBLive* aimed at serious archivists. That's how it roughly breaks down, but both are worth deeper exploration, because they are the best and easiest ways for fans to get their PhD in DMB.

Live Trax

The Dave Matthews Band organization began the *Live Trax* series in 2004, when it became clear that the hardcore fan base retained a hunger for live DMB material even after the steady stream of official releases. That year, *The Gorge* went into the Top 10, so there was a clear appetite for new live albums from Dave Matthews Band, so the group instituted *Live Trax* in response. Cleverly taking its name from the band's old haunt, Charlottesville's Trax nightclub, *Live Trax* debuted in November 2004 with a recording of a show in Worcester, Massachusetts, on December 8, 1998, sold only on the DMB website, in vinyl and CD formats. Later, it would be available as a digital download, and the *Live Trax* series as a whole became available as digital downloads and special-order CDs. Apart from the sixth volume, showcasing the July 2006 shows at Fenway Park, and a 2007 compilation of highlights distributed via Starbucks, none of these *Live Trax* releases appeared in brick-and-mortar stores.

A publicity photo of Dave Mattthews Band, taken at the group's mid-'90s peak. *Author's collection*

At first, the shows were primarily archival—the first five volumes dug through the vaults, finding shows that were as old as a decade or as recent as two years—but as the nature of the music industry shifted, the *Live Trax* series turned into something akin to a bulletin from the band to the hardcore, offering a speedy digital turnaround of gig recordings from the current tour. This began in 2007, when the June release of *Volume 9* presented a show recorded just three months earlier, at the MGM Grand Garden Arena in Paradise, Nevada. Archival releases remained an occasional feature of *Live Trax*—*Vol. 11* is an August 2000 show from Saratoga; *Vol. 12* a 1995 gig from Salem, Oregon—making the series a hybrid of brand-new albums and the DMB equivalent of the Grateful Dead's archival Dick's Picks.

Noteworthy *Live Trax* Releases

By the time the band closed out 2018, there were forty-six *Live Trax* volumes with the promise of more to come in the future. That's an intimidating number for the neophyte, so here are a few shows that stand out among the crowd.

DMB Live Trax, Vol. 1: Centrum, December 9, 1998

The first volume in the *Live Trax* series lifts off the ground thanks to guest spots from Béla Fleck and Jeff Coffin, not to mention a traveling Tim Reynolds.

DMB Live Trax, Vol. 2: Golden Gate Park, September 12, 2004

A benefit concert for Bay Area Charities, this roundly celebrated live show featured a guest spot from Carlos Santana and the debut of two previously unheard songs, "Joyride" and "Hello Again."

DMB Live Trax, Vol. 3: Meadows Music Theatre, August 27, 2000

A fan favorite due to its good vibes, this concert in Hartford, Connecticut, was the last of a three-night stint at the Meadows Music Theatre. There were no guests, but the band sounds inspired throughout.

DMB Live Trax, Vol. 6, Live at Fenway Park ‹2006›

The only *Live Trax* album to get a release in traditional stores—it wound up reaching #37 on the *Billboard* 200 in 2006—this set captures highlights from the group's two July 2006 shows at Fenway—a residency so well-received that the band rushed this out in September, and then pushed it into brick-and-mortar stores to satiate the demands of Bostonites.

DMB Live Trax, Vol. 7: Hampton Coliseum, December 31, 1996

A New Years Eve celebration that features all of the Flecktones onstage for five songs, with Béla Fleck guesting for nine, this is a good snapshot of the band at the time, featuring a heavy dose of songs from the band's first three albums.

DMB Live Trax, Vol. 9: Live at MGM Grand ‹2007›

Returning to the stage for the first time in 2007, Dave Matthews Band played two shows at Las Vegas's MGM Grand Garden Arena on March 23 and 24. *Live Trax, Vol. 9* is a four-disc set of these shows, highlighted by unusual covers of Neil Diamond's "Sweet Caroline" and the Zombies' "Time of the Season," in addition to the first performance of "I'll Back You Up" in a decade.

DMB Live Trax, Vol. 10: Lisbon, Portugal, May 25, 2007

A rare entry in *Live Trax*, considering that it showcases a concert recorded outside of the US, this show at the Pavilion Atlantico in Lisbon, Portugal, was a marathon show, lasting nearly three hours and highlighted by a guest spot from Tom Morello.

DMB Live Trax, Vol. 14: Nissan Pavilion, June 28, 2008

This fourteenth volume in the *Live Trax* series captures the last concert given by LeRoi Moore, which makes it important, but it's also a solid show, highlighted by the live debut of the band's cover of Peter Gabriel's "Sledgehammer."

DMB Live Trax, Vol. 15: Alpine Valley Music Theatre, East Troy, WI, August 9, 2008

Wisconsin's Alpine Valley Music Theatre is a favorite spot of Dave Matthews Band, and this muscular show is widely considered by one of the best sets DMB has given there, highlighted by a cover of Talking Heads' "Burning Down the House," which was just starting to enter regular rotation at the time.

DMB Live Trax, Vol. 16: Riverbend Music Center, Cincinnati, OH, June 26, 2000

Breaking the pattern of *Live Trax* releasing recent concerts, this installment was chosen by members of the Ants Marching forum, who chose this gig from 2000. Highlights include lengthy renditions of "Bartender" and "Crush."

DMB Live Trax, Vol. 19, Vivo Rio, Rio de Janeiro, Brazil, September 30, 2008

This set captures a Rio de Janeiro performance where the band accentuated its South American surroundings by bringing on Carlos Malta to play wood fife on "Say Goodbye."

DMB Live Trax. Vol. 28: John Paul Jones Arena, Charlottesville, Virginia, November 19–20, 2010

Dave Matthews Band announced it would be taking a break from touring in 2011, so this hometown stint on November 19–20, 2010, became a way to bid *adieu* for a little while. The band packed out the shows with guests—old mentor John D'Earth is here, as is Trombone Shorty—and hauled out a bunch of old favorites, including "The Spoon" and "Halloween."

This handbill promoting a concert at the Journal Pavilion in Albuquerque, New Mexico, on May 5, 2009, is notable because it is one of the few times Dave Matthews Band is presented as a quartet.
Author's collection

DMB Live Trax, Vol. 37: Trax, Charlottesville, Virginia, November 11, 1992

The thirty-seventh volume of *Live Trax* came as a complete surprise, presenting the first multitrack recording of Dave Matthews Band onstage: a show given at Trax on November 11, 1992. At this stage, keyboardist Peter Griesar was still part of the band, so this lengthy twenty-two-song set—heavy on early favorites—is quite rare and valuable.

DMBLive

Launched in December 2008, the *DMBLive* series isn't as splashy as its Live Trax cousin, nor is it as diligently maintained. Where *Live Trax* usually has four entries per year, the number of *DMBLive* releases varies, containing as many as three in a year and as few as one. Everything depends on the number of available tapes from the '90s, and their worthiness in terms of either show or audio quality.

Noteworthy DMBLive Releases

By 2018, the group had amassed quite a few of these—thirty, to be precise, including some interesting shows from DMB, Dave and Tim, and Matthews solo.

DMBLive: The Bayou, Washington, D.C., April 21, 1992

An incredibly early show that was rarely, if ever, circulated among fans, this set captures Dave Matthews Band with Peter Griesar in tow, playing twenty-one songs in a small venue called the Bayou.

DMBLive: The Flood Zone, Richmond, Virginia, January 27, 1993

An early show by Dave Matthews Band, again featuring keyboardist Peter Griesar, this was recorded at the Flood Zone, one of the key venues for the band in the early years. The band played twenty-three songs, which is enough time to get through most of its existing repertoire, including lengthy versions of "Jimi Thing" and "Two Step."

DMBLive: Trax, Charlottesville, VA, February 22, 1994

This show on February 22, 1994, was the last time Dave Matthews Band ever played Trax, the Charlottesville bar where it made its reputation.

DMBLive: Masquerade Night Club, Tampa, Florida, March 2, 1994

This show, from March 2, 1994, came during DMB's first tour of Florida, where the band found an enthusiastic reception for its high-energy sixteen-song set.

DMBLive: Irving Plaza, New York, New York, March 26, 1994

This club show from the spring of 1994 is a good portrait of Dave Matthews Band starting to gather its powers: the band is in front of a relatively small but eager crowd—one earned through word of mouth and indie releases, not a major-label push.

DMBLive: Town Point Park, Norfolk, Virginia, April 26, 1994

This recording captures a free concert given in Norfolk, Virginia; the group relies on its early repertoire, including strong versions of "Minarets," "Recently," and "Tripping Billies."

An all-access pass for Dave Matthews Band's summer tour of 2003.
Author's collection

DMBLive: Cameron Indoor Stadium, North Carolina, April 7, 1995

Recorded in the throes of the *Under the Table and Dreaming* tour, this *DMBLive* is spliced together from soundboard and multitrack recordings, but the efforts preserve a sinewy performance, along with an early version of "#41."

DMBLive: First Union Center, Philadelphia, PA 11–30-1998

This November 1998 show features the full band augmented by Tim Reynolds, plus Butch Taylor, who plays keyboard through most of the set; Béla Fleck also appears often, including on a long version of "Two Step."

DMBLive: Benaroya Hall, Seattle, Washington, October 24, 2002

This recording of an early solo acoustic show by Matthews captures his easygoing charm through his onstage banter.

29

Hunger for the Great Light

Key Concerts

There is no easy way to discern what the best concerts by Dave Matthews Band are. To begin with, no two people have the same taste, so they may prefer different eras of the band, or perhaps different songs mean more than others. "Best" always hinges on those particular details: personal preference, plus sheer timing and luck. So, the idea of determining a "best" Dave Matthews Band concert is something of a folly. A few concerts have wound up earning the designation of great or important shows, but that's often due to external factors: they might be easily heard shows, so people are drawn to them simply because they're available, or they've been gossiped about on forums and listservs, the conversation elevating their position.

Instead of wasting time debating what the best gigs are, it's better to look at what concerts from this quintessentially live band made a difference to the DMB story. Not all of these have been released commercially—a couple of them took place before such matters would be taken into consideration—but every concert here provides a crucial marker in the band's history.

Trax, Charlottesville, Virginia, March 14, 1991—First Gig

For many years, it was assumed that the first Dave Matthews Show arrived on April 21, 1991, during an Earth Day Festival, but Stefan Lessard posted on Twitter, on October 9, 2010, that the group—then consisting of him, Dave Matthews, Carter Beauford, and LeRoi Moore—played for the first time at Trax on March 14, 1991, as part of a benefit for the Middle East Children's Alliance. Considering this was both a debut gig and a charity show, it's no surprise that the set that March evening was rather short: just seven songs were played. Lessard posted a set list on October 10, 2010—having recently discovered his old tape of the show—and revealed that the group played "Typical Situation," "The Best of What's Around," "I'll Back You Up," "The Song That Jane Likes," "Warehouse," "Cry Freedom," and "Recently"—all songs that became standards over the years. Lessard is the only person who has a recording of the show, so it's not in circulation, but on March 14, 2016, the official Dave Matthews Band YouTube Channel posted a recording of "Recently" from the gig.

Earth Day Festival, Downtown Mall Amphitheater, Charlottesville, Virginia, April 21, 1991—First Show with Boyd Tinsley

Although Stefan Lessard has since debunked the notion that Dave Matthews Band made its public debut at this Earth Day Festival performance, this concert nevertheless played a crucial part in Dave Matthews Band history because it was the first time that Boyd Tinsley played with the group. He wasn't an official member yet, but this show helped establish the chemistry that became essential to the band's identity. No recording of the show exists, so nobody knows precisely what was played, but on Twitter, Tinsley said the group probably played "Tripping Billies," "Warehouse," and "Recently." It's also likely that Miguel Valdez appeared at the show.

The Flood Zone, Richmond, Virginia, May 6, 1992—First Headlining Show

The first indication that Dave Matthews Band was on the rise came when the band headed to Coran Capshaw's Richmond club the Flood Zone. DMB had played there once before, opening for Widespread Panic on November 4, 1991, but this is where the band established a residency, appearing every Wednesday night for the next two years. There are no complete recordings of the show, but according to what's survived, the band played most of its standard set of the time, including "What Would You Say," "Tripping Billies," "Warehouse," and "The Best of What's Around."

Big League Chew, Trax, Charlottesville, Virginia, March 23, 1993

This spring 1993 show was the last Peter Griesar played with the band. He had quit earlier, but honored his commitment to sit through two previously scheduled gigs, culminating in this one. The concert was dubbed Big League Chew because there was a promotion at the bar for the chewing gum that was designed to look like chewing tobacco. This helped distinguish the show from many other shows; it was easy for traders to give it a nickname. Playing its local haunt of Trax, Dave Matthews Band went through twenty-one songs—thirteen in the first set, eight in the encore—playing for a marathon two hours and thirty-five minutes.

A quirk of this show was that soundman Jeff "Bagby" Thomas decided to have a laugh by writing down funny alternate titles for songs: "The Best of What's Around" became "Best of What Is," "I'll Back You Up" is "Let's Get a Beer," "Dancing Nancies" is "Turtles Turtles and More Turtles," and so on and so forth.

The Flood Zone, Richmond, Virginia, September 28, 1994—*Under the Table and Dreaming* Release Show/ The Band's Last Show at the Flood Zone

This September 1994 show occupies two important slots in Dave Matthews Band history. It was a party to celebrate the band's major-label debut, *Under the Table and Dreaming*, and, not coincidentally, it happened to be the last show the group ever played at the Flood Zone, its home away from Charlottesville. As so often happens, one era begins when another one ends, but it's rarely as striking as it is here. There's certainly a sense of joyful celebration here—how could there not be, when the group was making the leap to the big leagues—but in retrospect, it seems bittersweet, the closing of an era. The group wound up playing almost all of the album—a full ten of the twelve songs—and reached back for a few songs from *Remember Two Things*, in addition to playing songs that would show up later on *Crash* and *Before These Crowded Streets*. The set list illustrates the transition, and shows how the band was poised for greater things.

Red Rocks, Colorado, August 15, 1995

This show at Red Rocks was pivotal in a couple of respects. To begin with, this is the show that was selected to be the first official live album from Dave Matthews Band, released by RCA on October 28, 1997. It was the second time the band headlined the venue, having previously also opened there for the Tragically Hip and the Samples in 1993, but this is when the group truly started to hit its stride. With *Under the Table and Dreaming* out for nearly a year, the band was in fine form, testing out the material that would wind up on *Crash* and generally sounding like a band that had begun to recognize its full power. Dave Matthews Band would return to Red Rock four more times—in 1997 and 1998, then for a four-night/two-weekend stand in 2005, and finally a show in 2008—but the concert released as a live album remains the most memorable, since it helps illustrate the distance the group had traveled in a short time.

Hampton Coliseum, Hampton, Virginia, December 31, 1996

Wrapping up an eventful year filled with touring and the release of *Crash*, Dave Matthews Band headed to Hampton Coliseum in Virginia for a New Years Eve set. There's a sense of triumph here, since the band had had such great success, but also of a new era, one that could possibly be considered DMB's Imperial Period—the time when DMB was the leading jam band in the United States, boosting the fortunes of all its peers. The group's prominence can be seen by how the entire lineup of Béla Fleck and the Flecktones guests for a rousing second set—Dave Matthews Band may have been welcoming guests onto the stage but, in doing so, showed how it was now at the top of the heap. (A recording of this New Years Eve show was released on December 12, 2006, as the seventh volume in the *Live Trax* series.)

The Gorge, George, Washington, September 6–8, 2002

The Gorge Amphitheatre is considered a special place by Dave Matthews Band and its fans. Located on the cliffs above the Columbia River in

Album art for *The Gorge*. The titular venue is considered one of the best places to see Dave Matthews Band. *Author's collection*

Washington, it's a picturesque, open-air amphitheater in the middle of nowhere—or close to the city of George, which is a small town with a population of five hundred. Because it's remote, visiting the Gorge is an event: it takes effort to get there, and, once you're there, you stay and camp through the weekend.

Dave Matthews Band played its first show at the Gorge on August 4, 1996, right in the middle of the *Crash* tour. It quickly became a favorite venue for the band, not just due to its pretty surroundings but the fact that the fans created their own little community. This became apparent by 1999, when the band returned to play its first multiple-night stand at the Gorge. The next year, it expanded to a full weekend, and soon the three-night stint became an annual event. In 2006, DMB and the Gorge settled on Labor Day Weekend as the regular time for the shindig.

Invariably, Dave Matthews Band fans enthuse about their experience at the Gorge Amphitheater—it is commonly accepted as the #1 "bucket list" item for the dedicated—but the year that is acknowledged as the best is 2002. Some of this is certainly due to the weekend's shows having been preserved as an official release—officially released albums are always easier to hear than traded tapes—but also because it was a killer set, capturing the musicians at their robust best.

Central Park, New York City, September 24, 2003

Regarded by many fans as the peak of Dave Matthews Band—a view that many within the organization share, too, since the DMB crew posted a note that day that "it was an absolutely amazing evening"—the band's show in Central Park on September 24, 2003, was later immortalized with an official live release, but this is not a case of a show being celebrated merely because it's on CD and DVD: this was a full-blooded portrait of the band's identity. New York City embraced Dave Matthews Band—Mayor Mike Bloomberg introduced the band—and the group responded in kind, playing a little bit of "Theme from New York, New York" during an eighteen-minute "Two Step." Warren Haynes was onstage for nearly a half-hour, playing on "Cortez the Killer" and "Jimi Thing," but the group remained the star.

The cover for *The Central Park Concert*, considered one of Dave Matthews Band's peaks.
Author's collection

Nissan Pavilion at Stone Ridge, Bristow, Virginia, June 28, 2008—Last Show with LeRoi Moore

Nobody knew it at the time, but this concert proved to be the last one the band ever played with LeRoi Moore. It's hard to view this show without that tragedy as part of the equation, but the concert—which was later released as the fourteenth volume of *Live Trax*—was a good one, distinguished by the live debut of a cover of Peter Gabriel's "Sledgehammer" and also the return of "The Space Between," which hadn't been played in four years. It was not a bad way for Moore to say goodbye, particularly considering how the show ends with "Thank You (Falettinme Be Mice Elf Agin)"—an unspoken tip of the hat to the audience that loved him and Dave Matthews so over the years.

Staples Center, Los Angeles, California, August 19, 2008—The Day LeRoi Moore Died

It's likely that this show, held on the day that LeRoi Moore died from complications following an ATV accident in June, may have been the hardest Dave Matthews Band ever played. Moore had returned to his Los Angeles home to do rehab following the accident, so everybody was in town that Tuesday, when he passed away at Hollywood Presbyterian Medical Center. According to a note that the DMB crew posted later that evening, when everybody was wondering whether they could go on with the show, Dave said, "There's no place I'd rather be than here with you guys right now." Wise words, as mourning is often better to do collectively than individually, so the group rallied and opened the show with "Bartender"—a performance that was later included on the iTunes collection *Live Trax 2008*—while Matthews told stories about LeRoi during the show. It was a wake for a dearly departed brother, something needed by both band and audience.

Madison Square Garden, New York City, April 14, 2009—Official Debut of the New Band Lineup

Although Tim Reynolds had been playing with Dave Matthews Band off and on for over fifteen years, although Rashawn Ross started playing with the band in 2005, and although Jeff Coffin had started sitting in for LeRoi Moore after his accident in June 2008, this Madison Square Garden show from April 2009 is when they all officially became part of the Dave Matthews Band. After Moore's tragic departure, this was the ideal time to revise the lineup, and while it wasn't necessarily a brand-new configuration, it nevertheless marked the opening of a new era. Additionally, it was the opening night of a new tour—one to support *Big Whiskey and the GrooGrux King*—so it's not a surprise that three of its songs make their debuts here: "Funny the Way It Is," "Spaceman," and "Why I Am." This may not have been a concert for the ages, but the show nevertheless opens up a new phase in the band's story.

Dave Matthews Band Caravan, Bader Field, Atlantic City, New Jersey, June 26, 2011

Atlantic City's Bader Field was the site of the first stop on the 2011 Dave Matthews Band Caravan—a touring festival that took place over three days. June 26 was the last of these concerts and, by popular consensus, represents the show where Dave Matthews Band Mk. II started to truly find its stride. The band gets into a grooved run through a two-hour set, digging back for a couple of old songs—"Kill the King" was played for the first time since 2006—but generally strutting, stretching, and showing its power. A recording of the show would be released on December 16, 2011, as *Live in Atlantic City*.

John Paul Jones Arena, Charlottesville, Virginia, May 7, 2016—Twenty-Fifth Anniversary Show

Not every band survives a quarter-century, so making that milestone is indeed something to celebrate, and Dave Matthews Band did it in a way that suited its style. The band held a show—loosely tied to the date of its first paying show, which was May 11, 1991, although the entire 2016 tour was framed around the anniversary—in its hometown of Charlottesville, Virginia, and had the proceeds go to its own charity, the BAMA Works Fund, which donated one million dollars to local charities.

The band also gave some nods to its past—this was the first time "The Song That Jane Likes" had opened a show since 1994, while John D'Earth came out onstage to play "Jimi Thing," which wound up taking a closing detour into "Sexy MF," in a salute to the recently departed Prince—but also to the future, debuting no less than three new songs: "Samurai Cop," "Bob Law," and "Bismarck." Accompanying this show was a "photographic retrospective pop-up gallery," teasing an exhibit that would open up at the Morrison Hotel Gallery in New York in June, which accentuated just how far the group had come while remaining rooted in the music and city that is at the core of its legacy.

Crush

Songs Covered in Concert

Ever since the beginning, Dave Matthews Band has threaded covers into its sets, but unlike many college bands, the group didn't entirely rely on covers when it first got off the ground. The band didn't play a single cover at its very first show, but by 1992 had threaded several covers into its repertoire, adding Bob Dylan's "All Along the Watchtower" as a regular set closer or encore, and also sometimes taking Bob Marley's "Exodus" into the wilderness, jamming on it for as long as forty minutes.

All bands have influences that they usually telegraph in covers, but for Dave Matthews Band, a choice of cover could mean something more than a simple tip of the hat. Sometimes, it would help signal the musical direction the band was pursuing on a tour; sometimes it simply served as a way to bring the crowd to its feet; sometimes it gave the band common ground with a guest. Sometimes the songs would become part of the band's longstanding repertoire—"All Along the Watchtower" has been played so often, it'd be forgivable if somebody figured Matthews wrote it himself—sometimes the songs would be aired once and then put away. Both approaches are interesting, and also revealing about Dave Matthews Band's musicality, how it's fluid while having deep roots—elements that come into view when examining the songs DMB covered regularly, in addition to a few of the interesting tunes that peppered its sets over the years.

"All Along the Watchtower"—Bob Dylan

This is the granddaddy of all Dave Matthews Band covers. It is, of course, a Bob Dylan song from 1968, a quiet miniature turned into an electric epic by Jimi Hendrix that same year. Hendrix popularized the song, turning it into a standard, and the Dave Mathews Band picked up on that version, turning down the electric howl but retaining a sense of drama and adding a hefty dose of elastic rhythm to the mix. This isn't to say DMB excised guitars from the song, however. "All Along the Watchtower" has remained a vital, sometimes necessary showcase for guest guitarists: a place where a friend can come in and wail. The number of six-string slingers to have played the song with DMB is voluminous, and there have been some heavy hitters among them, including Carlos Santana and Warren Haynes.

"Angel from Montgomery"—John Prine

One of the prettiest songs John Prine ever wrote, "Angel from Montgomery" has been the subject of many wonderful covers over the years—a particularly excellent one is by Bonnie Raitt—but in the hands of Dave Matthews Band, it turns a little bit funky. Much of this is due to how it's often performed as a solo spotlight by Boyd Tinsley, who not only uses it as a place for several solos but also cherishes turning Prine's words around in his mouth. Sometimes, Matthews has performed this song in acoustic sets with Tim Reynolds, and he's also been known to duet with Brandi Carlile on the song, too. The song was played often in the '90s, then put to rest after 2001, and has only appeared seven times since, including the duets with Carlile.

"Burning Down the House"—Talking Heads

Perhaps no other rock band of the '80s could really display what it meant for a college band to get loose and funky like Talking Heads. The group remade itself as a funk band at the turn of the '80s, finally scoring an undeniable hit with "Burning Down the House" in 1983; the song has since become a new-wave standard, played frequently in retro parties and playlists, long outlasting its run on the charts. Given its funkiness, it's a good fit for Dave Matthews Band, but the group started playing it relatively late, debuting it in the summer of 2008. From there, it worked its way onto set lists quite regularly during 2009 and 2010, then faded away for a couple of years before resurfacing between 2014 and 2016.

"Cortez the Killer"—Neil Young

One of Neil Young's churning, minor-key epics, "Cortez the Killer" was first played by Dave Matthews Band in 2000, when the group was joined onstage by the song's composer at that year's Bridge School Benefit concerts. The performances struck a nerve within DMB; the group revived it that December, but usually reserved the song for the occasions when guitarist Warren Haynes sat in. Haynes covers it with his own band, too, so when he teamed up with DMB, they were all ready to stretch out—as they do on the version featured on 2003's *Central Park Concert*, which is roundly celebrated as one of Dave Matthews Band's best live albums.

"(Don't Fear) the Reaper"—Blue Öyster Cult

The first members of the Dave Matthews Band universe to cover Blue Öyster Cult's eerie rock anthem "(Don't Fear) the Reaper" was Stefan Lessard in his busman's holiday group Yukon Kornelius, which played it at its first show. Dave Matthews Band first played it on the Caravan tour of 2011, at the group's beloved Gorge. It only became a regular in 2013, when it was played regularly throughout the summer. At the second show on that tour, Matthews said that the departed LeRoi Moore had always wanted to play the song, which may explain why it showed up during this tour.

"Down by the River"—Neil Young

As with "Cortez the Killer" before it, the first time Dave Matthews Band played Neil Young's epic "Down by the River" was at a Bridge School

Benefit concert. This one was in October 22, 2006, when Neil Young came on to close a set by DMB, and then Dave took it to a couple of shows with Tim Reynolds the following weekend. The song became a full-band number during the spring tour of 2007, and from there it has popped up on occasion—once in 2009, then four times in 2015.

"Exodus"—Bob Marley

Perhaps no other Bob Marley song speaks to his status as a Jamaican messiah than "Exodus," a song designed to push him and his people to the Promised Land. This song has a deeper message than something like "Three Little Birds" or "One Love"—both appealing paeans to world peace, yet both sometimes playing like schoolyard sing-alongs—and so it isn't much of a surprise that it appeals to Dave Matthews, who often grapples with larger issues within his songs. It may have been something of a formative influence for how the members of Dave Matthews Band interact with each other, which could be why it was heard primarily during the early years—it was played a few times in 1991 and 1992, hauled out again in 1994 and 1995, then served up as an occasional surprise between 1996 and 2007, but not heard since.

"Funny How Time Slips Away"—Willie Nelson

Willie Nelson's barroom standard was first popularized by Ray Price, but it's long been a country standard, withstanding innumerable covers over the course of the decades. Dave Matthews began playing the song in the summer of 2001, and he played it often during that year and the next, always as a solo feature, always sanding down the rural flair so it wound up seeing neat and a little genteel. It was revived a couple of times in 2010, both times performed in a full-band arrangement, with Zac Brown coming onstage to sing it as a duet with Dave.

An unused ticket from Dave Matthews Band's concert at the Arco Arena in Sacramento, California, November 12, 1996. *Author's collection*

"Hey Bulldog"—The Beatles

The Beatles may have been a big influence on Dave Matthews, but Dave Matthews Band rarely covered the Fab Four in concert. "Blackbird" showed up three times in 2005, and the band tried out "You Won't See Me" when starting out in 1991, but the one Beatles song Matthews has covered regularly in concert is an odd choice. A heavy-footed rocker from the *Yellow Submarine* soundtrack, "Hey Bulldog" is as gnarly as the Beatles every got, and Dave Matthews Band isn't really known for such heavy rocking. Maybe that's why he played it on his Dave Matthews and Friend tours, in a collective that featured Tim Reynolds, Trey Anastasio, and Brady Blade on the tour supporting 2003's *Some Devil.* Americana star Buddy Miller sometimes sat in on these shows, and would sing "Hey Bulldog" with the band, giving it a bit of a gut-level punch.

"If I Had a Boat"—Lyle Lovett

Lyle Lovett's exquisite, minimalist sketch is delicate and lyrical, an ideal choice for the intimate concerts given by Dave Matthews and Tim Reynolds. The pair played the song often throughout their winter tour of 1999, but then it was put in mothballs, never to be heard again. That's too bad, because these performances wound up underscoring how Matthews has an ear for nicely structured little narratives.

"Linus and Lucy"—Vince Guaraldi

Whenever Butch Taylor showed up to guest with Dave Matthews Band, he'd inevitably wind up throwing in a bit of "Linus and Lucy," the Vince Guaraldi holiday standard written for *A Charlie Brown Christmas* in 1965. It was a Taylor spotlight, but it also offered a nice boost of humor to a Dave Matthews Band show whenever it was heard—which it was during the holiday season of 1998, the summer of 1999, then finally three seasonal shows in 2005.

"Long Black Veil"—Lefty Frizzell

"Long Black Veil" is song that feels as if it was never written; a song to seems to be etched into the fabric of America. It was composed by Marijohn Wilson and Danny Dill back in 1959, the pair combining various American folk legends to create an indelible murder ballad. Lefty Frizzell first had a hit with it in 1959, and then in the '60s it became a standard in folk revival circuits, recorded by the likes of Joan Baez and the Kingston Trio, eventually leading to Johnny Cash's 1965 cover on the *Orange Blossom Special* LP. What really cemented the song as a modern standard was its appearance on the Band's landmark 1968 debut *Music from Big Pink*—the record that essentially invented Americana.

Despite this, Dave Matthews is on record claiming that he thinks of "Long Black Veil" as a Johnny Cash song, possibly because the first time he performed it was as a duet with Emmylou Harris at a tribute to Cash on April 6, 1999. From that point on, "Long Black Veil" was heard regularly through 1999 and 2000, but fell out of favor after 2003. It appeared only four times between 2004 and 2012, but was revived for a spell between 2013 and 2015. Like "The Maker" below, it is one of the rare songs Matthews has played with Dave Matthews Band, with Tim Reynolds, with Dave and Friends, and on his own.

"The Maker"—Daniel Lanois

One of the more obscure songs Dave Matthews has covered regularly—and he has, playing it with Dave Matthews Band, with Tim Reynolds, with Dave and Friends, and on his own, one of the few songs to be played in all incarnations—"The Maker" is a 1989 song by Daniel Lanois, best known as a producer for U2 and Bob Dylan but also an artist in his own right. It's easy to see the connection between "The Maker," from Lanois's 1989 solo debut, *Acadie*, and Dave Matthews: it's a funky yet moody piece about religion whose melody certainly suggests many Matthews songs yet to come. It's been performed regularly ever since 1991—some years it's put on the back bench, but it was heard a few times in 2016—and that is because it suits any incarnation of the band: it feels like a blueprint for all of Matthews's introspective moments.

Dave Matthews Band later covered another Daniel Lanois song, "For the Beauty of Wynona." Their version first started showing up in sets during the summer of 1997. Tonally, it provided a clue of where DMB would head on *Before These Crowded Streets*, and it became a fairly regular feature in the years following the release of that 1998 album. Matthews played it for a bit in 2002 and 2003, then it was put into storage.

"Me and Julio Down by the Schoolyard"—Paul Simon

Paul Simon is an undeniable influence on Dave Matthews Band, but Simon's songs have rarely entered the band's repertoire. Dave Matthews and Friends covered "American Tune" in 2003 and 2004, but that didn't say as much as the early covers of "Me and Julio Down by the Schoolyard," for which the band expanded the song and let Boyd Tinsley take a lot of space to solo. It was played a few times in 1991 and 1992, then abandoned for a decade until DMB revived it for when sharing a stage with Simon at the 2001 New Orleans Jazz and Heritage Festival; Simon himself played the song with the band there, albeit in a much tighter fashion than the group did in its earlier years. Later, in 2014, the group played it with Simon at a Children's Health Fund Gala in 2014, but its infrequent appearances only underscores how the song has become absorbed into DMB's vocabulary, reappearing only when it is time to pay tribute to a master.

"Money"—Pink Floyd

Pink Floyd's sneering broadside against cold hard cash is a good fit for Dave Matthews Band because it allows the musicians to showcase their rhythmic dexterity along with their jazz chops. It's a deceptive song, one that's elastic and complex in its structure, being one of the few popular songs to roll to a 7/4 time signature. It's classic rock song, but also quite jazzy, so it gives the band a lot of opportunity to stretch out—which it did throughout the summer of 2008, when DMB set lists were loaded with covers. The band's Alpine Valley show on August 9, 2008, was preserved on the fifteenth volume of *Live Trax*, suggesting that the song was played a little bit more often than it was: it was aired only in '08, then it disappeared.

"The Needle and the Damage Done"—Neil Young

Dave Matthews sang Neil Young's bittersweet ode to fallen addicts at the MusiCares Person of the Year gala on January 29, 2010—it showed up on the home-video release *A MusiCares Tribute to Neil Young*—and, afterward, he played it quite frequently as a solo spotlight throughout 2010. A recording of one of these shows, a concert in Chicago on September 17, showed up as *Live at Wrigley Field*, giving the impression that it was played perhaps a little more frequently than it actually was. For the next three years, it wasn't played at all, then it showed up on four 2014 dates and five 2015 shows.

"Rye Whiskey"—Pete Seeger

Dave Matthews began performing "Rye Whiskey"—a traditional song that's usually known as "Jack of Diamonds" but was recorded as "Whiskey, Rye Whiskey" by Pete Seeger in 1954—in the spring of 2009, warming up with a few Dave Matthews Band performances before showing up at the Clearwater Concert in celebration of Seeger's ninetieth birthday on May 3, 2009. Matthews's performance didn't necessarily garner raves—Jon Caraminca, writing in the *New York Times*, called it "overly precious" and one of show's "moments of overindulgence"—but the song became a regular in 2009 and appeared again in 2010. It showed up a few more times over the next four years before appearing frequently in the summer of 2015.

"Still Water"—Daniel Lanois

Like "The Maker," "Still Water" comes from Daniel Lanois's 1989 debut *Acadie*, and is another slow-burning piece that seems to tie directly toward the quieter, more atmospheric moments of Dave Matthews Band. Whereas DMB had been kicking around "The Maker" from the beginning, "Still Water" started sliding into Matthews's set lists during his 2007 duet tour with Tim Reynolds. Often, it was played in fragments, as a bit of mood music, accentuating other colors in a set or perhaps acting as a segue.

"Sledgehammer"—Peter Gabriel

Dave Matthews may have picked up on the moodiness within Peter Gabriel's solo work—not to mention the embrace of lively, cross-cultural rhythms—so it's slightly surprising that the Gabriel song Dave Matthews Band chose to cover was "Sledgehammer," a carnal number arranged as an ode to Otis Redding. The chillier, more deliberate aspects of Gabriel's work would seem like the idea fit for DMB, but "Sledgehammer" also fits due to its sheer carnality. Matthews often wrote about sex in a thinly coded way, so this would up being a natural fit, too—plus, this is a party tune, guaranteed to rile up a crowd. Like "Burning Down the House," another MTV chestnut from the '80s, "Sledgehammer" first debuted in Dave Matthews Band set lists in 2008, then showed up semi-regularly over the next few years. It didn't show up every year, but it was played late into the 2010s.

"Solsbury Hill"—Peter Gabriel

Peter Gabriel's testament to the moment that he decided it was time for him to leave Genesis is a natural fit for the Dave Matthews for one simple reason: it deals with questions of mortality. Such navel-gazing is a specialty of Dave Matthews's—questions of life and death have been present in his songs from the start—so "Solsbury Hill" wound up sounding comfortable within his hands. Dave Matthews Band never played the song; rather, Matthews brought it to his Dave Matthews and Friends tour of 2003 and 2004, while supporting *Some Devil.* Those shows gave "Solsbury Hill" a somewhat funkier and tighter rendition: there are more polyrhythms, so it feels hemmed in instead of rapturous.

"Sugar Man"—Rodriguez

After Rodriguez became a household name following the release of the Oscar-winning 2012 documentary *Searching for Sugar Man*, Dave Matthews Band began playing his "Sugar Man" in concert, adding it to sets late in 2013 and playing it throughout 2014. During a performance on May 16, 2014, Matthews claimed that he knew Rodriguez from his days in South Africa, adding that when he first saw Tracy Chapman, he told anybody who would listen that she reminded him of Rodriguez, but that all fell on deaf ears. That all may be true, but the reason why "Sugar Man" worked its way into the sets is because, in 2013 and 2014, audiences would now know who Rodriguez and his tunes were. Either way, "Sugar Man" works as a Dave Matthews Band song, since it shares a similar cross-cultural sensibility and an easy rhythm—something DMB nailed when playing it for a few months in the middle of the 2010s.

"Take Me to Tomorrow" —John Denver

Dave Matthews covered John Denver's "Take Me to Tomorrow" on *The Music Is You*, a 2013 tribute to the departed singer/songwriter. He started to test out the song onstage, playing it four times in the fall of 2012—once

A handbill promoting a concert in New Mexico on August 31, 2006.
Author's collection

with Tim Reynolds but usually as a solo act at rallies for President Barack Obama. Over the next three years, Matthews's introspective rendition of the Denver tune found its way into the band's concerts, often as a solo showcase.

"Thank You (Falettinme Be Mice Elf Agin)"—Sly and the Family Stone

This Sly and the Family Stone chestnut gives Dave Matthews Band a chance to stretch its funk muscle, letting the band open up the rhythms. The group first started playing it in the winter of 2003 and 2004, all in the lead-up to the recording of the soul-influenced *Stand Up*, but it was heard more often in 2008—a year when the group loaded up its set lists with familiar covers. From that point on, it wasn't necessarily a song that would regularly be heard, but it's been pulled out semi-frequently on summer tours.

"A Whiter Shade of Pale"—Procol Harum

The Procol Harum classic carries a majestic, classical sweep—something that's baked into its neo-operatic crawl. It's not something that is necessarily an easy fit with the loose-limbed jazz-funk grooves of Dave Matthews Band, so it's not much of a surprise that when Matthews decided to cover the show, he did it as a solo spotlight, usually at the beginning of a show or at the end of it. This helped spotlight the delicate nature of the song, making it a successful cover.

Covers of Dave Matthews Band Songs

Dave Matthews is an idiosyncratic songwriter, but that hasn't stopped other musicians from covering his songs. During the 2000s, he racked up several notable covers by Stevie Nicks and Mika—versions that paid tribute to his songs—but he also fell victim to one of the oddest trends of the decade: style-specific tributes by studio groups. Some of these records were awkward, some were fine, but they all demonstrate one thing: the reach of Dave Matthews Band stretched far and wide in the 2000s, during which time the group became a cultural touchstone.

Mika—"Satellite" (2007)

Added to certain retailer-exclusive editions of his 2007 debut *Life in Cartoon Motion* and included as a B-side to his hit single "Grace Kelly," Mika's version of "Satellite" remains faithful to the intimate sprit of Dave Matthews Band's original, but the feel is much different. Where DMB's version feels earnest, Mika's has a bit of arch theatricality to it, accentuated by his keening falsetto—an affect that's much showier than Matthew's murmuring—and the result is appealing. The showiness isn't showboating; it winds up highlighting the emotions that flow through the song.

Stevie Nicks—"Crash into Me" (2009)

The Fleetwood Mac singer recorded *The Soundstage Sessions* in October of 2007, but it wasn't released as an album until 2009. When it was, it was preceded by the single of "Crash into Me," a cover of the 1996 Dave Matthews Band hit. Nicks stays faithful to the arrangement—it's all hazy and anchored on acoustic guitar—but she sings the song with more force than Matthews, bending it to her will, so it sounds more like a Fleetwood Mac song than a Dave Matthews Band tune.

Boyce Avenue—"Crash into Me" (2009)

The Sarasota, Florida–based band of brothers Boyce Avenue, led by Alejandro Luis Manzano, covered "Crash into Me" the same year Stevie Nicks's version appeared. The version showed up not on the group's 2009 debut, *All You're Meant to Be*, but on the same year's *Influential Sessions* EP. It's a straight coffeehouse cover of the tune, delicate and quivering—a song that begs for affection instead of earning it.

Josh Groban—"Satellite" (2013)

On *All That Echoes*, his second mainstream pop album, classically trained vocalist Josh Groban recorded with producer Rob Cavallo, who produced *Big Whiskey and the GrooGrux King*. Perhaps that's why Groban recorded "Satellite" as a bonus track for the Target-specific edition of *All That Echoes*. In Groban's hands, the gently plucked acoustic guitars are swapped for a string section, so the music becomes softer and stuffier, yet it remains a sweet love song that exudes warmth.

31

Joyride

Satellite Tours

While Dave Matthews Band has toured almost every year, almost ever summer, Matthews himself has often filled his downtime with tours that could be described as satellite tours—a combination of solo gigs, duo tours with Tim Reynolds, and sometimes shows where he's surrounded by fellow spirits. The latter happened in the wake of the 2003 release of *Some Devil*, when he launched a tour called "Dave Matthews with Friends," which saw the singer/songwriter performing with a group of musicians fronted by Phish guitarist Trey Anastasio, who also played on the album. With the exception of Dave Matthews Band Caravan—a 2011 festival that was something different than the usual Dave Matthews Band tour, announced when the group was purportedly on a break—these are projects that belong to Dave on his own, but these are the byways of the official Dave Matthews Band tours, the concerts that might not quite be canon, yet still count among the group's main shows.

Dave Matthews and Tim Reynolds

Clearly, the biggest side tours away from Dave Matthews Band are the ones that Dave Matthews has embarked on with Tim Reynolds, his old guitar mentor, whom he met for the first time when he was tending bar at Miller's. Matthews wound up forming his own band, but he never lost sight of Reynolds, who in many ways remained his idol. In 1993, when Dave Matthews Band started to gain some traction, the duo started to play acoustic shows, and this became an annual winter event, although the pair took a hiatus during the difficult years of 2000–2002, when Matthews was still figuring how to move forward with DMB. Reynolds returned to the fold in March of 2003, as Matthews was prepping his solo debut, *Some Devil*. That month, he revived the concerts with Reynolds, and he never completely abandoned them from that point forward—even if, in some years, there would only be a handful of gigs.

Reynolds became a permanent member of Dave Matthews Band in 2009, but even though he was now part of the acknowledged crew, he and Dave still played shows together—an acknowledgment of the strong bond between the two. DMB fans were well aware of the connection the two had. Matthews helped push Reynolds into a position of prominence

A VIP badge for Dave Matthews Band's summer tour of 2004
Author's collection

through their joint tours, along with the release of live albums of these shows. In 1999, when the band was at the peak of its popularity, it was a recording of a duo gig at Luther College in Deborah, Iowa, on February 6, 1996, that became the second official live album released by Matthews, following *Live at Red Rocks 8.15.95*. This helped introduce Tim Reynolds to a wider audience—it was a help that his name appeared in bright yellow on the cover, popping out against the blue background, while Dave Matthews receded into the saturated warmth—and, from that point on, shows by Matthews and Reynolds would become cherished events for dedicated Dave Matthews fans.

Dave Matthews and Friends

To support his 2003 solo album, *Some Devil,* Dave Matthews assembled a new group called Dave Matthews and Friends. He took two old friends—guitarist Tim Reynolds plus Phish guitarist Trey Anastasio, whose relationship with Matthews dates back to 1993—and added bassist Tony Hall, keyboardist Ray Paczkowski, and drummer Brady Blade. Some of them had a shared past—Paczkowski and Anastasio had been playing together since 2001—and others would have a shared future (Trey would bring Hall into his Trey Anastasio Band later in the decade).

Fittingly, for a tour featuring Reynolds, the shows started with an acoustic set by the two old friends, and then the rest of the band showed up afterward. Usually, the band would then work through much of *Some Devil,* sometimes threading in *The Lillywhite Sessions* outtake "Sweet Up and Down." At the longer shows, there was another acoustic segment, this time bringing Trey to the stage, where he would sing Phish's "Bathtub Gin" or "Waste," trading verses with Matthews; they'd also sing DMB's "Everyday," with Anastasio singing part of the song.

The Dave Matthews and Friends tour was small, lasting just a dozen dates in the winter of 2003, augmented by a November 8 appearance on *Saturday Night Live.* Subsequently, Dave Matthews and Friends played the 2004 Bonnaroo Festival and the 2005 Vegoose festival, then wound up going out on a three-day cruise in February 2005 and 2006. These cruises helped pave the way for semi-regular private shows on cruise ships by Dave Matthews Band—events that weren't held every year, but were revived in the fall of 2009.

Dave Matthews Band Caravan

Dave Matthews Band Caravan was a series of four festivals held during the summer of 2011. Unlike some touring festivals, which usually stick with the same group of bands throughout their run, Dave Matthews Caravan changed from date to date—something that makes sense, because the anchor always was Dave Matthews Band. This may have been a splashy way to spend the summer of 2011, but it also had the effect of cutting down the band's workload; there may have been five big dates, but that was considerably fewer than the band would do on a solo tour, which may be why the group members decided to busy themselves with this roving festival during a summer they were allegedly going to sit out.

Bader Field, Atlantic City, New Jersey

The first stop on Dave Matthews Band Caravan was at Bader Field in Atlantic City, New Jersey, between June 24 and 26, 2011. The last show here wound up getting preserved in a December release called *Live in Atlantic City*, a live album that's considered among the group's best, but the festival overall was filled with other heavy hitters. Over the course of the three days, ATO singer/songwriter David Gray also was on the bill, along with Ray LaMontagne, the Flaming Lips, Damian Marley, Dr. Dog, O.A.R., Michael Franti and Spearhead, Grace Potter and the Nocturnals, Guster, Carolina Chocolate Drops, Punch Brothers, Dawes, and the Warren Haynes Band—a nicely diverse selection of bands that underscores just how much musical ground Dave Matthews Band covers.

Lakeside, Chicago, Illinois

When Dave Matthews Band Caravan set up shop at South Works—a site that was called Lakeside by the Dave Matthews Band organization, and has since been demolished—the show retained a fair amount of acts from the Atlantic City show, but also wound up adding some new ones. The carryovers included David Gray, the Flaming Lips, Ray Lamontagne, O.A.R., and Michael Franti and Spearhead; new to the bill were Chicago native Liz Phair—who released an album on ATO—Umphrey's McGee, Edward Sharpe and the Magnetic Zeroes, Emmylou Harris, rapper Kid Cudi, Amos Lee, Ben Folds, G. Love and Special Sauce, Gomez, Drive-By Truckers, the Jayhawks, Soulive, Sharon Jones and the Dap-Kings, the Dirty Dozen Brass Band, Gary Clark Jr., and fellow ATO act Amos Lee.

Randall's Island, New York, New York

Due to Hurricane Irene, this concert, originally due to take place at Governors Island on August 26–28, wound up being canceled and rescheduled for September 16–18. This meant that the band's three days at the Gorge—the true spiritual conclusion to the tour, since it is such a beloved place in Dave Mathews Band lore—weren't the finale, but rather that this rescheduled show at Randall's Island was.

The acts featured at Randall's Island differed slightly from the Governors Island lineup. At Randall's, DMB and Dave Matthews and Tim Reynolds played, along with a solo set from Warren Haynes, a set by Tim Reynolds's group TR3, Brandi Carlile, Trombone Shorty and Orleans Avenue, Dispatch, Josh Ritter and the Royal City Band, and the Tangiers Blues Band. Dropping out from the Governors Island set were the Roots, Gogol Bordello, Béla Fleck and the Flecktones, the Head and the Heart, O.A.R., and Robert Randolph and the Family Band.

The Gorge, George, Washington

Dave Matthews Band Caravan set up shop at the Gorge in Washington, one of the band's favorite places in the United States. DMB sell out this venue every year, so didn't necessary need a lot of assistance in making this a big deal; as such, the lineup for this particular Caravan was a lot smaller than those in Chicago or New Jersey. Here, the bill included the Roots, Dispatch, Gogol Bordello, Edward Sharpe and the Magnetic Zeroes, Josh Ritter and the Royal City, Lindsay Fuller, Blind Pilot Moon Taxi, Brandi Carlile, JD McPherson, Dumpstaphunk, Blind Pilot, Shovels and Rope, and David Ryan Harris.

Dave Matthews Solo

Dave Matthews doesn't necessarily launch solo shows as much as he grabs a slot every so often, whether at gala events or a stolen moment during a Dave Matthews Band show. During the 2000s, these became more frequent, with shows either opening or ending with Matthews strumming or singing covers or originals, but he has also popped up at charity gigs and political rallies, including a number of events for Bernie Sanders during the Democrat primary race of 2016.

32

Save Me

Guest Appearances

Collaboration is a mainstay of Dave Matthews Band, and the road runs both ways. DMB has invited plenty of guests onstage, and Dave Matthews has returned the favor, popping up in concerts and on records by superstars and colleagues alike.

Some of these gigs are certainly a reflection of Matthews's stardom. When he sang with the Rolling Stones in 1997, it was an acknowledgment that his star was on the rise—a situation that's very different from Matthews singing with compatriot Béla Fleck in 1998. By that point, the bond between Béla and Dave was evident, so their collaboration was no surprise, but Matthews's celebrity has sometimes meant that he's teamed up with musicians that don't seem to be in his wheelhouse. Take country superstar Kenny Chesney: there is no direct line between the breezy, beachy good times of Chesney and Matthews, but due to their mutual stardom, they became a natural pairing: both had huge followings, both liked to bend the rules of their genres, so they wound up being simpatico crossovers.

Although some of Matthews's cameos reveal similar calculations at their root—certainly, the fact that he showed up on Santana's 1999 blockbuster *Supernatural* is an acknowledgment of his commercial potential—usually, he has lent his name and time to projects that are directly connected to the music that inspired him as an aspiring musician. This makes his guest appearances fascinating to examine as a whole: they illustrate both his loyalty and his increasing status.

Dave Matthews Guest Appearances

Plenty of musicians sat in with Dave Matthews Band over the years, and Dave Matthews was usually inclined to return the favor. Often, Matthews joined these musicians onstage, but on occasion he would sit in on studio sessions. Here are some highlights of these guest appearances from Matthews over the years.

Danny Barnes—"Caveman" (2010)

On *Pizza Box*, the 2010 album by banjoist Danny Barnes, Dave Matthews sings harmony vocals on the grinding "Caveman." Barnes showed up on *Big Whiskey and the GrooGrux King*, so this is Dave paying back a favor, but this funky roots-rocker suggests a little of the limber rhythms of DMB.

Blue Man Group—"Sing Along" (2003)

Performing artist collective Blue Man Group entered the mainstream in the early years of the 2000s; 2003's *The Complex* was its bid at a hit album. Dave Matthews played a part in the attempt to push the group over the line, singing on "Sing Along," the first single from the album. Its lazy, cheerful groove suggests Matthews, so it's a bit a surprise he didn't have a hand in writing the song, but that speaks to the smarts of Blue Man Group, which wrote a solid little Dave Matthews Band song and then invited its leader to sing the tune.

Kenny Chesney—"I'm Alive" (2008)

Kenny Chesney's 2008 album *Lucky Old Sun* is one of the country singer's mellow efforts—it's not as ruminative as *Hemingway's Whiskey*, but it proceeds at a steady, easy gait. "I'm Alive," his duet with Matthews, sets the stage with its lazy pace. Originally recorded by Willie Nelson for his 2008 album *Moment of Forever*, the tune turns into a song of middle-aged gratitude when sung by Chesney and Matthews; they trade off verses, both men happy to be where they are, despite their respective struggles.

Mike Doughty—"Tremendous Brunettes" (2005)

The Soul Coughing singer signed to ATO Records in 2005, and Dave Matthews helped give his new signing a boost on *Haughty Melodic*, his first album for the label, by singing a verse and providing harmonies on "Tremendous Brunettes." Early, bootlegged versions of the song did not feature Matthews, which suggests his presence was indeed a way to raise the album's profile. Dave is fine, but the song was clearly meant to be sung by one person alone.

Béla Fleck and the Flecktones—"Communication" and "Trouble and Strife" (1998)

Released in June of 1998, right around the peak of Dave Matthews Band's popularity, *Left of Cool* features two appearances from Dave Matthews. He sings the bridge on the funky, fluid pop song "Communication," and provides harmonies on the cloistered, nervous "Trouble and Strife." At this point, the bond between DMB and the Flecktones was strong—that year, Béla appeared on *Before These Crowded Streets*—and *Left of Cool* almost feels like the flip side of where Dave Matthews Band was in 1998: it's ambitious but light, a record of a band settling into its skin.

Herbie Hancock—"Tomorrow Never Knows" (2010)

A sequel to *Herbie Hancock's River: The Joni Letters*, an album that unexpectedly won the Grammy for "Album of the Year" in 2007, *The Imagine Project* was more ambitious than that subdued, well-manicured set. Hancock decided to make *The Imagine Project* into a cross-cultural interpretation of a number of pop standards, drafting stars from several different cultures in for a duet. Dave Matthews was brought in to sing "Tomorrow Never Knows," the second of two John Lennon songs on this collection. This version of dispenses with the madness of Ringo Starr's beat on the Beatles original, so the psychedelic swirl is softened, and Matthews's vocals get swallowed up by a gentle pull.

Emmylou Harris—"My Antonia" (2000)

Emmylou Harris wound up winning a Grammy for "Best Contemporary Folk Album" in 2001 for *Red Dirt Girl*, the 2000 LP that picks up where *Wrecking Ball*, her Daniel Lanois–produced album of 1995, ended. Indeed, "My Antonia"—a duet between Dave Matthews and Harris—feels indebted to Lanois, as it sways to a gentle, muddied rhythm. "My Antonia" is one of Matthews's best vocal performances: he's restrained and empathetic, playing off of Harris's keening lead.

Jimmy Fallon—"Walk of Shame" (2012)

Despite having won the Grammy Award for "Best Comedy Album" in 2013, *Blow Your Pants Off* is a somewhat forgotten album from Jimmy Fallon. It was his second record, released two years before he started hosting *The Tonight Show*, but he still had considerable pull, which is why the album is album is packed with cameos, including Justin Timberlake, Eddie Vedder, Bruce Springsteen, Big and Rich . . . and Dave Matthews, who sings "Walk of Shame" with the comedian. Dave had nothing to do with the song's composition—Fallon wrote it with Mike DiCenzo and Gerard Bradford—and he barely appears on the track, showing up only for some harmonies toward the end of the tune.

Jurassic 5—"Work It Out" (2006)

A single from Jurassic 5's 2006 album *Feedback*, "Work It Out" features Dave Matthews Band, but the hip-hop group's production distills whatever DMB contributed into a lithe, funky groove. This means that Dave Matthews himself makes the biggest impression, singing the lengthy chorus hook. "Don't stop your dreamin' . . . we gonna make it right now," he pleads, with a seize-the-day spirit familiar from his own songs, and even if Jurassic 5's video, featuring a George W. Bush lookalike, was sly satire, "Work It Out" preaches personal change, not political. As it was a Jurassic 5 single, DMB never performed "Work It Out" live, and the single didn't chart.

Gov't Mule—"Forsaken Savior" (2013)

Gov't Mule designed its 2013 album *Shout!* as a way to reel in new listeners. It's a double album where the songs are presented twice—first with leader Warren Haynes on lead vocals, then with a host of guests singing the very same songs. It's an eclectic bunch, filled with idols and colleagues, from Elvis Costello and Toots Hibbert to Grace Potter and Glenn Hughes. Dave Matthews seems right at home here, singing the slow-burning blues "Forsaken Savior," a song that suits his own meditative sensibilities like a glove.

Angelique Kidjo—"Iwoya" (2002)

The Beninese singer/songwriter received a considerable promotional push when she signed with Columbia/Sony in 2002 and released *Black Ivory Soul*. Part of that push included the invitation to collaborate with such stars as Dave Matthews, who sings on the cheerful "Iwoya." Matthews takes most of the verses, with Kidjo effectively acting as something of a guest on her own song, but the end result is a bright ray of sunshine: it's the kind of song that piques curiosity, which is what the recording was certainly designed to do.

Little Feat—"Fat Man in the Bathtub" (2008)

Little Feat recorded a star-studded tribute to itself in 2008, and brought Dave Matthews in to sing "Fat Man in the Bathtub," one of the group's greatest numbers. Toning down the wild New Orleans syncopated rhythms from the Feat's original version, this update feels somewhat subdued: the groove is mellow, and, suitably, Matthews doesn't sing with the leer and howl of the song's author, Lowell George. This isn't a party, nor is it a hangover; it's music for a two-beer barbecue on a Sunday afternoon.

Taj Mahal—"Shake a Tail Feather" and "Land of 1,000 Dances" (1997)

Eclectic modern day bluesman Taj Mahal cut a children's album called *Shakin' a Tailfeather* in 1997, just as Dave Matthews Band was near the peak of its popularity. *Shakin' a Tailfeather* didn't strictly follow the contours of a conventional children album. In addition to originals and some old kids tunes, Taj Mahal threads in a bunch of old R&B chestnuts, sprucing them up for a family-friendly audience. Two of these covers feature Dave Matthews: the *de facto* title track, "Shake a Tail Feather"; and Ruth Brown's "Land of 1,000 Dances." Dave doesn't have a prominent vocal performance here: instead, he provides willowy, chicken-scratch guitar, helping to keep the groove going.

Vusi Mahlasela—"Sower of Words" (2007)

Vusi Mahlasela appeared on *Everyday*, so Dave Matthews returns the favor by singing in "Sower of Woods," a crucial track on Mahlasela's 2007 album *Guiding Star*. Matthews didn't have a hand in writing this reassuring piece of world pop, but it feels of a piece with his own openhearted folk-pop, even if Mahlasela's acrobatic melody is distinctly his own.

Robert Randolph and the Family Band—"Colorblind" (2006)

On Robert Randolph and the Family Band's 2006 album *Colorblind*, Dave Matthews plays guitar and sings on "Love Is the Only Way," a song he co-wrote with Mark Batson, the producer of *Stand Up*. Batson is one of handful of producers here, and he not only brought in Matthews but also persuaded LeRoi Moore and Rashawn Ross to play on this song plus "Angels," another Matthews collaboration that, like "Love Is the Only Way," logically might have its roots in *Stand Up*. "Love Is the Only Way" is big and bright, a celebration of good vibes, but "Angels" is a funky blues workout that might be even better, since it showcases the earthy interplay of the Family Band.

The Rolling Stones—"Memory Motel" (1998)

About twenty years after the release of *Black and Blue*—a transitional album for the Rolling Stones, recorded when the group was auditioning new guitarists—Dave Matthews strolled onstage to duet on "Memory Motel" with Mick Jagger. On *Black and Blue*, this is one of the rare songs where Jagger trades vocal lines with his partner, Keith Richards, but on this live version, Keith doesn't abandon his parts; instead, Dave takes over parts of Mick's verse. He pours his heart into it, just as he did on a live version of "Wild Horses" that didn't show up on the 1998 live album *No Security*. That earnestness illustrates the divide between Matthews and the Stones: he's determined to spill his heart all over the stage, but Jagger keeps something in reserve.

Santana—"Love of My Life" (1999)

Santana's Clive Davis–engineered comeback *Supernatural* is rampant with guest stars, but Dave Matthews receives a prominent spotlight on the album. Although "Love of My Life" wasn't released as a single, it is the second song on the album, and also features the dexterous drumming of Carter Beauford—a move that underscores the jazz-fusion sensibility that flows through both Santana and DMB. "Love of My Life" swings harder than most Dave Matthews Band songs, and it also has Latin-flavored breakdowns, so it winds up existing at the cross-section of the two bands: it has the rhythms of Santana and the pop sensibility of Dave Matthews Band.

Soulive—"Joyful Girl" (2002)

When Soulive covered Ani DiFranco's "Joyful Girl" in 2002, the group turned the song into a slow, funky groove and invited Dave Matthews to sing it. It's one of Matthews's best vocals: he's restrained and sexy, riding the rhythm but never pushing too hard. Rashawn Ross was playing in Soulive's horn section at this time, but he's not featured here; Matthews is the center, and he smolders like he rarely does elsewhere.

Chris Whitley—"Radar" (2001)

Chris Whitley signed to Dave Matthews's label, ATO, in 2001, and Matthews attempted to boost his signal by appearing on "Radar," the second song on Whitley's *Rocket House*. Matthews simply adds color—at times, his presence is imperceptible, his voice blending nicely with Whitley's—but it's enough to give the performance a lift, even if it didn't pay off on the charts.

33

Ants Marching

Online Fan Sites

The rise of Dave Matthews Band coincided with the rise of the internet, and, in many respects, it's difficult to separate the group's increasing popularity in the '90s from the web. In the middle of the '90s, thousands of fans flocked to e-mail listservs to discuss DMB and trade live tapes. Soon, this became an invaluable resource for diehards—a place where they could exchange information and also trade rare live performances.

Not every website that surfaced the '90s would survive the years. Some faded away, some changed into permanent resources, and others were a bridge between the ragged grassroots movement of the '90s and the streamlined information exchange of the twenty-first century. When examining online DMB resources, the key thing to remember is this: without the pioneers of the early days of the internet, so much information would never have been preserved. Maybe they didn't get it right, but they laid the groundwork for such serious resources as the DMBAlmanac, which examines the work of Dave Matthews Band at a level of detail no other band has ever had.

Minarets Digest

If tape trading was ground zero for early Dave Matthews Band fans, the Minarets Digest was the pivotal point in the transition from snail mail to the internet. In the early days, tapes were traded via word of mouth—hand to hand, college to college, the way that Grateful Dead live tapes used to work their way across America. The Minarets Digest, however, pushed this community into the nascent internet. It was one of the early message boards—and message boards happened to coincide with the rise of Dave Matthews Band.

The Minarets Digest effectively transferred the tape trees to e-mail, becoming one of the first fan-oriented music mailing lists on the internet—a place where fans could trade set lists while offering live tapes. Compared to the quick-fire dissemination of information in the age of Twitter, this seems archaic, but it was a considerable leap forward; prior to this, it would take months for this kind of information to spread across the country. The mailing digest also helped consolidate a fan base: local communities were now connected through the internet.

Naturally, the Minarets Digest was started in 1993 by groups of collegiate Dave Matthews fans based at the universities in Virginia and Vermont, and at Union College of Schenectady, New York. Minarets was an e-mail list, so it didn't need to be centralized in one place. However, the fact that all three colleges were aligned along the Eastern Seaboard suggests the strength of Dave Matthews Band's following in this area of the country, so this became the foundation of the fandom that soon spread out from coast to coast. Because DMB did not yet have an official web presence, this became the easiest way for connected fans to learn about where and what the group was playing.

To Nikki Van Noy, in her book *So Much to Say: Dave Matthews Band—20 Years on the Road*, fan Bill Lakenan underscored how important this was. "At that point it was somewhat of a novelty to be in an online community. Most of the people that were participants were college students through the mid-Atlantic and Northeast. It wasn't a huge group of people, and you go to know who the regular posters were. It was really the only way to get in touch with people for analog tape trade-in at the time because there was no way to transfer music over the web and people weren't really burning actual CDs yet."

If it wasn't possible to spread the actual music, the Minarets Digest nevertheless let fans dictate and design the rules for taping the music. They picked up on a lot of the Dead's ideas about trading, underscoring that this was never to be for profit; when this was combined with the ability to tell others what was actually played at certain gigs, it helped establish a blueprint for taping that lasts to this day.

The success of the Minarets Digest cut both ways. It helped form the thriving fan culture that Dave Matthews Band maintains to this day, but it was so successful that DMB's own organization, Red Light Management, soon started to pick up on things Minarets did well, particularly the sharing of set-list information. That became the bread and butter of fan trading, but what the message board did especially well is creating a community. It was one thing to present raw information but quite another to have a bunch of fans trade thoughts and ideas about this music—the very thing that would keep DMB's popularity alive for years. Also, within the records of the Minarets Digest it's possible to see the wider jam-band community evolve—there were people pushing regional bands like Jackopierce, too.

Looking back at these posts now, it's interesting to see how popular opinion about Dave Matthews Band started to develop. These early posts provide fascinating insight into the thoughts of the first guard of DMB fans. At this point, the standards were not yet enshrined, so people were happy to complaining about "Jimi Thing" or "Ants Marching," grousing that they were played too often. Similarly, there were complaints about covers—one poster notes, "The name of the song in question is 'Angel from Montgomery,' a song written by John Prine, DMB does not do justice to Prine's version"—and that level of comfortable criticism differs from the twenty-first century's online discourse, which seems determined to rally around consensus. It's also interesting to see how fans did not know the names of certain band members—one post calls Boyd Tinsley "Mr. Fiddle" and LeRoi Moore "Mr. Woodwind," with the author refusing to consult the FAQ for their names because he is simply too enraptured by the show itself—because it signals that fandom had yet to be codified: people were just grooving on the band.

Naturally, the number of posts on the Minarets Digest increased in the wake of *Under the Table and Dreaming*. Early in 1994, a week could produce as little as five posts, but by the end of the year there were often over one hundred messages a week—a volume of posting that increased through 1995. Not long afterward, the golden age of the internet mailing list started to recede, first with official band pages and e-mail lists supplementing the most basic services of the digest, and then with other more ambitious websites digging deeper into areas the digest couldn't. Over the course of 1996, the Minarets Digest morphed into another listserv called the DMBML. This mailing list stayed strong until 2002, by which point band e-mail lists started to seem archaic. DMBML made the leap from listserv into website in '02, becoming the online resource www.antsmarching.org.

This is not where the old archives of the Minarets Digest are preserved, however. A competing website called DMBAlmanac—a virtual warehouse of information, including detailed set lists and song analytics—wound up becoming the host of the old posts from the '90s. Dan Cheatham, one of the primary organizers of DMBAlmanac, helped move the Minarets Digest over to DMBAlmanac, preserving a valuable archive of early insights and firsthand reporting from the initial wave of diehard Dave Matthews Band fans.

www.antsmarching.org/DMBML

If Minarets Digest started Dave Matthews Band's online presence in 1993, the DMBML—an acronym for the Dave Matthews Band Mailing List—is where this fan discourse started to mature. Minarets evolved into the DMBML in 1996, just as Dave Matthews Band's second album, *Crash*, arrived in stores. The DMBML was the primary Dave Matthews Band internet repository in the mid-'90s. Like a lot fledgling fan sites of the period, it was a hybrid of fan community, news, and MP3 trading.

At this point in time, the DMBML wasn't alone on the internet. There were plenty of Dave Matthews Band fan sites—including Nancies and Moosey's DMB Palace—that hosted a similar blend of fan services and news, while www.minarets.net tended to be the repository for tape trading. That was the site that dove deep into live shows, but DMBML pioneered the hosting of individual MP3s. During the late '90s, most users' internet bandwidth was too small to facilitate the trading of full shows, but live MP3s of individual songs could be spread with relative ease, which is what DMBML did.

In addition to MP3s and tour information, the site hosted message boards—including one devoted to tape trading—a java chat applet, a game called Hangdave (Hangman with DMB Songs), and Davelibs, where users could "become Dave Matthews' new lyricist." This captures the freewheeling spirit of the early days of the internet, when there was a fair amount of serious hardcore information along with a bunch of silly stuff.

Operating roughly at the same time were dmbonirc and www.greystreeet.org, both of which covered similar territory to DMBLB. The other big site was www.nancies.org; www.greystreet.org morphed into www.dmbservers.com, and then www.dmbforums.com, which then became one of the biggest DMB fan sites, www.antsmarching.org. This website was inaugurated in 2002, with refugees from www.dmbforums.com, which by that point had usurped DMBML.

Not all users wound up going to over to www.antsmarching.org. Many of the fans from the early days migrated to www.anyoneseenthebridge.com later, then www.thesedayscontinue.org, which continued to run into the new millennium. This was a rarity, because most sites started to wither in the late 2000s; www.nancies.org went under in 2008, and there was a fair amount of churn at other DMB fan sites, too, due to differing personal animosities and competition over the same audience.

Through it all, www.antsmarching.org wound up triumphing as the place where many fans turned for discussion and information. One of the things that set it apart from its competitors was that it wasn't afraid to change with the times, as evidenced by the addition of a podcast in the 2010s. By comparison, www.thesedayscontinue.org turned into a staid message board designed for private members; it's useful for this dedicated community, but it doesn't welcome outsiders. The www.antsmarching.org site is explicitly designed to facilitate conversation, offering posts, news, user comments, downloads, and columns. Some of these features are relatively stale. The regular column hasn't been updated since 2012, abandoned in favor of podcasts, but the forums remain active as a place to trade tapes, exchange tickets, and talk about all matters Dave Matthews Band, along with related (or not so related) issues. Where the DMBAlmanac is constructed as an information clearinghouse, www.antsmarching.org is a forum for discussion—the podcasts allow the hardcore to banter back and forth, and they'll also find room for one-shot posts from fans, such as a defense of the much-derided "Mercy."

Warehouse Fan Association

An outgrowth of MusicToday, a website founded by manager Coran Capshaw, Warehouse is the official Dave Matthews Band website, providing a community in addition to selling merchandise and live albums.

Deadhead that he was, Coran Capshaw recognized the potential in marketing music directly toward the biggest fans of Dave Matthews Band. He certainly helped stoke the fires of tape trading among the dedicated, and he monitored the legions of hardcore fans on the burgeoning internet, realizing that there was a deep, vast collection of hardcore DMB heads waiting to acquire as much music and information about their favorite band as possible.

All this provided the impetus for the launch of the Warehouse Fan Association on December 4, 1998. Like many fan clubs, the Warehouse provided hardcore fans with access to the band, but Capshaw jury-rigged the outfit to benefit from the connectivity of the internet. For a modest fee—$30 a year, which would rise in time to $35—fans would be purchasing access to their favorite band, with the most enticing element being early access to concert tickets.

Through a convoluted system, Warehouse put fan requests into a lottery, with a slight emphasis on Warehouse members who had been in the club the longest. This started to change in 2002 and by 2003; seniority

A CD insert promoting Warehouse, Dave Matthews Band's official fan club. *Author's collection*

was no longer a factor in distribution, and this was the first step toward the Warehouse Fan Association becoming something of a standard fan club site.

In 2018, it cost $35 for an annual membership—or $40 for fans residing outside of the United States—and that brought several benefits for fans. First and foremost among these would be opportunities to purchase tickets early; sometimes, it could also result in early entry into the venue. Exclusive live recordings on what are called Warehouse 7 CDs—a single CD containing seven exclusive live performances—are given to each member; the site was also offers access to other recordings and meet-and-greets with the band.

Perhaps more important than all of this is how Coran Capshaw managed to spin what he learned with Warehouse into the powerhouse website MusicToday, which hosted various other fan clubs that all operated similarly to Warehouse, offering members exclusive first shot at concert tickets. By 2005, MusicToday was so large that it had expanded into in-venue retail, becoming the official merchandise vendor for Madison Square Garden. The next year, Live Nation acquired MusicToday, turning it into a live music and music merchandise behemoth.

www.dmbalmanac.com

Of all the various Dave Matthews Band websites on the internet—either currently active or from the past—DMBAlmanac provides the most thorough deep dive into the particulars of the band's history. Formed in 2001 by Rob Bokon, the DMBAlmanac was initially part of the www.justdmb.com site, but the following year Matias Nino turned it into a searchable database. Bokon was assisted by researcher Henry Hart; together, they turned DMBAlmanac into a comprehensive website offering detailed examination of Dave Matthews Band set lists throughout the years, offering instant updates of new concerts and shows stretching back to the beginning.

The DMBAlmanac is the titan of all unofficial Dave Matthews Band fan sites. While the Warehouse is essential for fans—it does, after all, provide early access to tickets—and www.antsmarching.org provides community discussion and news, DMBAlmanac processes what happens at those shows, keeping track of the songs that are played and the songs that are not, and providing set lists that date back decades. Additionally, the site swallowed up the original DMB mailing list, the Minarets Digest, so it is now the repository for all aspects of the group's history and provides an essential resource for any scholar of the group.

One of the best things about the DMBAlmanac is that it offers multiple angles for something as seemingly mundane as a set list. It arranges these set lists by year, venue, and guest stars, providing intense stats on how often certain songs have been played and in what contexts. This also includes solo shows by Dave Matthews, along with duet shows with Tim Reynolds, and even times when a DMB member guested with another act. No aspect of the DMB universe is ignored. If the group played a song, it's here. There are also running tallies of songs that need to be "liberated"—meaning, songs that have been out of circulation for years. Such features speak to the obsessiveness of the people that run the DMBAlmanac, but also to the band's fans: since the beginning, they've kept track of what the group has and has not played, so having all this material in one meticulously maintained site is something of a godsend.

34

One Sweet World

Philanthropic Work

Dave Matthews Band played its first show at a benefit concert, so charity was in its DNA right from the start. Once the band members became stars, they developed their own charity, the BAMA Works Fund, while also working with several other organizations. Often, they'd align with long-standing charities like Farm Aid, but whenever a new disaster occurred, there was a good chance that either Dave Matthews or DMB were involved in rebuilding.

What's interesting is how Matthews viewed his philanthropic work as existing on a separate plane from politics. In 2000, he told *Rolling Stone*, "I try not to become too preachy. If you want people to look at something, you have to make the seeing of it somewhat attractive. It doesn't have to be pretty. You can't make land mines in Cambodia a pretty thing. But you can make it seem less a source of guilt and accusation, and more a situation that needs to be dealt with. I try to make people feel powerful in the telling of a situation, rather than chaining myself to a tree." He also explained that he'd chosen to shine a spotlight on causes, not protests. "If I'm going to scream about something, it's going to be about something like the decimation of the rain forests or the ancient forests in the Northwest, or land mines in Cambodia, or the plight of Indians in Guatemala."

Over the next decade and a half, Matthews proved he was a man of his word through charitable work by himself and his band.

BAMA Works Fund

Dave Matthews Band established BAMA Works Fund in 1999, just after *Before These Crowded Streets* cemented the group's superstardom. With stardom comes a lot of money, so DMB decided to spread the wealth, particularly because, as Boyd Tinsley said in a 2015 interview with the Tom Tom Founders Festival, "We all wanted to give back." This included DMB manager Coran Capshaw, who started the ball rolling in establishing the BAMA Works Fund.

The charity's name is an inside joke for the band. Tinsley relates, "'Bama' is short for Alabama. There were two members of the band (I won't mention their names) who were somewhere like New York, and someone yelled out, 'Look at those two 'Bamas.' It just stuck. We embraced Bama. It's part of us." The group already used the term for its merchandise arm, so when it came time to establish the charity, BAMA was a logical choice for the group. The BAMA Works Fund was set up as a partnership with the Charlottesville Area Community Foundation and established with a donation of more than one million dollars. From that point on, a portion of every Dave Matthews Band concert ticket went to the BAMA Works Fund, while the group would also hold concerts specifically to benefit the charity.

BAMA Works primarily supported a variety of local Charlottesville charities with an emphasis on organizations that concentrated on underprivileged youth, arts, environmental and disabilities. BAMA Works would also sometimes dip into major international and national issues. Since its inception, the fund has raised over forty million dollars and made over twelve hundred grants. In 2016 alone, it gave $569,422 to the Charlottesville Area Community Foundation—in the previous year, it donated $422,500—whose president Anne Scott said in a statement, "The generosity of Dave Matthews Band is amazing. They wanted to have a way to give back to the community that they care about very much."

Dreaming Tree Wines

Dave Matthews's line of wine, the Dreaming Tree, has wound up donating a half-million dollars to environmental causes, including the Wilderness Society—a longstanding institution dedicated to conserving American wild lands—and Living Lands and Waters, an environmental organization that concentrates on cleaning up rivers and other bodies of water.

Farm Aid

Picking up on Bob Dylan's comment at Live Aid that it would be wonderful if somebody held a similar fundraiser for the American farmer, Willie Nelson, John Mellencamp, and Neil Young founded Farm Aid in 1985. It became a lasting tradition, held every year over the next three decades. Dave Matthews Band first played Farm Aid for its tenth anniversary in 1995, returning in 1997 and 1999. Dave played it solo in 2001, and, from that point on, he never missed a year, sometimes playing in conjunction with Tim Reynolds, sometimes in a duet set with Neil Young, but usually solo. These frequent performances came hand in hand with Dave Matthews joining the Farm Aid Board of Directors in 2001.

The Haiti Relief Project EP

Following the devastating earthquakes in Haiti in 2010, Dave Matthews Band founded the BAMA Works Haiti Relief Fund to help the citizens of that nation island. To help raise awareness for that charitable service, they released *The Haiti Relief Project* in 2010. The EP contains five previously unreleased live tracks—one of which, "Butterfly," features Dave Matthews solo—and, additionally, a T-shirt was produced to help raise awareness and funds.

Live 8

The July 2005 Live 8 concerts were designed as a continuation to Bob Geldof and Midge Ure's legendary 1985 event Live Aid, which was created to combat Ethiopian famine. Live 8, while not strictly a sequel, was designed to raise awareness and funds to combat global poverty. Dave Matthews Band, supported by Butch Taylor, played the Philadelphia portion of the show. As it happens, Dave Matthews was one of only two artists on the lineup of African descent; the other was Youssou N'Dour.

A media pass for Dave Matthews Band's AOL Concert for Schools—one of many benefit concerts the group has played over the years. *Author's collection*

New Orleans Habitat Musicians Village

The New Orleans Habitat Musicians' Village is a project from Habitat For Humanity that intended to build three hundred homes in the Upper Ninth Ward for residents, especially musicians, who were displaced in the aftermath of Hurricane Katrina. Dave Matthews Band issued a $1.5 million challenge grant, encouraging fans to meet that goal with the hopes that the charity would match its funds—hopes that were fulfilled.

Vote for Change

The MoveOn organization came to be in the years following the 1998 impeachment of President Bill Clinton. It was a progressive activist coalition that gained some strength during 1999, but it truly started to gain strength in the wake of the controversial Supreme Court decision to award the 2000 US election to George W. Bush. During the early years of the 2000s, www.moveon.org received even greater strength due in large part to opposition to the Iraq War. This was the impetus for the organization's strong support of John Kerry in the 2004 election.

Part of the support included Vote for Change, a tour that started in October 2004 designed to benefit the get-out-and-vote organization America Coming Together. Vote for Change targeted swing states in the United States—the states that could potentially change the course of the election. Officially, the tour was nonpartisan, but the politics of www.moveon.org leaned left. This includes Dave Matthews Band, whose members often did lean left. The group played several dates on the tour, in University Park, Fairborn, Auburn Hills, Madison, Ames, Gainesville, and Washington. D.C. At these gigs, the band would be joined by My Morning Jacket, Ben Harper, and Jurassic 5, with Neil Young sitting in at the Ames date as well. The D.C. show was a big blow out, featuring all of the above minus Neil, but also Bruce Springsteen.

It's impossible to tell whether the concerts worked. They didn't really move the needle in terms of the winners. Every state the Vote for Change tour played went to the candidate who was leading the state prior to the concerts. Nevertheless, it was a noble endeavor, and perhaps the most explicitly political act Dave Matthews Band has taken.

Belly Belly Nice

Dave Matthews Band and Food

Belly" is a favorite word of Dave Matthews, popping up frequently in his lyrics and song titles. Often, he sings "belly" in a carnal context, but he's equally enamored of culinary delights, if his extracurricular projects from Dave Matthews Band are any indication. At the dawn of the 2000s, he and Dave Matthews Band started to dabble in various gastronomical excursions, starting with lending the group's name to an ice cream flavor by Ben and Jerry's. Several years later, Dave hired winemakers to develop Dreaming Tree Wines from his Blenheim Vineyards, and his fans have followed his cue. Over time, beers and pizzerias have been named in homage to DMB, plus early keyboardist Peter Griesar opened his own restaurant—a sign that a passion for food wasn't limited to the group's singer/songwriter, and also a reflection of how Dave Matthews Band created its own ecosystem to sustain such endeavors.

Ben and Jerry's: One Sweet Whirled and Magic Brownies

Vermont ice-cream maker Ben and Jerry's first named a flavor after a rock star in 1987, when it paid tribute to Grateful Dead leader Jerry Garcia with Cherry Garcia. Not only is this the most famous flavor Ben and Jerry's ever released, it also established a precedent for the ice creamery to release other quirky flavors named after rock-and-roll bands. Phish Food, a chocolate ice cream with marshmallow and caramel swirls, appeared in 1997, and many others have followed over the years—including Dave Matthews Band's.

In 2002, Ben and Jerry's unveiled One Sweet Whirled, an ice cream named after a song from *Remember Two Things*, with "world" swapped out for a "whirled" of coffee ice cream and caramel and marshmallow swirls. Proceeds from sales of the ice cream were set aside for the organization Save Our Environment, which was right in line with all of DMB's charitable works.

Everything started with the best intentions, but One Sweet Whirled only survived for two years before being retired. On the Ben and Jerry's Flavor Graveyard—a place to celebrate styles of the past—One Sweet Whirled is memorialized with the following poem:

Working hand in hand with the band
Creating global warming awareness
We kinda forgot about the flavor, in all fairness.

This suggests that One Sweet Whirled wasn't particularly distinctive, and that may be true. The flavors of coffee and caramel pair well together, but marshmallow doesn't add much texture or notable taste; it's just sweetness. It's something pleasant and diverting, a little bit of a diversion that's not as earnest as its cause. Ultimately, that good intent was the lasting legacy of One Sweet Whirled: though perhaps the ice cream is somewhat forgotten even by its makers, its very existence proves that the band's heart was very much in the right place.

Everybody involved seemed to think One Sweet Whirled was a bust, so they decided to give it another shot in 2007. Subtitled the "Encore Edition"—an acknowledgment that the first flavor didn't quite click—Magic Brownies was a black raspberry ice cream with brownies and sweet, creamy ice cream swirls. It was much bolder and more distinctive, and that's what made it a hit. It stuck around for four years, and, since its retirement, has popped up on lists of flavors that should be revived. On the Flavor Graveyard, Ben and Jerry's seems fond of the flavor as well:

Some thought the original "too vanilla,"
So in 2006 we deep-sixed it
Fans then declared it raspberrily better
After we re-mixed it.

Blenheim Vineyards

Blenheim Vineyards is the vineyard owned by Dave Matthews, who established it in 1999 with craftsman William Johnson. Its Virginia location has a rich history, reportedly being a place where Thomas and Martha Jefferson took refuge after a snowstorm. Andrew Stevenson, a Speaker of the House and rector of the University of Virginia, acquired the property in 1846, and it remained notable, with chapels, schools, libraries, smokehouses, and laundries all standing on the property. In 1975, the location entered the Virginia Landmarks Register; months later, it joined the National Register of Historic Places.

About thirty years later, it became a winery owned by Dave Matthews. Blenheim Vineyards opened in 2000 with the assistance of winemaker Brad McCarthy, who steered the vineyard through its first two plantings before Kirsty Harmon came in as the winemaker and general manager for the establishment in 2008. Under Harmon's direction, Blenheim Vineyards has produced several varieties of white wines—one specialty was viognier, a wine that isn't nearly as popular as chardonnay—which were sold through a wine club. The winery itself became a local destination, hosting food trucks for the public, while also being made available for private parties and weddings.

Dreaming Tree Wines

With his first vineyard under his belt, Dave Matthews moved into the rich wine country of Sonoma County, California, to open a vineyard called Dreaming Tree, naming it after a pivotal song on 1998's *Before These Crowded Streets*. Launched in 2011, Dreaming Tree Wines debuted with a 2009 cabernet sauvignon, a 2010 chardonnay, and a 2012 red blend, all designed by a University of California graduate called Steve Reeder who previously worked at Fosters Wine Estates and Simi Winery but didn't last long at Dreaming Tree. By the end of 2011, Matthews had hired Sean McKenzie, a native of New Zealand, to design the wines for Dreaming Tree. According to the company's web site, "They realized they had a few things in common, like a passion for making wine at least as strong as their passion for drinking it." That sentiment was reduced to the axiom "Great minds drink alike," but the distinguishing characteristic of Dreaming Tree wines—apart from how they're environmentally friendly, poured into thinner, lighter bottles and bearing recycled labels that feature original artwork and poetry from Dave Matthews—is that they're easy to enjoy. This fact was confirmed by a 2016 review for *Paste Magazine* by Amy Glynn, who proclaimed, "They're solid as hell. I find them less risk-taking than some wines from the northern fringe of the Californian wine country, and whether that's good or bad is absolutely a matter of perspective. . . . The worst thing I can say about them isn't really a bad thing: they are mainstream. They're people pleasers. If your jam is generally beer and you want to know what to bring to a dinner party—these guys won't let you down."

Crush, a red wine blend, is the signature offering from Dreaming Tree Wines.
Author's photo

Dreaming Tree took a little while to get to the point of delivering such solid wines. Early on, in 2013, the vineyard debuted a white blend called Everyday, but this "bright and aromatic wine" was abandoned a few years later. Crush, another blend named after a Dave Matthews Band song, lasted much longer. On the vineyard's website, Matthews claims, "I swallowed it before I put the glass down. There wasn't any opportunity to spit." He's not exaggerating: it's a bold wine, not too sweet and not too aggressive. It's similar to a zinfandel, a wine that is quite large in its flavor profile, but Crush is also very drinkable: it's

The back label of the Dreaming Wine Chardonnay features art by Dave Matthews. *Author's photo*

smooth but relatively a complex, a very nice bargain considering its price point. Generally, red wines seemed to be a specialty of Dreaming Tree. Its chardonnay, which the site claims has "baked pear and peach flavors that jump out of the glass," is a sweetness bomb, the tart citrus hit giving way to a sugar rush. Much better is the sauvignon blanc, which is billed as "fresh and juicy," but it's much lighter and subtle than the chardonnay. Still, the Crush blend, the pinot noir, and the cabernet sauvignon are richer experiences, with the cabernet being nearly as good as Crush: it's flavorful yet smooth—a wine that would go well with a meal or parties.

Warehouse Pils from Starr Hill Brewery

As Dave Matthews Band celebrated its twenty-fifth anniversary in 2016, Starr Hill Brewery commemorated the occasional with Warehouse Pils, a pilsner beer that was available on tap in Charlottesville, Virginia, during the weekend of May 7, which is when the group played its anniversary concert. The Warehouse Pils is a dry-hopped German pilsner designed to be a light, drinkable potable to accompany the good times of a Dave Matthews Band concert. In a statement released at the time, Jack Goodall, the marketing manger at Starr Hill, claimed, "Starr Hill Brewery was born out of the local music scene here, and this beer commemorates another Charlottesville original."

The Warehouse Pizza Parlor

It's with some irony that Chicago, the site of Dave Matthews Band's infamous Poopgate, also happens to be the site of a Dave Matthews Band–inspired restaurant. Carmelo Scalzo opened up the Warehouse Bar and Pizzeria at 14919 W. Fullerton Avenue, the former location of Via Carducci—which just happened to be operated by Scalzo's uncle. The restaurateur says he and his partner Augie Femminella always intended to start a bar named "Warehouse," telling www.dnainfo.com, "We're both really big Dave Matthews fans. We bought the URL seven or eight years ago knowing we'd open up this bar." Despite naming their establishment after a celebrated Dave Matthews song, Scalzo and Femminella resisted the temptation to clutter up the menu with a bunch of items cutely titled after DMB songs. They chose instead to turn it into a straightforward pizza place specializing in craft beer and showing sports—the kind of thing that would appeal to Dave Matthews fans, but not *only* Dave Matthews fans.

I Did It

Dave Matthews Onscreen

Prior to forming Dave Matthews Band, Dave Matthews performed as an amateur actor. This skill served him well once the band became a major label act, since he could ham it up to the camera, but Matthews also pursued acting after he became a star, appearing as a guest on *House M.D.* and showing up in several Adam Sandler films. All of these performances showcase Matthews's acting chops, but his charisma was just as evident whenever Dave Matthews Band appeared on television.

Since Dave Matthews Band was at its peak during the 1990s and 2000s, when there were many outlets for live music on network and cable television, the group was a mainstay on certain shows, appearing on late-night television on a regular basis. This golden era began to wane in the late 2000s, just as Dave Matthews Band transitioned to a heritage act, so there is a lot of footage of the band in its prime in easy circulation.

Dave Matthews, the Actor

Dave Matthews revived his interest in acting in 2003, which is by no coincidence the same year he released his first solo album, *Some Devil*. Dave Matthews Band was at something of a crossroads, not sure how to proceed after achieving stardom, so it made sense that he began to branch out in several different areas, opening up a vineyard, making music on his own . . . and returning to his first love: acting. From this point forward, he'd return to film whenever the opportunity would arise, but tellingly, since 2008, his interest in acting appears to have waned, and his appearances on screen have been sporadic.

Where the Red Fern Grows (2003)

In this family film released by Disney, also starring Dabney Coleman, Dave Matthews stars as Will Coleman, the father of Billy, a young boy who desires his own hunting dog. A remake of the 1974 film of the same name, *Where the Red Fern Grows* is set in the Ozarks during the depression and co-stars Kris Kristofferson and Mac Davis, so there are plenty of musicians-turned actors here.

Because of Winn-Dixie (2005)

In his second major motion picture, Dave Matthews once again co-stars with a dog. Matthews signed up for the film because director Wayne Wang "did that movie *Smoke* and I thought that was pretty exceptional." If *Where the Red Fern Grows* is essentially a boy's adventure movie, *Because of Winn-Dixie* is a heartwarming comedy about how a quirky dog changes the fortunes of not just the girl who adopts her but the town in general.

House M.D., "Half-Wit" (2007)

In one of the better episodes of the long-running medical mystery series, Dave Matthews guest stars as Patrick Obyedkov, a preternaturally gifted pianist who is stricken with muscle spasms during a concert. While hospitalized at Princeton-Plainsboro, Obyedkov is treated by Dr. House, who discovers that the pianist's skill is tied to a bus accident from childhood that left him severely mentally handicapped.

I Now Pronounce You Chuck and Larry (2007)

In the first in a string of cameos in Adam Sandler films, Matthews plays a salesman who encounters Sandler and Kevin James as they're passing themselves off as a gay married couple.

Lake City (2008)

A thriller starring Troy Garity, *Lake City* casts Dave Matthews in a rare villainous role as Red, the man who pursues Garity's Billy in hopes of finding a large stash of drugs.

You Don't Mess with the Zohan (2008)

In another cameo in an Adam Sandler film, the bizarre and spirited *You Don't Mess with the Zohan*, Matthews is featured as James, a racist terrorist.

Just Go with It (2011)

The final installment in his Sandler trilogy, *Just Go with It* finds Matthews as Ian Maxine Jones—a role that is considerably more than just a cameo. Here, he plays a rich inventor married to Nicole Kidman, who he winds up dumping for another man.

A Child's Garden of Poetry (2011)

An animated film in which the classic children's text is brought to life by a variety of actors and musicians, *A Child's Garden of Poetry* features some major actors—including Philip Seymour Hoffman, Carrie Fisher, Claire Danes, and Julianne Moore—as well as a clutch of musicians making cameos. Matthews belongs that latter group, along with Ziggy Marley and Natalie Merchant.

The Being Experience (2013)

In this psychological drama exploring the deep recesses of the mind, Matthews appears alongside Terrence Howard, Alan Cumming, and Famke Janssen, as well as fellow musicians Moby and Questlove.

The Last Stop

Poopgate

Stick around long enough, and a band is bound to have a scandal of some sort. Dave Matthews Band is no exception to this rule. In fact, the band wound up with one of the most embarrassing scandals in rock history with the scatological accident that quickly became known as "Poopgate."

What Is Poopgate?

"Gate" became the preferred suffix to attach to any scandal after the legendary 1972 burglary of the Democratic National Committee headquarters at the Watergate hotel and office complex in Washington 1972. Following the escalation of the scandal—an escalation that ultimately lead to President Richard M. Nixon resigning in 1974—nearly any scandalous moment in popular culture has had "-gate" attached to it. For instance, when Bill Clinton became embroiled in some minor controversy with the White House travel office in 1993, it was called Travelgate.

The phrasing would be applied to many other scandals, political or otherwise, over the years. And so it was with Poopgate, an infamous incident on August 8, 2004, involving a Dave Matthews Band tour bus accidentally depositing over eight hundred pounds of human waste into the Chicago River. It wasn't just that the waste was sent into the river itself: feces showered a bunch of tourists on Chicago's Little Lady who were taking a sightseeing tour of Chicago River architecture.

How Did This Happen?

It certainly wasn't intentional. The bus driver pushed the button to release the contents of a tour bus's septic tank. He didn't realize he happened to be by the Kenzie Street Bridge, and the contents of the tank all went showering into rivers and the tourists below. Nearly one hundred passengers were subjected to the steady brown stream, which they reported to ruin their clothes—and the stench then transferred over to their automobiles, dirtying their cars on the drive home—and made them sick. Once the boat docked, the passengers were given refunds, and several passengers were taken to the hospital, although no serious injuries were reported.

Whose Bus Was It?

The bus was part of the Dave Matthews Band's touring entourage, but it was not specifically the band's bus. Indeed, Matthews wasn't even in Chicago when he heard about the incident. He was in a plane, flying to DMB's next location, so he wound up having a laugh when he heard a bunch of unsuspecting tourists being showered with poop, not yet realizing that a bus in his employ was responsible. "It would be funnier if it was anyone else but me," Dave Matthews admitted in a podcast interview with WTMX's NBC Chicago Street Team's Cara Carriveau in 2009.

Aftermath

Not surprisingly, spraying eight hundred pounds of fecal matter onto unsuspecting tourists and the river they were touring did not make for great press for Dave Matthews Band. Although the group had received a handful of negative reviews over the years, DMB never experienced anything like the onslaught of negative press it received in the wake of the incident that quickly became termed Poopgate.

The story provided rich material for puns from across the world. *NME*'s headline was "A Shit Dave Matthews Band Story!" *Entertainment Weekly*'s was "What a Dump!" *Chicagoist* wrote "Human Waste Linked to

Dave Matthews?" *Mocking Music*—a forgotten music blog—played with the idea of this being reflective of the group's music: "Dave Matthews Band Release More Crap."

Dave Matthews Band didn't immediately take responsibility for the action. The band's bus driver, forty-two-year-old Stefan Wohl—who had been friends with Boyd Tinsley for years—first denied any charges of wrongdoing when interviewed by the police, but almost a year after the incident he turned himself in. In March 2005, he was sentenced to eighteen months of probation, 150 hours of community service, and a $10,000 fine after pleading guilty to misdemeanor charges of water pollution and reckless conduct. According to an article in the *Chicago Tribune* dated March 10, 2005, this was the first time anybody within the Dave Matthews Band organization had taken responsibility for the incident.

Cook County Assistant State's Attorney Robert Egan was responsible for the case, and called the plea deal fair. The Tribune reported that Egan said, "I have been in touch with many of the people who were on the boat, and none of them suffered any lasting health effects."

Wohl's $10,000 fine was donated to the Friends of the Chicago River, an organization that also received a $50,000 donation from Dave Matthews Band in the fall of 2004. The band donated a further $50,000 to the Chicago Park District, intending these gestures to "begin the healing process." On May 2, 2005, *Billboard* reported that as part of a settlement with the City of Chicago, Dave Matthews Band agreed to pay a further $200,000 to an environmental fund, and to record where and when its buses emptied their septic tanks.

In addition to these settlements with the city, Dave Matthews Band also had to settle several personal injury lawsuits. The healing process lasted years. During the podcast with Carriveau, Matthews immediately said, "I'll apologize for that as long as I have to." The singer knew that words only go so far. "I regret that enormously, and I know some people there accept my apology and other people don't, but I can't do anything about it now." Even when Dave put the blame on somebody else, he accepted responsibility. "The bus driver lost his job, and I didn't have my finger on the button, but it was one of our buses—wasn't mine—but it was one of the buses in my employment, and so I feel bad about it."

Anniversary

Nobody easily forgot Poopgate—it was too rich, silly, and vulgar a scandal to be forgotten. That said, the anniversary has been celebrated in odd ways, such as a time in 2015, when journalist John Walaszek decided to revisit the site of the Kenzie Street Bridge for an article for *Pigeons and Planes* published June 5, 2015. In his piece, the former Dave Matthews Band fan tried to imagine the circumstances of Poopgate, both from the tourists' perspective and from that of the bus driver. He overplayed his hand a little bit, but he also was clever enough to leave behind a homemade plaque, claiming, "In August 2004, at This Very Location, a DMB Tour Bus Dumped Pounds of Poo on Some People #NeverForget #AlwaysRemember."

Walaszek's remembrance was strangely timed. Not only was the eleventh anniversary an odd one to celebrate—very few people ever spend time remembering an eleventh anniversary; it's not as clean or simple as a tenth or twentieth—but it was also posted in June 2015, not August, which is the month it happened. It was trolling designed for a viral story, and it succeeded: the image showed up on Reddit and then spread like wildfire, resulting in a succession of articles that only served as a reminder that

The memorial for Poopgate set up by John Walaszek. *John Walaszek*

for some people, Dave Matthews Band and Poopgate remain something worthy of plenty of chuckles and snorts, even if it was an incident caused genuine pain to a number of poor unfortunate souls.

Finally, Dave Matthews Band isn't the only band to have had problems dispensing with its fecal matter. Five years after Poopgate, Keith Urban wound up dispensing gallons of waste on East 11th Street in New York—it didn't hit any tourist but wound up taking over a day to clear up. Despite this Urban incident, Poopgate remains associated with Dave Matthews Band, and always will be seen as the most embarrassing event in its history.

Bibliography

Books

Browne, David. *So Many Roads: The Life and Times of the Grateful Dead.* Boston: Da Capo, 2015.

Budnick, Dean. *Jambands: The Complete Guide to the Players, Music, and Scene.* San Francisco: Backbeat Books, 2003.

Conners, Peter. *JAMerica: The History of the Jam Band and Festival Scene.* Boston: Da Capo, 2013.

Delancey, Morgan. *Dave Matthews Band: Step into the Light.* Winnipeg: ECW Press, 2001.

Marell, Nevin. *Music for the People: Dave Matthews Band.* New York: Pocket Books, 2004.

Rodgers, Jeffrey Pepper. *Rock Troubadours.* San Anselmo: Sting Letter Publishing, 2000.

Sclafani, Tony. *The Grateful Dead FAQ: All That's Left to Know About the Greatest Jam Band in History.* Milwaukee: Backbeat Books, 2013.

Sokolowski, Lynda Jo Mykkanen. *Dave Dances . . . Life, Love, and Art Inspired by the Music of the Dave Matthews Band.* New York: LJMS Art, 2008.

Van Noy, Nikki. *So Much to Say: Dave Matthews Band—20 Years on the Road.* New York: Touchstone, 2011.

Newspaper, Magazine, and Internet Articles

Apczynski, Dan. "Dave Matthews Interview and Lesson." *Acoustic Guitar.* October 2009.

Associated Press. "Dave Matthews Band Settles Bus Waste Case." www.billboard.com. May 2, 2005.

Aswad, Jem. "Boyd Tinsley, Accused of Sexual Harassment, Is 'No Longer a Member' of Dave Matthews Band." www.variety.com. May 18, 2018.

Bailey, Jack. "On the Road . . . with the DMB, Part 1." *C-Ville Weekly*. June 30–July 13, 1993.

Beller, Bryan. "Still Learning: From Stadiums to the Studio, Stefan Lessard Isn't Done Exploring." www.basssplayer.com. September 1, 2009.

Bloom, Mina. "The Warehouse, a Pizza Spot in Lincoln Park, Named After Dave Matthews Band." www.dnainfo.com. October 20, 2015.

Blumberg, Perri O. "25 Years Later, Dave Matthews Band Gets a Beer." *Men's Journal*. May 4, 2016.

Bonar, Samantha. "Dave Matthews Introduces Line of Wines: The Dreaming Tree." www.laweekly.com. November 21, 2001.

Borzillo, Carrie. "Matthews Shows a Darker Side." *Billboard*. March 18, 1998.

Browne, David. "Dave New World." *Entertainment Weekly*. May 8, 1998.

Caulfield, Keith. "Dave Matthews Band Scores Seventh No. 1 Album on Billboard 200 Chart With 'Come Tomorrow.'" www.billboard.com. June 17, 2018.

Colapinto, John. "The Salvation of Dave Matthews." *Rolling Stone*. March 15, 2001.

Considine, J. D. "Songs Come First for Band Inspiration: Dave Matthews' Writing Is Influenced by His Bandmates' Strengths." *Baltimore Sun*. August 31, 1996.

Currin, Grayson Haver. "On the Dave Matthews Band and When Old Bands Should Break Up." www.indyweek.com. December 5, 2012.

Eckhardt, Kai. "Dave Matthews Band—Stefan Lessard." *Bass Player Magazine*. July 2001.

Farley, Christopher John. "And the Band Plays On." Time. March 5, 2001.

Fox, Brian. "Stefan Lessard Shows His Street Smarts with the Dave Matthews Band." *Bass Player Magazine*. September 2005.

Fricke, David. "Dave Matthews Band: Back in the Groove." *Rolling Stone*. August 8, 2002.

Gordinier, Jeff. "Dave Matthews Band Reaches Out." *Entertainment Weekly*. May 1, 1998.

Glynn, Amy. "Dave Matthews Makes Wine, and Damn It, We Like It." *Paste Magazine*. January 27, 2016.

Hackney, Suzette. "Life as a Black Dave Matthews Band Fan." *Washington Post*. July 26, 2013.

Harrington, Richard. "The Secret of the Dave Matthews Band." *Washington Post*. August 16, 1998.

Hirshey, Gerri. "The Wine World's No. 1 Rock Star: Dave Matthews." *Food and Wine*. October 1, 1995.

Kot, Greg. "Dave Matthews: On the Road Again." *Rolling Stone*. August 17, 2000.

Marchese, David. "Dave Matthews: In Conversation." *New York Magazine*. May 14, 2018.

Moss, Corey. "Dave Matthews Digs Up a Video for His First Solo Single." www.mtv.com. August 7, 2003.

Newcomb, Ming Lee. "Dave Matthews Band Announces First New Album Since 2012, 'Come Tomorrow,' Due Out in June." www.liveforlivemusic.com. April 25, 2018.

Norlander, Matt. "Under the Table at 20: Revisiting Dave Matthews Band's Most Important Record." www.relix.com. September 26, 2014.

Norris, Chris. "Fanfare for the Common Man." *Spin*. July 1998.

O'Keeffe, Kevin. "What We Talked About When We Talked About Dave Matthews' Poop-Bus Incident." www.theatlantic.com. August 8, 2014.

Parales, Jon. "Dave Matthews Sings to the Next Generation on 'Come Tomorrow.'" *New York Times*. June 6, 2018.

Partridge, Kenneth. "An Honest Defense of the Dave Matthews Band's First Album." www.refinery29.com. June 17, 2014.

Rovzar, Chris. "Keith Urban Steals Tour-Bus-Turd Title from Dave Matthews." www.nymag.com. April 6, 2009.

Scaggs, Austin. "The Devil in Dave Matthews." *Rolling Stone*. June 23, 2011.

Seidenberg, Robert. "The Gospel According to Matthews." *Entertainment Weekly*. June 2, 1995.

Semigran, Aly. "Dave Matthews Band Turns 25: Celebrate with 10 Essential Live Tracks." www.billboard.com. February 2, 2016.

Semigran, Aly. "Dave Matthews Band's New Album 'Come Tomorrow': Ranking the Songs from Worst to Best." www.billboard.com. June 18, 2018.

Serpick, Evan. "Dave Matthews Shares the Stories Behind 'Big Whiskey and the GrooGrux King.'" *Rolling Stone*. June 10, 2009.

Sinclair, Tom. "'Crash' Landing." *Entertainment Weekly*. May 3, 1996.

Slater, Rob. "Boyd Tinsley: Reflections with BT." www.jambands.com. March 27, 2014.

Symonds, Jeff. "Dave Matthews Bootlegs Himself." *E News*. November 1, 1997.

Vineyard, Jennifer. "Julia Roberts Is a Literal 'Dreamgirl' in Surreal Dave Matthews Band Clip." www.mtv.com. August 18, 2005.

Waddell, Ray. "Dave Matthews Band's 'Big Whiskey' Is a Toast to LeRoi Moore." www.billboard.com. April 10, 2009.
Walaszek, John. "Dave Matthews Poopgate: Revisiting the Bridge." www.pigeonsandplanes.com. June 5, 2015.
Willman, Chris. "Busted Stuff." *Entertainment Weekly*. July 19, 2002.
Zaleski, Annie. "Dave Matthews' 'Eh Her': What the World Really, Really Doesn't Need." *Riverfront Times*. September 4, 2007.
——. "Looking to Fans for Setlist Ideas." *Billboard*. July 1, 2007.
——. "Dave Matthews Band to be Featured on Neighborhood Sessions Series on TNT, 9/11." www.broadwayworld.com. August 16, 2016.
——. "Rocker Dave Matthews' Sustainable Winery Is Truly the 'Best of What's Around.'" www.cultureist.com. April 30, 2012.
——. "Brazos Tacos Takes a Permanent Space at IX and More Local Restaurant News." www.c-ville.com. June 9, 2005.
——. "Dave Matthews on His Band's 'Unique Sort of Love Affair.'" www.npr.org. September 8, 2012.
——. "The Space Between DMB Markets Hollywood." www.readthehook.com. February 21, 2002.
——. "Plan for Old Have a Nice Day Cafe/Flood Zone Building Does Not Include Music." www.wtvr.com. December 5, 2014.
——. "Boyd Tinsley: Founding Member, Dave Matthews Band and the BAMA Works Fund." www.tomtomfest.com.
——. "Taping Enthusiasts Make the Dave Matthews Band the World's Most Publicly Traded Group." Yahoo Music. July 11, 2014.

Websites

www.allmusic.com
www.antsmarching.org
www.blenheimvineyards.com
www.dmbalmanac.com
www.dreamingtreewines.com
www.minarets.net mailing list archive: www.dmbalmanac.com/minarets/
www.riaa.com
www.wikipedia.com

Selected Discography

Studio Albums

- *Remember Two Things*: October 13, 1993, Bama Rags Records (reissued in 2014 by RCA/Legacy)
- *Under the Table and Dreaming*: September 27, 1994, RCA
- *Crash*: April 30, 1996, RCA
- *Before These Crowded Streets*: April 28, 1998, RCA
- *Everyday*: February 27, 2001, RCA
- *Busted Stuff*: July 16, 2002, RCA
- *Stand Up*: May 10, 2005, RCA
- *Big Whiskey and the GrooGrux King*: June 2, 2009, RCA
- *Away from the World*: September 11, 2012, RCA

Official Live Albums

- *Live at Red Rocks 8.15.95*: October 28, 1997, RCA
- *Listener Supported*: November 23, 1999, RCA
- *Live in Chicago 12.19.98 at the United Center*: October 23, 2001
- *Live at Folsom Field, Boulder, Colorado*: November 5, 2002, RCA
- *The Central Park Concert*: November 18, 2003, RCA
- *The Gorge*: June 29, 2004, RCA
- *Weekend on the Rocks*: November 29, 2005, RCA
- *Live at Piedmont Park*: December 11, 2007, RCA
- *Live at Mile High Music Festival*: December 16, 2008, RCA
- *Europe 2009*: December 22, 2009, RCA
- *Live in New York City*: November 9, 2010, RCA
- *Live at Wrigley Field*: May 31, 2011, RCA
- *Live in Atlantic City*: 2011, RCA

EPs

- *Recently*: May 17, 1994, Bama Rags
- *The Haiti Relief Project*: January 29, 2010, RCA

Compilations

- *The Best of What's Around, Vol. 1*: November 7, 2006, RCA
- *Live Trax*: July 31, 2007, RCA

Singles

- "What Would You Say": September 1994, RCA
- "Jimi Thing": 1995, RCA
- "Typical Situation": 1995, RCA
- "Ants Marching": September 1995, RCA
- "Satellite": 1995, RCA
- "Too Much": April 1996, RCA
- "So Much to Say": August 1996, RCA
- "Crash into Me": December 3, 1996, RCA
- "Two Step": January 1997, RCA
- "Tripping Billies": March 1997, RCA
- "Don't Drink the Water": 1998, RCA
- "Stay (Wasting Time)": 1998, RCA
- "Crush": September 8, 1998, RCA
- "Rapunzel": 1999, RCA
- "I Did It": January 3, 2001, RCA
- "The Space Between": April 16, 2001, RCA
- "Everyday": November 15, 2001, RCA
- "Where Are You Going": July 16, 2002, RCA
- "Grace Is Gone": 2002, RCA
- "Grey Street": 2002, RCA
- "American Baby": March 17, 2005, RCA
- "Dreamgirl": August 8, 2005, RCA
- "Everybody Wake Up (Our Finest Hour Arrives)": 2006, RCA
- "Funny the Way It Is": April 21, 2009, RCA

- "Why I Am": July 13, 2009, RCA
- "You and Me": 2009, RCA
- "Mercy": July 16, 2012, RCA

Dave Matthews Solo Discography

- Tribe of Heaven, *Imagine We Were*: March 15, 2005, Fear of the Atom (recorded in 1989)
- *Live at Luther College*: January 19, 1999, RCA
- *Some Devil*: September 23, 2003, RCA
- *Live at Radio City*: August 14, 2007, RCA
- *Live in Las Vegas*: February 9, 2010, RCA

Singles

- "Gravedigger": 2003, RCA
- "Save Me": 2003, RCA
- "Oh": 2004, RCA
- "Eh Hee": 2007, RCA

Index

<Above: "Everywhere." no period?>

THE FAQ SERIES

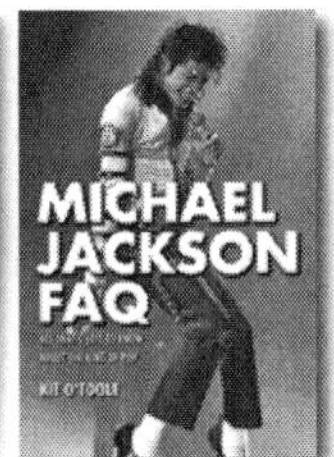

AC/DC FAQ
by Susan Masino
Backbeat Books
9781480394506..................$24.99

Armageddon Films FAQ
by Dale Sherman
Applause Books
9781617131196..................$24.99

The Band FAQ
by Peter Aaron
Backbeat Books
9781617136139 ....$19.99

Baseball FAQ
by Tom DeMichael
Backbeat Books
9781617136061..................$24.99

The Beach Boys FAQ
by Jon Stebbins
Backbeat Books
9780879309879..................$22.99

The Beat Generation FAQ
by Rich Weidman
Backbeat Books
9781617136016 ....$19.99

Beer FAQ
by Jeff Cioletti
Backbeat Books
9781617136115 ....$24.99

Black Sabbath FAQ
by Martin Popoff
Backbeat Books
9780879309572..................$19.99

Bob Dylan FAQ
by Bruce Pollock
Backbeat Books
9781617136078 ....$19.99

Britcoms FAQ
by Dave Thompson
Applause Books
9781495018992 ....$19.99

Bruce Springsteen FAQ
by John D. Luerssen
Backbeat Books
9781617130939..................$22.99

A Chorus Line FAQ
by Tom Rowan
Applause Books
9781480367548 ....$19.99

The Clash FAQ
by Gary J. Jucha
Backbeat Books
9781480364509 ....$19.99

Doctor Who FAQ
by Dave Thompson
Applause Books
9781557838544..................$22.99

The Doors FAQ
by Rich Weidman
Backbeat Books
9781617130175..................$24.99

Dracula FAQ
by Bruce Scivally
Backbeat Books
9781617136009 ....$19.99

The Eagles FAQ
by Andrew Vaughan
Backbeat Books
9781480385412..................$24.99

Elvis Films FAQ
by Paul Simpson
Applause Books
9781557838582..................$24.99

Elvis Music FAQ
by Mike Eder
Backbeat Books
9781617130496..................$24.99

Eric Clapton FAQ
by David Bowling
Backbeat Books
9781617134548..................$22.99

Fab Four FAQ
by Stuart Shea and Robert Rodriguez
Hal Leonard Books
9781423421382..................$19.99

Prices, contents, and availability subject to change without notice.

Fab Four FAQ 2.0
by Robert Rodriguez
Backbeat Books
9780879309688..................$19.99

Film Noir FAQ
by David J. Hogan
Applause Books
9781557838551..................$22.99

Football FAQ
by Dave Thompson
Backbeat Books
9781495007484..................$24.99

Frank Zappa FAQ
by John Corcelli
Backbeat Books
9781617136030..................$19.99

Godzilla FAQ
by Brian Solomon
Applause Books
9781495045684 ....$19.99

The Grateful Dead FAQ
by Tony Sclafani
Backbeat Books
9781617130861..................$24.99

Guns N' Roses FAQ
by Rich Weidman
Backbeat Books
9781495025884 ....$19.99

Haunted America FAQ
by Dave Thompson
Backbeat Books
9781480392625..................$19.99

Horror Films FAQ
by John Kenneth Muir
Applause Books
9781557839503..................$22.99

James Bond FAQ
by Tom DeMichael
Applause Books
9781557838568..................$22.99

Jimi Hendrix FAQ
by Gary J. Jucha
Backbeat Books
9781617130953..................$22.99

Johnny Cash FAQ
by C. Eric Banister
Backbeat Books
9781480385405 .... $24.99

KISS FAQ
by Dale Sherman
Backbeat Books
9781617130915 .... $24.99

Led Zeppelin FAQ
by George Case
Backbeat Books
9781617130250 .... $22.99

Lucille Ball FAQ
by James Sheridan and Barry Monush
Applause Books
9781617740824 .... $19.99

M.A.S.H. FAQ
by Dale Sherman
Applause Books
9781480355897 .... $19.99

Michael Jackson FAQ
by Kit O'Toole
Backbeat Books
9781480371064 .... $19.99

Modern Sci-Fi Films FAQ
by Tom DeMichael
Applause Books
9781480350618 .... $24.99

Monty Python FAQ
by Chris Barsanti, Brian Cogan, and Jeff Massey
Applause Books
9781495049439 .... $19.99

Morrissey FAQ
by D. McKinney
Backbeat Books
9781480394483 .... $24.99

Neil Young FAQ
by Glen Boyd
Backbeat Books
9781617130373 .... $19.99

Nirvana FAQ
by John D. Luerssen
Backbeat Books
9781617134500 .... $24.99

Pearl Jam FAQ
by Bernard M. Corbett and Thomas Edward Harkins
Backbeat Books
9781617136122 .... $19.99

Pink Floyd FAQ
by Stuart Shea
Backbeat Books
9780879309503 .... $19.99

Pro Wrestling FAQ
by Brian Solomon
Backbeat Books
9781617135996 .... $29.99

Prog Rock FAQ
by Will Romano
Backbeat Books
9781617135873 .... $24.99

Quentin Tarantino FAQ
by Dale Sherman
Applause Books
9781480355880 .... $24.99

Robin Hood FAQ
by Dave Thompson
Applause Books
9781495048227 .... $19.99

The Rocky Horror Picture Show FAQ
by Dave Thompson
Applause Books
9781495007477 .... $19.99

Rush FAQ
by Max Mobley
Backbeat Books
9781617134517 .... $19.99

Saturday Night Live FAQ
by Stephen Tropiano
Applause Books
9781557839510 .... $24.99

Seinfeld FAQ
by Nicholas Nigro
Applause Books
9781557838575 .... $24.99

Sherlock Holmes FAQ
by Dave Thompson
Applause Books
9781480331495 .... $24.99

The Smiths FAQ
by John D. Luerssen
Backbeat Books
9781480394490 .... $24.99

Soccer FAQ
by Dave Thompson
Backbeat Books
9781617135989 .... $24.99

The Sound of Music FAQ
by Barry Monush
Applause Books
9781480360433 .... $27.99

South Park FAQ
by Dave Thompson
Applause Books
9781480350649 .... $24.99

Star Trek FAQ (Unofficial and Unauthorized)
by Mark Clark
Applause Books
9781557837929 .... $19.99

Star Trek FAQ 2.0 (Unofficial and Unauthorized)
by Mark Clark
Applause Books
9781557837936 .... $22.99

Star Wars FAQ
by Mark Clark
Applause Books
9781480360181 .... $24.99

Steely Dan FAQ
by Anthony Robustelli
Backbeat Books
9781495025129 .... $19.99

Stephen King Films FAQ
by Scott Von Doviak
Applause Books
9781480355514 .... $24.99

Three Stooges FAQ
by David J. Hogan
Applause Books
9781557837882 .... $22.99

TV Finales FAQ
by Stephen Tropiano and Holly Van Buren
Applause Books
9781480391444 .... $19.99

The Twilight Zone FAQ
by Dave Thompson
Applause Books
9781480396180 .... $19.99

Twin Peaks FAQ
by David Bushman and Arthur Smith
Applause Books
9781495015861 .... $19.99

UFO FAQ
by David J. Hogan
Backbeat Books
9781480393851 .... $19.99

Video Games FAQ
by Mark J.P. Wolf
Backbeat Books
9781617136306 .... $19.99

The Who FAQ
by Mike Segretto
Backbeat Books
9781480361034 .... $24.99

The Wizard of Oz FAQ
by David J. Hogan
Applause Books
9781480350625 .... $24.99

The X-Files FAQ
by John Kenneth Muir
Applause Books
9781480369740 .... $24.99